T0013463

SCHOOL CLOTHES

A COLLECTIVE MEMOIR OF BLACK STUDENT WITNESS

JARVIS R. GIVENS

Beacon Press, Boston

BEACON PRESS
Boston, Massachusetts
www.beacon.org

Beacon Press books
are published under the auspices of
the Unitarian Universalist Association of Congregations.

Printed in the United States of America

26 25 24 23 8 7 6 5 4 3 2 1

This book is printed on acid-free paper that meets the uncoated paper
ANSI/NISO specifications for permanence as revised in 1992.

Text design and composition by Kim Arney

Library of Congress Cataloguing-in-Publication Data is available for this title.

ISBN: 978-0-8070-5481-9
Ebook: 978-0-8070-5474-1; audiobook: 978-0-8070-0842-3

African American children are not without history, though discussions about them are often ahistorical—as though the children just arrived on the educational scene in the 1970s with nothing but a plethora of problems.

—VANESSA SIDDLE WALKER,
Their Highest Potential

Contents

Preface

"School Clothes" and the Black Vernacular

I got shoes, you got shoes,
All God's chillun got shoes;
When I get to heaven, gonna put on my shoes
And walk all over God's heaven

I got a robe, you got a robe,
All God's chillun got a robe;
When I get to heaven, gonna put on my robe
And shout all over God's heaven

—"All God's Chillun Got Shoes,"
African American spiritual

WHEN I WAS A YOUNG STUDENT, my family referred to "school clothes"—uniforms or clothing purchased with the specific intent of being worn to school. Shopping for school clothes before the new academic year was an occasion of major significance. If I stayed over at a cousin's house between Monday and Friday, I had to "pack some school clothes," just as I knew to "pack some church clothes" if I visited my grandmother for the weekend. When my cousins and I came home in the afternoons, we had to take off our school clothes before going outside and were usually instructed to "put on some play clothes," or specifically "play shoes"—we were not to wear newer shoes or "good" shoes reserved for school or events where we had to look our best. We needn't worry about "play clothes" getting dirty or "play shoes" getting scuffed: they were already, by definition, "messed up." Embedded in such routines and usage were values about school, church, and play, although this knowledge was rarely explicitly articulated.

These sartorial politics reflect distinct ways of being in African American vernacular culture, a culture held and cultivated internally, where black people expressed their own aesthetic judgments, "their own ways of seeing the world, its history, and its meanings."[1] And those sartorial politics are not unique to my family, nor are they new. As Monica Miller writes, "The spiritual has always had a sartorial dimension for black people in America."[2] While churches have been a major site for these sartorial practices, schools have long been a locus for expressions of black spirituality, and sites where African Americans have "worked on ourselves as canvases of representation," to borrow from Stuart Hall.[3] Immediately following Emancipation, black communities all over the United States went to school as a means of putting distance between themselves and the conditions of a slave past that constantly threatened to contaminate their lives as free people. I found accounts of students dressing up for school—and for freedom—in the nineteenth and twentieth centuries to be particularly beautiful and endearing.

I encountered portraits of students in the first days of freedom trying to look the part. Take E. D. Tilghman, for instance. After this formerly enslaved young man was admitted to Hampton Institute in July 1868, he asked for time to get his affairs in order. He made only $5.50 per week, but he was determined to find a way to pay for school—and the appropriate clothing! "You may relie on my coming," he assured them, "for I am coming without I dies or sickness prevents, *as soon as I get my clothes look out for me*."[4] Black students dressed in ways that made them and their people feel proud, striving to put on attire commensurate with their mission.

More than raiment, school clothes were something akin to ceremonial garb. At least, that is how I think of it when I reflect on the black farmers near Maysville, South Carolina, who held high ambitions for one of their own: a Miss Mary Jane McLeod (Bethune). In October 1888, they halted all work operations to send a thirteen-year-old Mary Jane off to Scotia Seminary. Some gifted her with clothes for the journey. "We used to have little cracker boxes. We kept our clothes in them, so my father went down and got me a little trunk," Bethune recalled. "Some neighbors knitted a pair of stockings, some gave me a little linsey dress, little aprons, this that and the other, and when that October day came I can see myself now, going down to Maysville to take the train for the first time in my life." The black farmers "stopped work that afternoon, got out the wagons, mules, ox-carts; some riding, some walking. They were going to Maysville to put me on the train to go to school," she recounted.[5] Mary Jane was their proxy, a young student striving to make freedom a real thing, for herself and her people.

Bethune's story about school clothes is a favorite of mine, in part because it was the first to jump out at me. I stumbled on the anecdote while reading an interview with Bethune in the archives at Fisk University. I was supposed to be searching for Carter G. Woodson in the papers of southern black teachers and black teacher organizations for my first book, *Fugitive Pedagogy*. But as always, my mind started wandering around in the archive. And such wandering often leads to me wondering about new questions, new traces; often I see things that have nothing to do with what I am searching for, but I find myself unable to turn away from them. After sitting with Bethune's story of those black farmers *stopping work* to send her off to school and providing her with new clothes, as well as her descriptions of the particular articles of clothing, I decided to take what I had seen with me. My eye would catch more and more sartorial metaphors in black student narratives. Such stories appear post-Emancipation, but they are intimately connected to African American experiences during slavery.

School clothes became part and parcel of African Americans' efforts to undo the harms inflicted on black youth during slavery and its afterlives. A young Booker T. Washington helps elucidate this point. Washington named "the wearing of a flax shirt" as the "most trying ordeal" he endured "as a slave boy" in Virginia. He explained, "It was common to use flax as part of the clothing for the slaves. That part of the flax from which our clothing was made was largely the refuse, which of course was the cheapest and roughest part." Washington detailed his memory of that dreadful slave shirt: "I can scarcely imagine any torture, except, perhaps, the pulling of a tooth, that is equal to that caused by putting on a new flax shirt for the first time. It is almost equal to the feeling that one would experience if he had a dozen or more chestnut burrs, or a hundred small pin-points, in contact with his flesh. . . . The fact that my flesh was soft and tender added to the pain." To mitigate the pain of that awful shirt, Washington's older brother John "performed one of the most generous acts" he had "ever heard of one slave relative doing for another." Whenever Booker was forced to wear a new flax shirt, John offered to wear it first, for several days, until the shirt was "broken in." Washington was about nine years old when slavery ended, but this experience did more than mark his flesh. The memory left an impression on him.[6]

Black youth like Tilghman, Bethune, and Washington covered themselves in new clothes to go to school after Emancipation—often with the care of parents and community—seeking redress for the "stolen childhoods" of years past, as historian Wilma King described the realities of enslaved youth.[7] School clothes were often armor, forms of protection just as much as assertions of dignity and self-worth for young black people whose childhoods continued to be threatened, even after slavery was legally abolished.

Quite often, black learners were elaborately adorned, with "decorations on the decorations," to borrow from Zora Neale Hurston.[8] Some enjoyed the pleasure derived from the luxury of choice in self-fashioning. Annette Gordon-Reed details this in her memory from the first grade, when her great-great-aunt, who was born on a Texas farm in the late nineteenth century, gifted her several new dresses as she embarked on the journey of desegregating an all-white school in Conroe, Texas, in the mid-1960s. Gordon-Reed writes: "My great-great aunt . . . bought boxes and boxes of dresses, tights, blouses, skirts, and hats from the most upscale department store in the city at the time, Sakowitz. . . . Making sure I was dressed to the nines was her contribution to the civil rights movement."[9] Gordon-Reed's experience was shared by many African American female students, who made up most of the black youth to stand on the front line of school desegregation; they were often the first students chosen by their communities or to volunteer.[10] Black students' will to adorn was a disruptive force, challenging past and present threats seeking to violate their dignity, as learners and as human beings.

African Americans' deep reverence for education expressed itself in how they showed up to learn. And while rigid social norms about clothing could certainly be limiting, aesthetic and sartorial politics, acts of adorning the body, could also be about soulcraft, cultivating an internal vision and virtues that one might express externally in the world. For a great many of them, education was the starting place for thinking up and creating that world, where everyone could have what they needed to live a life of dignity and human flourishing—a world where they could pursue the desires of their hearts without being barred because of who they were. Knowing beauty to be a method, black students dressed themselves in dreams that emerged over generations of African Americans striving within the veil.[11] This book is about that journey, and black students bearing witness to it.

Such recollections were intimate encounters for me. I experienced them as connected to my own identity as a learner and researcher, and I found myself drawing on personal experiences to interpret the stories unveiled in *School Clothes*, just as I have done in this preface. And I quickly learned that I wasn't the only one to find such stories familiar, as evidenced by the archive of historical sources informing this book. I found myself combing through letters, memoirs, eulogies, unexpected email correspondences, poems, newspapers, interviews with my former African American teachers, and more as I pieced together this continuum of black student life—experiences of harm, of beauty, of resistance, and of deep learning. When I received emails from black people around the country describing how parts of *Fugitive Pedagogy* resonated with their own experiences with black teachers, I understood such acts as part of a long tradition of black students working to claim their place in the historical record. When I stumbled across references by African American scholars and artists about their precollegiate education and how it marked them, I transcribed their words, or I contacted them directly. I have attempted to hold on to the plurality of textures represented by their voices, and I often retain their ways of saying, integrating their words with my own, even when they defy "standard" conventions in the English language. For black speech acts do indeed have layered meaning. I have learned to take that meaning seriously.

Introduction

Living and Learning Behind the Veil

Persons born with the veil were, if not clairvoyants, at least clearseeing. They could see through guise and guile. They were considered wise, weird, blessed, tetched, or ancient, depending on the bent of the describer.

—TONI CADE BAMBARA,
"Deep Sights and Rescue Missions"

A Georgia Negro . . . having been born with a caul, attributed to this fact his possession of two spirits, one that remained in his body and one that went about aiding him.

—MELVILLE HERSKOVITS,
The Myth of the Negro Past

MY EIGHTH-GRADE TEACHER shared a story that left an impression on me. Miss Paige, fifty-three years old at the time, explained that she was born with "a caul," what she also referred to as "a veil." I had never heard the term before. In fact, I was unclear how to distinguish it in spelling or meaning from the word that immediately registered in my mind: *a call*, the way people said preachers were called to the pulpit. My face wore a puzzled look, likely squinted eyes and a tilted head. The writer Toni Cade Bambara seemed to have the same reaction when she encountered this folk knowledge as a young girl in New York City during the 1940s. "Some said 'caul,' which I heard as 'call' as in having a calling," Bambara wrote.[1]

Reflecting back on this now, perhaps there is some relation between the homonyms; maybe the caul begets the call. Whatever the case, Miss Paige clarified her statement, having noticed the confused expressions on the faces of twenty-five seventh and eighth graders staring back at her while sitting on either side of the classroom—boys in blue slacks, white shirts, red sweaters and ties, and the girls wearing a combination of plaid jumpers or blue pants, along with white blouses and matching red sweaters and ties. Looking back at us over her glasses, Miss Paige explained, "It's a kind of mask over the baby's face when they're born."

Miss Paige was a black woman from Lake Providence, Louisiana. All her life, she learned that children born with a veil possessed the gift of sight. Those born with a caul were likely to have intuitive abilities about spiritual aspects of the world. Historians and anthropologists documented how some enslaved Africans believed children born with a caul were "gifted with the ability *to see* haunts and spirits," or that they possessed "two spirits, one that remained in [their] body and one that went about aiding [them]."[2] Those born with a veil could sense and detect bad things before they happened. Miss Paige's anecdotes about seeing things—deaths, untrustworthy characters, students who misbehaved when she stepped out of the classroom, but also the near-fatal car accident of her son and his wife—implied the theory was true. I was intrigued. While I was skeptical when Miss Paige initially shared the story, part of me believed her.

I inquired about this encounter in 2019, some eighteen years later, as Miss Paige and I sat in her living room for an interview. Our conversation focused on her journey as a student in Louisiana, where she grew up picking cotton with her parents and siblings, and her lifelong career as an educator at the small black parochial school I attended in Compton, California, from 1992 until 2002. Miss Paige laughed and was utterly surprised. "You remember that?!" she asked, then she proceeded to tell the story in what felt like the exact way she told it when I was twelve years old. Secretly, I wished that I too had been born with this mystic veil. In my twelve-year-old mind, seeing things about the world that others could not seemed like a worthy gift. Though the image of a child coming into the world with their face completely covered by part of the amniotic sac seemed distressing, possibly even deadly, I nevertheless found the mystery of it all quite fascinating.

Miss Paige's classroom would not be the last time I had heard of the veil. The concept returned during my first semester at UC Berkeley in 2006. My African American studies professor assigned W. E. B. Du Bois's *Souls of Black Folk* as our first reading. I immediately thought of my former principal and teacher when I encountered Du Bois's conceptualization of "the veil," which was the psychic manifestation of the socially and materially manifested antiblack color line. The veil caused black people to see with a second sight. Du Bois described it as a "peculiar sensation . . . , this sense of always looking at one's self through the eyes of others, of measuring one's soul by tape of a world that looks on in amused contempt and pity." The connection to Miss Paige's narrative of her own second sight immediately pulled me in to Du Bois's literary brilliance, though I was also amazed with the beauty of what he did between the first and final word of the book. Like many, I immediately found Du Bois's frame for thinking about the interior world of black life to be generative. He helped me reach new depths of understanding about my individual life as tethered with a collection of striving souls in a world of antiblack domination. It helped me see things about my life as an African American learner on new terms, with a fresh perspective.

Like me, Du Bois encountered the veil in a classroom. This small fact was not lost on me. His experience in the racially mixed New England classroom in Great Barrington, Massachusetts, during the 1870s invites an examination of the veil and second sight that considers their distinct meaning for black student life. Du Bois's social alienation sets in after a white female classmate refuses his friendship because of his known difference as a black student. This peer encounter caused the veil to descend. Du Bois described the event as follows:

> I remember well when the shadow swept across me. I was a little thing, away up in the hills of New England. . . . In a wee wooden schoolhouse, something put it into the boys' and girls' heads to buy gorgeous visiting-cards—ten cents a package—and exchange. The exchange was merry, till one girl, a tall newcomer, refused my card,—refused it peremptorily, with a glance. Then it dawned upon me with a certain suddenness that I was different from the others; or like, mayhap, in heart and life and longing, but shut out from their world by a vast veil. I had thereafter no desire to tear down that veil, to creep through; I held all beyond it in common contempt, and lived above it in a region of blue sky and great wondering shadows.[3]

Du Bois gradually realized what his difference, as a black student in New England, meant to those around him. He explained, "I realized that some folks, a few, even several, actually considered my brown skin a misfortune; once or twice I became painfully aware that some human beings even thought it was a crime." And as he came of age, Du Bois would continue to live his life in the shadow of the veil.[4]

Miss Paige's caul became the context for my comprehension of Du Bois's abstractions regarding black spiritual strivings. Every time I read about double consciousness, I am transported back to the story shared by Miss Paige and generally reminded of the role education has played in conditioning the veiled existence of black people. What's more, Du Bois's use of history, empirical data, autobiography, and fiction to unmask the embattled realities of black life in *Souls of Black Folk* also became instructive for my own studies, in college and beyond; the convergence of Du Bois's writing and Miss Paige's story gave me permission to collapse false dichotomies of high and low knowledge, academic and folk ways of knowing—knowledge in school and knowledge that black folks carried with them. Parsing through the intricacies of black life as it is lived—in the interstices between such divergent, often adversarial realms of the world—gradually became my subject and mode of study.

Born within the veil, black Americans' psychosocial existence derives much of its character from the political economic realities of the antiblack color line, a partitioned social order in which African-descendant people have been perpetually relegated to the outermost margins of society. As the black studies scholar Sylvia Wynter observed, W. E. B. Du Bois, and others like the Caribbean historian Elsa Goveia, "emphasized the way in which the code of 'Race' or the Color Line, functions to systematically *pre-determine* the sharply unequal re-distribution of the collectively produced global resources; and, therefore, the correlation of the racial ranking rule with the Rich/Poor rule."[5] Such stratification occurred in material terms—via segregated schools and water fountains, racialized poverty, and police violence—but it also persists through limited access and opportunity in more elusive and symbolic ways. As a people forged through this persecution—of racial chattel slavery and its ever-unfolding aftermath—black people had a distinct way of seeing and knowing the world. As Du Bois explained in 1903, the veil's interior was "a spiritual world in which ten thousand thousand Americans live and strive."[6]

From this place, black people operate from their gifts of second sight, from their twoness: "an American, a Negro . . . two unreconciled strivings." And this double consciousness had important implications for the identity of African American scholars and black studies. For the purposes of this book, the classification might be restated in terms particular to black learners: *a student, a Negro; two unreconciled strivings*. Writing about the souls of black students explicitly, Du Bois observed, "And yet in this wide land to-day a thousand thousand dark children brood before this same temptation, and feel its cold and shuddering arms. For them, perhaps, some one will some day lift the Veil."[7] Writing more than a decade later, he recalled the work of noble educators in his own life who worked to bring about some relief. Writing of his late teen years, when he was a student at Fisk University, Du Bois explained, "I studied eagerly under teachers who bent in subtle sympathy, feeling themselves some shadow of the Veil and lifting it gently that we darker souls might peer through to other worlds."[8]

But the veil would never be fully lifted. Black students continue to bear witness to their lives on the black side of the color line. And per tradition, they have had to use and repurpose their experiences as armor for protection. Here, I am following black cultural critic Kevin Young, who insists that we not think of the veil as only a burden or hindrance: "The gift may also be a curse, but second sight is one of the qualities necessary for being . . . critical in our reading of the culture all around us. It is important for us not just to lift the veil, or look behind the curtain, but also to embrace the powerful notion of vision and the vantage point the caul provides."[9]

Like Young, Toni Cade Bambara explained that as a girl, she "learned early on through Eldersay, namely, that the seventh son . . . who was born with a 'veil' . . . was enhanced by it, was gifted, not afflicted (unless the parents or godparents failed to perform particular rites with the caul, in which case the cauled might see ghosts)." But for Bambara, even this seemed to be no big deal, "for a people who've come through the Middle Passage are surely predisposed to see ghosts, right?"[10]

School Clothes: A Collective Memoir of Black Student Witness is a book that sits with the repository of knowledge gained from first-person accounts of black students—what they saw and documented as learners living behind the veil. Black students' witness has long been cultural armor: protection for themselves and those that were to come after, aiding black students to notice haunts and violent forces in this world, that they might be clear-seeing. This kind of witness might provide covering and help black students see through guise and guile in their efforts to navigate a world that is often more hostile than hospitable.

This book is a modest attempt to follow Du Bois and black students behind the veil, as a site for excavation and sociohistorical insight, and to render an account of black students' legacy as learners and strivers. Such an account is offered as a collective endeavor. In form it is the cobbling together of individual narratives of black students across generations. Until now, there has yet to be a single historical work devoted to the study of black students' experiences, where their voices are privileged as the primary source for historical interpretation. And yet, such a work is necessary to clarify their peculiar relationship to American education. *School Clothes* provides resources not only for black students themselves as they construct their academic identities but also for those who love and care for them.

Foundational to this book is a simple premise: black students have a way of *seeing* school and education in the United States that is distinct and distinguishable. Looking out from this historically situated perspective reveals a story of educational domination and, simultaneously, one of fugitive learning: a countervailing educational tradition set against an antiblack status quo in American schooling. This way of seeing education, indeed of seeing the world, is part of a rich tradition among black students, even as it continues to be muffled and omitted in dominant story lines—even while some attempt to drown out its memory, noisily disrupting the transmission of said tradition.

The black pupil has a particular gift of second sight. Their witness is the point of entry for this book: a looking from the eyes of those who left some record of what they saw, of their teachers, of their own actions as participatory learners, of the worlds within and beyond the veil. Black students' witnessing constitutes a privileged perspective for the historical scholar but also for those concerned with what it means *to be* a black student: their watchfulness to document, their looking at the world in critical ways because of an awareness of their collective subjugation as individual learners. Such posture continues to carry important meaning. To borrow from poet and scholar Elizabeth Alexander, black students carry a historian's sense about the need to correct the record. Their insistence on remembering was also their way of saying, "*I am black alive and looking back at you.*"[11] The insights that motivated black students' critical posture of "looking back" are stories that might clothe those who continue to know school and the world as a place of antiblack persecution but who are also committed to envisioning and pursuing educational justice.

Black students' witness provides equipment for living—school clothes—cultural armor for a world fraught with deceit and shallow visions of who we are and the crises we face.

THE BLACK STUDENT BODY

The black student body carries distinguishable marks. African Americans are the one group of learners for whom education and criminality were deemed equal transgressions, by both laws and lawlike social customs. Eighteenth- and nineteenth-century antiliteracy laws, which targeted free and enslaved black people in the South, similar to the violent resistance and surveillance of black education in northern states, reflected deeply engrained antagonisms in American education. This sociolegal history, which amounted to an ambient antiblackness in laws and educational policies, mattered greatly to the development of black student identities then, and this legacy of educational domination continues to have lived consequences today.

Through this history and social forces, "the black student" has been constructed as a distinct subject position—one defined through competing narratives on both sides of the veil. This subject position is made and remade through images documenting black students being escorted by the National Guard to desegregate schools while facing violent white mobs—images shown ritualistically on an annual basis. It is also reproduced through ongoing debates about race and achievement, among other educational "crises," that construct black students as *the* problem population in schools. Such contemporary discourses are always informed by and interacting with the aforementioned historical metaphors and scripts. Simply put, no other group of students must contend with (or make sense of themselves relative to) such a long history of their education being criminalized through laws and violently suppressed.

Suppression of black American education is older than the United States itself. Colonial South Carolina passed its Slave Code of 1740 in response to the Stono Slave Revolt of 1739, where it was believed that the rebel slaves used the written word to organize their insurrection. Writing was listed among the Slave Code's many prohibitions. South Carolina legislators expressed, "The having of slaves taught to write, or suffering them to be employed in writing, may be attended with *great inconveniences*." The law was extended to include free blacks in 1800. Colonial Georgia also made reading and writing illegal for the enslaved in 1770.[12] These laws thus set an important precedent for what were to be the riddled lives of black students—a crucial precedent indeed.

Such laws and anti-literacy sentiments proliferated in southern states leading up to the Civil War. Virginia's law, as revised in 1831, declared, "That all meetings of free negroes or mulattoes, at any schoolhouse, church, meeting-house or other place for teaching them reading or writing, either in the day or night, under whatever pretext, shall be deemed and considered as an unlawful assembly." For this offense, the law authorized whippings, "at the discretion of any justice of the peace, not exceeding twenty lashes."[13] Missouri's General Assembly passed an act in 1847 stating that "no person shall keep or teach any school for the instruction of negroes or mulattoes, in reading or writing, in this State."[14] Some slaveholding Native American tribes also established anti-literacy laws. In 1841 the Cherokee Nation declared: "*Be it enacted by the National Council*, That from and after the passage of this act, it shall not be lawful for any person or persons whatever, to teach any free negro or negroes not of Cherokee blood, or any slave belonging to any citizen of the Nation, to read or write."[15]

Such fierce opposition to black education over the years was accompanied by equally hostile—though contradictory—speculations about black intelligence. Generation after generation of black students have had to *prove* their intellectual capacity as representatives of their race. Such was the case for the prodigious Phillis Wheatley, author of *Poems on Various Subjects, Religious and Moral*, a groundbreaking text that made her the first black person and woman in the United States to publish a book of poems. The specter of Wheatley's 1772 literary trial continues to haunt black student life.

A panel of eighteen distinguished white men in Boston—the majority of whom enslaved black people—examined Wheatley in October 1772. The enslaved girl would have been in her late teens. The panel's charge was to verify whether Wheatley possessed the intellectual capacity to have written the poems her owner sought to publish in her name. But, of course, Phillis Wheatley's individual intellect was not the only thing on trial. A specimen to be picked and prodded, the girl represented the whole of the Negro world in the white imagination. As Henry Louis Gates Jr. aptly noted, such "rituals of validation scarcely died with Phillis Wheatley."[16] Just over a decade later, a soon-to-be president Thomas Jefferson classified Wheatley's poetry as "below the dignity of criticism." As he saw it, blacks were "in reason much inferior" to whites, and in imagination they were "dull, tasteless, and anomalous." By nature, Jefferson explained, African-descendant people were incapable of producing anything that could be called real poetry, and the same for arts and sciences more broadly. Jefferson, who created the precursor to tax-supported universal schooling, insisted that black students' minds were inferior to those of their white (and Native) counterparts in the newly formed United States.

George Allen faced an examination similar to Wheatley's as a twelve-year-old student at New York's African Free School in

1828. Charles Andrews, the white schoolmaster, tasked students with writing essays for the "American Convention for Promotion of the Abolition of Slavery" in Baltimore. He would select the best writings to represent the school. But Allen's essay was so stellar that Andrews questioned whether the student produced the prose independently. Andrews required Allen to prove he was capable of such literary composition.

Ironically, in his original essay, Allen referenced frequent visits to his school "by gentlemen from the South, and other parts of the country," during which he and his schoolmates were regularly "called upon and examined by them upon the several branches that [they] were acquainted with."[17] They were regularly called on to perform their intelligence before skeptical audiences. As historian Crystal Lynn Webster explains, since the early nineteenth century, New York's African Free School "introduced public examinations in which the brightest and most agreeable students would present speeches and scripted readings in front of an audience of benefactors and interested guests." Webster documents how some abolitionists encouraged naysayers to "perform a pilgrimage to New York and at the shrine of education recant their principles and confess that the poor despised African is as capable of every intellectual improvement as themselves."[18]

But Allen expressed hope for more than convincing individual spectators that black students were equal to whites. He set his eyes on a larger prize. He hoped he and his classmates' academic performances would help the cause of abolition. In his essay, he conveyed a dream that one day "the blessings that we enjoy, shall be the happy portion of all our colored brethren."[19]

Andrews mailed the student's essay along with a letter signed by reputable white men authenticating that "the said Address is the genuine, unaided production of George R. Allen, *a very black boy of pure African descent*, who is now between twelve and thirteen years old, and was born in this city." In addition to this letter, signed by five white men from the New York Manumission Society, the schoolmaster described a special examination he administered to assess Allen's intellect. Andrews "required the boy to take a slate and pencil, and in half an hour to produce a piece of poetry on any subject he pleased. The boy took the slate *with a good deal of trembling*, and said he would try to write a verse on 'Slavery.'" Allen was then "locked up in a room alone, by the Master," where he would produce this poem.

ON SLAVERY.

Slavery! oh, thou cruel stain,
Thou dost fill my heart with pain:
See my brother, there he stands
Chain'd by slavery's cruel bands.

Could we not feel a brother's woes,
Relieve the wants he undergoes;
Snatch him from slavery's cruel smart,
And to him freedom's joy impart?

—GEORGE R. ALLEN,
aged 12 years, Oct. 21st, 1828

The content of Allen's poem is inspiring, but the form is also striking: a lyric poem of two stanzas, both composed of four lines and each taking a distinct analytical mode. The first quatrain is a moment of apostrophe—the young man addressing the subject of slavery directly, as though it were itself a person—whereas the second quatrain switches to an interrogative and philosophical mode—in which Allen turns to the subjunctive (*Could we . . . ?*). A gifted reader and a dreamer, the young man moves from *what is* to *what might be*—a perceptive analysis of the present to a utopian striving for a world after slavery. Interesting to note, the poet moves from seven syllables per line in the first stanza to eight syllables per line in the second quatrain, changing meters to make more room for his own wonderings. A little more space for his own meditations. Simply put, this twelve-year-old black boy could write. And it seems that Allen's poem met the standard. But white suspicion of black intelligence reappeared across the generations.[20]

In 1834, Noyes Academy was founded in Canaan, New Hampshire, as a coed institution, permitting white and black students to enroll. To cultivate public approval, the school's administrators framed its admission of black scholars as an experiment. They insisted, "If, as some assert, they are naturally and irremediably stupid, and incorrigibly vicious, then the experiment we propose will prove this fact; and will in any event furnish valuable data."[21] Despite such intentions, white members of the town destroyed the school in July 1835. Black students were violently attacked and subsequently forced to leave the state.

While violent repression of black education was particularly pronounced in the US South because of anti-literacy laws and ideology, cases like that of Noyes Academy reveal that the strategic underdevelopment of black education was never confined to any particular region. In 1831 New Haven residents, including Yale professors and students, protested and successfully blocked the founding of a black college in their city. They urged that "the founding of colleges for educating colored youth is an unwarranted and dangerous undertaking . . . and it ought to be discouraged."[22]

African American students' awareness of their people's ongoing persecution in education, and in society more broadly, played a central role in the formation of their academic identities. This is particularly evident in the life of Charlotte Forten, who dreamed of being an anti-slavery lecturer in her teenage years during the 1850s. Forten took comfort in poems by Phillis Wheatley while witnessing the daily insults made on black people, even in Massachusetts, where her Philadelphia family sent her to attend a racially mixed school. Writing in her diary on July 28, 1854, Forten recorded the following: "This evening read 'Poems of Phillis Wheatley,' an African slave, who lived in Boston at the time of the Revolution. She was a wonderfully gifted woman, and many of her poems are very beautiful. *Her character and genius afford a striking proof* of the falseness of the assertion made by some that hers is an inferior race."[23] Forten recognized that, like Wheatley, the condition of her color meant that she was always on trial. She engaged Wheatley's poems with second sight, one framed by an awareness of her shared vulnerability with the poet and, likewise, her role in a shared struggle against the ongoing condemnation of black life.

The noise of antiblackness caused Forten to struggle with the impulse to always criticize herself and other black people for falling short, even as she knew it was human nature. After listening to a black woman's public reading of Shakespeare in November 1855, with which Forten was "not very much pleased," she offered: "I wish colored persons would not attempt to do anything of the kind unless they can compare favorably with others.—But I know that I should not presume to criticize; and most sincerely hope if she has talent, it may be cultivated,—and that she may succeed in her vocation—reflecting credit upon herself and her race."[24] The burden of representation was one shared by black students during and after Forten's time. This they understood to be their reality. The load was heavy and the stakes were high.

White hostilities persisted after the Civil War, a time when African Americans made unprecedented strides in education, having led the charge to establish the first public education system in the southern states. This hostility manifested in a variety of ways, not the least of which were school burnings. More than six hundred black schools were burned in the South between 1864 and 1876.[25] And angry white Americans continued to burn down black schools well into the twentieth century. Novelist Alice Walker, born in 1944, learned how her father, Willie Lee Walker, a sharecropper, organized the first African American school in their town of Eatonton, Georgia—the Wards Chapel School—before it was set ablaze. She learned "how he walked everywhere talking to parents" and raising support to build the school before it was "burned down by whites."[26] Walker learned how her father "had to humble himself to get use of an abandoned shack for the school to be in until another school was built." How her father had to appeal to the white people in town as African Americans in Eatonton worked to rebuild—like so many other black communities—explaining that "without knowing how to read black people could not properly care for white people's children. If a child needed medicine, an illiterate person might not be able to read the label on the medicine bottle." Walker learned that her father, like many before and after him, attempted to narrate a vision of African Americans' interest in education in a manner that converged with the interest of white people, as a strategy of making some progress, as some measure of protection—hoping the newly built school would not be burned down like the previous one.

Black education also faced strategic ideological underdevelopment by white elites, beginning in the nineteenth century and continuing well into the twentieth, as the number of African American schools continued to grow. Rich white philanthropists and social reformers gradually gained near complete control over the institutional development of black education by the end of World War I. They advocated for a practical education, one focused on menial work as opposed to higher intellectual training and political leadership.[27] As historian Horace Mann Bond explained, public education for black Americans "depended upon the social and economic utility which this education was thought to have for the class of white persons in control of legislation and finance."[28] He continued: "Whether this control has been that by slave-owners, humanitarians, planters, financiers, or white farmers and workers, it is obvious that each has wished to provide for Negroes an education designed to meet its own concept of Negro status in the social and economic order." Though Bond writes specifically about Alabama, his observation speaks to the general manipulation and underdevelopment of black education, particularly after Reconstruction, across state and regional boundaries.

Consider what these circumstances meant for the educational goals of black students and their families. Learning, for African American people, has been a distinct task because antiblackness is so endemic to the ecological context of the national educational landscape. African American students' education was burdened by having to "prove" they had human souls, that they were reasoning, rational subjects, but these scholars also had to navigate ongoing, irrational hostilities directed toward their individual and collective strivings. These hostilities manifested time and again, as Du Bois pointed out, in "ashes, insult, and blood"—ongoing physical and symbolic forms of violence, both during slavery and in the periods that followed. What might this living history mean for students then and now, as they come to understand the form and function of their education in the American social order? What exactly does it mean to know oneself as *a black student* against the backdrop of this past propping up the present?

Black students carry the weight of this past with them. Whether named or unnamed, the marks of this past function as resources—good, bad, or otherwise—that condition students' developmental process. They influence how black students come to know themselves as racialized learners—identities that are always historically situated.[29] As historian Vanessa Siddle Walker writes, "African American children are not without history, though discussions about them are often ahistorical—as though the children just arrived on the educational scene in the 1970s with nothing but a plethora of problems."[30]

I am reminded here of a student writing of his family's history of enslavement in 1935. Bill Parker wrote a poem about his great-great-grandfather during a ten-week unit of study on "Progress of the Negro" in his third-grade class in Hampton, Virginia. Reflecting on the legacy of slavery, Parker pointed to the suppression of black education as having been a key feature of the peculiar institution. He notes how the denial of black education was bound up with violence, forced labor, and the disruption of black families.

> *They made him carry cotton by the ton,*
> *And even shipped his little son,*
> *They didn't teach him to read or write,*
> *Or even let him out of sight.*

In addition to their written assignments, Parker and his classmates interviewed the grandmother of their teacher, one of the oldest members in their community and a formerly enslaved woman. Slavery and educational suppression were not merely part of the racial past shared by Parker and his classmates but discernable aspects of family lineage—both for the students and their teacher, Miss Tamah Richardson. This legacy was part of the stories that marked them, contributing to the substance of their racialized and academic identities.[31]

Black students' individual aspirations were always bound up with the larger struggles of their race. They learned from family members, and often black teachers, that their mission was to pursue education because it would help them refute the lies told about them and their people. As evidenced by George Allen's and Charlotte Forten's writing in the antebellum North, and Bill Parker's in the Jim Crow South, black students understood the frame of their individual journeys to be part of a broader collective striving for freedom and justice. A disposition that resonates for black students across time and place.

To be clear, black students' mood and orientation toward their collective mission were not only somber but often struck a celebratory chord. African American learners were proud to stand in the gap and relished the idea of their education being used in service of their people. In their 1929 yearbook, students at Washington,

DC's National Training School for Women and Girls identified classmates who were most likely to be leaders in the fight for racial justice. Katherine Allen gained the confidence of her peers for this superlative category. Inspired by their lessons in Negro history, Katherine became a "race agitator." In fact, "Many race agitators have been discovered," the young women explained, and "Miss Allen, a senior, is sure to be another Sojourner Truth."[32] Heroic figures like Truth were introduced to students through the alternative scripts of knowledge passed on by black teachers.

Such stories and systems of representation implied a countervailing tradition that also marked their mission as budding scholars. While dominant school curricula studiously excluded references to black historical figures, especially the stories of fugitive slaves and abolitionists like Sojourner Truth, the National Training School's founder, Nannie Helen Burroughs, introduced students to textbooks by the black historian Dr. Carter G. Woodson, which he began publishing in 1922. Woodson also founded Negro History Week in 1926 (celebrated today as Black History Month). According to Burroughs's students, they had been "helped" and "inspired" by their studies of black people's persistent struggle for freedom. They likely found the story of Truth, as it appeared in Woodson's textbook, to be encouraging. Truth was a fugitive and fierce abolitionist who "acquired miraculous power" through her ability to "stir audiences with her heavy voice, quaint language and homely illustrations." Truth's contributions to the cause of black freedom went beyond the words she uttered. She also "served the Union army as a messenger and spy."[33] Thus, contrary to the American curriculum, black people played an active role in the war to achieve their emancipation. The training school students understood their education and their mission as Negro youth through the frame of black folk heroes like Sojourner Truth. Evidence of this tradition clarifies that the black student, as a distinct subject position, is marked by more than antiblack persecution. A continuum of resistance formed an equally forceful tradition shaping black lifeworlds behind the veil, and it contributed greatly to the substance of African American education.

Remember these names: Minnijean Brown (16 years old). Elizabeth Eckford (15 years old). Ernest Green (16 years old). Thelma Mothershed (16 years old). Melba Joy Pattillo (15 years old). Gloria Ray (15 years old). Terrence Roberts (15 years old). Jefferson Thomas (14 years old). Carlotta Walls (14 years old). These students are collectively known as the Little Rock Nine. The image of the National Guard, bearing rifles, escorting nine black students up the steps of Little Rock's Central High School in 1957, and the white mobs terrorizing them all the while, was televised for all the world to see. Ruby Bridges of New Orleans followed in their steps. The iconic image of that six-year-old child taunted by hateful chants and killed in effigy by white bystanders as she attempted to desegregate a New Orleans elementary school in 1960 forms part of a collective truamatic historical memory. While news cameras revealed the clash between antiblack hatred and African Americans' spiritual striving, the camera's aperture could not capture the vantage from within the veil. Only the witness of black students can do that.

Such stories, and the historical images that circulate and depict them, form a visual narrative that cannot be unseen. The Little Rock Nine and Ruby Bridges are just two of many spectacles where we see black students passing through "the bloodstained gate," to borrow from Frederick Douglass. For many, it is difficult to imagine how and where these children found the courage to accept such a mission. But parsing becomes easier when we listen to black students give their own accounts—when we listen to voices like that of Carlotta Walls. As one of the Little Rock Nine, she emphasized: "We were standing on the shoulders of others. . . . We had Negro History Week in the segregated Black schools. And I was always proud to read more and hear about what African Americans or Negroes or Coloreds did for this country. . . . I knew I was standing on their shoulders."[34]

Black students' lives were wedged in the interstices of competing visions. The antiblack color line took on real, material, political, economic form. It was an unavoidable reality, one their parents and teachers could scarcely protect them from. It was deafening, always working to outspeak any other vision of the world. Such realities in the physical world had psychic implications: there was no way for students to completely block out the noise. Corresponding with the physical partitioning of the world—black codes, the racialized allocation of resources, separate schools—was also a psychic veil, behind which students saw the world from their distinct positionality. From this place, black students were tasked with mastering an art of learning that included an awareness of this world-structuring form of persecution while being adamantly set against it. For black students, learning and study were tasks marked by their color and condemnation in this way.

Learning the rudiments of reading, writing, and arithmetic; the art of rhetoric; or classic languages and literature were never their singular curricular object. Black students had to learn *how to see the world*, by necessity, from a distinctly black perspective. Their learning was also about unlearning. Their veiled perspective had to be honed to see through an upside-down world wrought by racism—a way of seeing informed by an awareness of the close interlockings of chattel slavery, black dispossession, and the established orders of knowledge—learning objectives set apart from the standardized protocols of the American school. This of course had to do with disrupting white conceptions about who could achieve mastery of knowledge, who could be sources of knowledge, who had the authority to interpret and express truth about the conditions of human life, but also whose aesthetic judgment could determine what was and was not beautiful. Black students' mission was to live a life in refusal of such established systems of knowledge in a world of white supremacy—a world that marked them as the antithesis of reason, beauty, justice, and all that was perceivably good in and for humanity. Given this, their education had to be about seeking out and modeling new ways of being in and toward the world. Their task was about worlding: crafting an image for life on earth, informed by their insights from behind the veil.

From Phillis Wheatley in the eighteenth century, to Charlotte Forten and George Allen in the nineteenth century, to Katherine Allen and Bill Parker in the twentieth century, as well as many unnamed and unheralded before and after them, black students have had to learn how to strive for a new world while marked by such powerfully competing social and intellectual forces in education. It is this history that coheres what might be thought of as *the black student body*: a distinct constituency of learners whose shared past of criminalized education, then confinement in materially inferior segregated schools, and finally contemporary experiences of school violence and neglect, engenders a suspicion and necessary vigilance of the "official" curriculum and protocols of the American education system.

This book is about their witness and their traditions.

A COLLECTIVE MEMOIR

The witness requires an audience. Thus, I am compelled to listen to and take seriously what black students have had to say. Heeding Du Bois, I approach black students as more than "their captious critic," as more than their "cold and scientific investigator, with microscope and probe."[35] For so long, black students have been written about; they have been picked at and prodded as specimens for study. They have been held in prolonged gaze, and rarely have those gazing felt the risk of black students writing or looking back.[36] Meanwhile, black students have always been watching, and speaking, and writing, and singing—striving to give an account of themselves as well as the entangled relations and social dynamics conditioning their worlds. I find black students insisting that they have always been not just mere objects of history but instead its subjects. Their narratives take the form of a "communal utterance." Given their shared vulnerability and how it has structured their experiences, the black student witness across generations renders "a collective tale, rather than merely an individual's autobiography."[37] *School Clothes* foregrounds this chorus.

This book takes the form of what I have come to call "collective memoir." There are two primary reasons for framing it as such, the first being methodology. The book is composed of a patchwork of more than one hundred first-person accounts by African Americans about their primary and secondary school experiences across the nineteenth and twentieth centuries. Their stories are stitched together and emplotted into a general narrative that transcends any individual perspective. In this way, the form intentionally blurs lines between particular stories to emphasize themes generalizable toward an articulation of the black student as a historically derived and socially distinct subject position. I rely on black students' memoirs, autobiographies, poems, diaries, oral histories, and inscriptions in yearbooks, as well as a variety of miscellaneous sources containing their voices, as portals into their interior worlds. By taking story elements from various autobiographical and historical accounts, then fashioning them in a thematic arrangement, I offer a "redescription" of these events in relationship to one another.[38] Through these accounts, we get at the essence of what black students have articulated about their experiences of school and the world from behind the veil. They leave a concrete record with intentionality. They insist their version of events be part of the historical transcript. They trust their own interpretations. And so do I.

Black students' witness is a gift. As a scholar of history, I am interested in student witnessing as an expansion of the archive. It is the research subject at hand, but it is also reflective of my own mode of study. This latter point brings me to the second motivation for framing the work as collective memoir.

There is no way to write such a narrative account, which amounts to something like a biography of black student life without it also being in some way autobiographical. Thinking with black women scholars who have long insisted on naming your place as a site from when and where one enters the room—to riff on Anna Julia Cooper—I allow my personal insights to function as an extension of the historical record that is the subject of this book, because that is exactly what it is.[39] Indeed, I have written this book from what philosopher George Yancy has called the "site of exposure."[40] My particular experiences as the student of nearly all African American teachers, in all-black or predominantly black schools my entire life, until college, are deeply instructive for how and why I study the history of black education.

I came of age studying not only what was required by our schoolbooks but also the stories my teachers shared about black people's persecution *and* protracted struggle in education and society. To suggest that I am reasoning from nowhere or only from the printed words that populate historical sources would simply be untrue. Similar to this introduction, small moments will appear where my own first-person accounts or those of my teachers are woven into the narrative. My experience adds to the historical record of black student voices and also acts as an interpretive resource.

Memoir and autobiography are never solely about an individual author in isolation. In their attempt to construct a narrative of the self ("I"), such literary forms are always tasked with giving an account of the social relations that produced the subject.[41] Just as my own story is always one that precedes me, the same can be said for each of the black students whose narratives appear in this book. Our individual stories are part of a continuum of consciousness. I oscillate between the individual and collective voices because either alone is insufficient. Weaving them together clarifies the depth and breadth of black student experiences. To truly appreciate their individual stories requires that we also listen to the chorus.

Memory, at its best, is a shared enterprise. The students appearing in this book deftly name and account for the social conditions that shaped their individuated experiences as a collective group—as a black student body. They explicitly name their experiences as part and parcel of a collective journey of black students or "the race." They render accounts of their emergence as always deeply embedded in social relations of their group, bounded by their collective striving and their shared vulnerability. But this articulation of a shared experience does not come at the expense of their own individual styles, talents, and dreams. The marks they carry are shared, but there are distinctions in how they communicate and name them. At times, I intentionally emphasize such distinctions and individuality. Black students are not fungible objects, and there is no desire to flatten them into one-dimensional characters. In fact, my intention is quite the opposite.

School Clothes is made up of hand-me-down stories, pieces of memory that have been passed on, stitched together, and offered as something to be taken up again, as though for the first time. Every generation of black learners must rediscover the beautiful and the terrible realities of black education for themselves, just as every generation of African Americans must rediscover the legacy of slavery for the first time.[42] This is a fact of blackness. Such stories are more than events of the past. They constitute living history: a past always sitting in the classroom beside us. Black students' educational strivings have always had to do with more than just the here and now. By necessity, they have been forward- and backward-looking in the same breath.

True to this tradition, black students have been summoned into the room and asked to revisit the past. This includes those who lived during the time of slavery, including free blacks like Charlotte Forten Grimké and Alexander Crummell, as well as children who were chattel, like Susie King Taylor and William Sanders Scarborough; students of the first generations born in "the afterlife of slavery," like William Holtzclaw and Mary McLeod Bethune; and students who came of age during the era of Jim Crow: Zora Neale Hurston, Malcolm X, Yvonne Hutchinson, Ralph Ellison, Ida Mae Holland, Richard Wright, Angela Davis, and John Bracey.[43]

Bearing witness is always a ritual of return. One returns to the past, to what happened, to help achieve justice in some way. Weighing their narratives against one another—my own insights against theirs, and vice versa—I hope to move toward some elevated understanding about the relations that have sutured the divergent experiences of black students in our nation's schools. In full disclosure, *School Clothes* offers no simple prescriptions for what to do in classrooms *to fix* black students or the problems they face. It makes no recommendations for school policy. It does, however, bring complex dynamics in black student life to the fore. It recognizes intimate knowledge black scholars accumulated about themselves, the world as they found it, and, indeed, the world as they desired it to be.

Chapter 1

Going to School North of Slavery

There are many public school systems in the North where Negroes are admitted and tolerated, but they are not educated; they are crucified.

—W. E. B. DU BOIS, "Does the Negro Need Separate Schools?"

GEORGE GARNET JUMPED from a second-story window, clinging to a freedom as fragile as it was life-giving. It was late summer 1829 when he made this split-second decision to evade the slave catcher's grip, landing in the narrow alley between his family's residence at 137 Leonard Street in New York City and the Crummell family's home. Feet scrambling, George ran through the yard, and to his surprise, the neighbor's dog—usually scrappy, "ill-tempered," and "the terror of the neighborhood"—was dead silent and thankfully caused no disruption to the fugitive's escape.[1]

So many thoughts flashed through George's mind: his wife, Elizabeth; his children, Henry and Eliza. But in the moment all George could do was try, as best he could, to refute the property claims grasping at his life, even as his former master, Colonel William Spencer of Kent County, Maryland, was dead and in the grave. Colonel Spencer, who owned George, just as he'd owned George's father, died in March 1822. Enslaved people on the Darby plantation knew separation from their families was eminent as

Spencer's estate was divided among his heirs. It took only a short while for the Garnets to plot and execute their escape. The family gained permission to attend the funeral of a slave on a nearby Delaware plantation. They never returned. The Garnets escaped via the Delaware River, first to Philadelphia and eventually to New York City. As early as May 1822, the colonel's brother, Isaac Spencer, paid slave catchers James Woodall and John Newcombe and his brother, Jervis Spencer, to find those who absconded and the horses they took with them. All property was to be recovered and accounted for. By January 1825 five of Spencer's runaways had been apprehended.[2] News of these captures reached the Garnets, causing them to constantly look over their shoulders. So on that summer day in 1829, after seven years, the Garnets' freedom continued to require the activity of escape.

Garnet—the family's new name—was part of the plot—their effort to be known as something more than what was recorded in the estate ledger and records of Colonel Spencer and the Darby plantation. George and Henrietta Trusty became George and Elizabeth Garnet to conceal their identity and assert control over their bodies. The threat of capture haunted George even before his family's escape. As a child, George learned that his father "was an African chief and warrior, and in a tribal fight he was captured and sold to slave-traders who brought him to this continent." Fragmented pieces of this family history likely circled in George's mind as he jumped out of that window, twenty feet from the ground. George, in such a state of desperation, hoped no one but that silent dog had seen or heard him.[3]

Alexander Crummell, then a ten-year-old black boy, spotted the white men approaching the Garnet family's Leonard Street residence. Having some awareness of the Garnets' status as fugitives, Crummell got an uneasy feeling while playing in front of his home. Status aside, unfamiliar white men approaching the home of a black family looked and felt out of place under any circumstance. Moments later he saw Mr. Garnet—the father of his friend and schoolmate, Henry Highland Garnet—jumping from a window. The spectacle of that "fearful leap" was terrifying for Crummell. Mr. Garnet was "a perfect Apollo, in form and figure" and someone the boy deeply respected. The scenario impressed itself on Crummell's memory, marking him for the remainder of his life.[4] To see an adult who held such a towering position in a child's mind reduced to such despair because someone claimed them as their property, but also because they had no legal recourse on which to stand and defend themselves, was crushing.

Henry Highland Garnet, fourteen years old at the time, was away when the white slave hunters came to claim him and his family. He worked as a cabin boy aboard a ship traveling between New York City, Alexandria, Virginia, and Washington, DC. His parents allowed him to take this role because being on the ships kept him moving and out of sight. Being stationary could be dangerous. Henry's mother and sister were in New York City when the slave catchers arrived. His mother successfully slipped away having recognized one of the men approaching her home. She was later apprehended and released only after abolitionists purchased her freedom. Henry's teenage sister did not share his luck.

Eliza Garnet was apprehended from the African Free School on Mulberry Street—no more than a ten-minute walk from Leonard Street—where Alexander Crummell and Henry Garnet were also enrolled (though male and female students attended separate classes).[5] Eliza stood trial and was released after community members successfully defended her. They testified that Eliza resided in New York at the time the men claiming her as property declared she was enslaved in Maryland, and that she had been enrolled in school for more than two years prior to the event in question. Irrespective of the outcome, Eliza's encounter was surely horrifying for her and her classmates. Some were fugitives themselves, and others had family members who had "illegally" escaped slavery.[6] Both home and school were violated by the intrusion of the slave master's reach, even in the North. The Garnets' encounter disrupts notions that the borders between "slave states" and "free states," North and South, were anything more than prosthetic.

In fact, when the Garnets arrived in New York, slavery was still legal in the state. Prior to the completion of New York's gradual emancipation plan in 1827, there were more slaves in New York City than any other urban center outside the southern states. The state moved toward complete emancipation while putting in place mechanisms to control and contain the free black population. "Through the provisions of the gradual emancipation laws and the 1821 suffrage law that disenfranchised the majority of the black community," writes historian Leslie Harris, "white New Yorkers selectively enforced republican virtues. By the end of the period of emancipation in 1827, whites had legally, economically, and socially designated black people as a separate, dependent, and unequal group within the New York City community."[7]

What happened to the Garnets was legitimized by the antiblack political landscape outlined above, and it was far from uncommon. James McCune Smith, another student at the African Free School, recalled that while New York abolished slavery in 1827, the state continued to be "slave hunting grounds." He described how "there went prowling about the State, in one-horse buggies, or in sloops on the rivers, wretches in abundance who would snatch up a colored child and run down to Virginia and make a handsome sum by the operation." Smith described such conditions of black life from a very personal place, having himself been emancipated through New York law only two years prior to the Garnet family's encounter. Yet Smith's mother continued to be enslaved as she had been brought to New York with her master—who was also Smith's father—from South Carolina prior to him being born. Smith laments, "Nor were these operations confined to children; men would be coaxed away from home on various pretences and as suddenly transferred to the Slave States." Whether or not these hunts were a daily occurrence, they were frequent enough to have shaped the way in which blacks—free, fugitive, or enslaved—moved about the city. "The whole colored population were more or less either directly from the South," Smith explained, or they were "linked by ties of marriage or consanguinity with their Southern brethren, a majority of whom had escaped from slavery." As such, the condition of blacks in free states "was one of constant apprehension and jeopardy."[8]

Like Smith, Alexander Crummell also understood the Garnets' misfortune as intimately related to his own life. He recalled stories about his father, Boston Crummell, a minister who harvested and sold oysters, being captured as a child and suffering through the Middle Passage.[9] Alexander Crummell explained, "My father was born in the Kingdom of Timanee," but "he was stolen thence at about twelve or thirteen years." Boston Crummell was stolen from his family, reduced to human cargo, and shipped across the Atlantic when he was just two years older than his son had been during that summer in 1829. The closeness to the Middle Passage, but also their African heritage, is something to keep in mind about both Crummell's and Garnet's personal stories; their father and grandfather, respectively, had been born on the other side of the Atlantic. Their family histories imply not only the harsh realities of people being reduced to property but also the rupture of culture and identity.

Alexander Crummell recalled how his father stoked dreams in his young mind about the beauty and wonder of his life before bondage. "From my early childhood," Crummell recalled, "my mind was filled with facts and thoughts about Africa and my imagination literally glowed with visions of its people, its scenery, and its native life." His father's "burning love of home, his vivid remembrance of scenes and travels with his father into the interior, and his wide acquaintance with diverse tribes and customs, constantly turned his thoughts backward to his native land." Crummell loved "listening to his [father's] tales of African life" as a child, and they made him "deeply interested in the land of our fathers." These stories made Crummell resolve early in life that one day he would go back to the land of his father.[10] Even for those living as "free" blacks, dreams of escape continued to occupy their interior lives, as captivity for black people was both a physical and a psychic phenomenon.

Mr. Garnet's fearful leap along with intimate knowledge of his father's own story framed Alexander Crummell's outlook about his standing in the world. His was a precarious position shared by his schoolmates. Crummell might have presumed he was "doomed to be both a witness and a participant" in this web of terror and struggle.[11] This was his bloodstained gate: a violent initiation of sorts—like so many other distinct but fundamentally similar moments in black students' lives. As such, the subject position of the black student in this book, as witness, implies more than spectatorship. Witnessing involves coming into awareness of how the violence and mistreatment of other individual black people could potentially be visited on oneself. For the developing mind of young Alexander Crummell, witnessing the attempted capture of the Garnet family was an early lesson about the shared vulnerability of black people in an antiblack world. The very idea of *black life* in the United States—a society ordered by racial chattel slavery—had long been a contradiction in terms.

Henry Highland Garnet returned days after the incident with the slave catcher. He was overcome with rage after learning that his family had been hunted down and forced into hiding. Everything about his reality seemed spiteful. Freedom in the North appeared to be a sham. These events led to a deeper awareness that he, like all black students, carried distinguishable marks as they lived and strived behind the antiblack color line.

Garnet could remember how he, Crummell, Smith, and every other black person joined in the great celebration on July 5, 1827, when slavery was formally outlawed in the state. They lined the streets in New York City to commemorate their crossing over from slavery to freedom. James McCune Smith recalled that those assembled were a diasporic bunch. They represented "every State in the Union, and not a few with gay bandanna handkerchiefs, betraying their West Indian birth: neither was Africa itself unrepresented, hundreds who had survived the middle passage, and a youth in slavery joined in the joyful procession." Smith proclaimed: now "that was a celebration!" It was "a real, full-souled, full-voiced shouting for joy, and marching through the crowded streets, with feet jubilant to songs of freedom!" Yet, as they all experienced firsthand, it was a riddled emancipation: Garnet's experience, his sister's trial, the family's hiding. It made the jubilation feel like a mockery.[12]

For Garnet, black emancipation felt like a travestied affair. He felt foolish for believing it was true. Crummell recalled his friend purchasing a clasp knife, walking up and down Broadway Avenue "expecting and prepared for an attack from the slave hunters." His friends rallied together to "hurry him out of the city, and for a time he was concealed on Long Island."[13] Garnet, who took after his father in his tall stature and muscular build, sustained a terrible injury to his leg while in hiding. The injury caused him to have a permanent disability, eventually leading to his leg's amputation in 1841. The injury became a constant reminder of his family's plight, and that of his race.

But it was the educational experience of Henry Highland Garnet and Alexander Crummell that caused them to see their mission in the world on tortured yet truer terms. Their school days would be years of hopeful striving met by fierce opposition. Crummell and Garnet experienced most of these events alongside one another.

Alexander Crummell, Henry Highland Garnet, and James McCune Smith went as far as they could with the primary and grammar school education offered at the African Free School, only to be left without any opportunities for higher learning. The African Free School was established in 1787 and was the product of the revolutionary spirit that led to American independence. But fiery pronouncements of "freedom for all" shortly waned, at least as pertaining to black people.

The ideology undergirding the African Free School's curriculum by the 1820s and 1830s borrowed heavily from the American Colonization Society, whose white members argued that black people could

Drawn by Patrick Reason, age thirteen,
a student at the African Free School.

only experience freedom if they immigrated to Haiti or West Africa, particularly Liberia. Writing of the antebellum era, one historian explained, "When whites did promote African American education, it was often with an eye toward preparing them for deportation to Africa."[14] Blacks and whites could never live as equal in the United States, they insisted—not simply because of white opposition but also because of their belief that blacks were intellectually and culturally inferior. This belief was evidenced by an incident that enraged black parents in 1832: the principal, Charles Andrews, severely beat a student referred to as "Sanders" with a cane because he called an African American male visitor a gentleman. The principal's refusal to see the black man as a gentleman reveals the limited visions of equality held by some white allies. Furthermore, the caning reflected a long history of racially motivated discipline black students experienced at the hands of white teachers in northern schools.[15]

Black parents rejected the mission of colonizationists. They eventually boycotted the school, demanding that the white schoolmaster be replaced and black teachers hired. White benefactors eventually defunded the African Free Schools, leading to their absorption into the New York public school system by the mid-1830s. This transition introduced its own problems, not the least of which was school authorities replacing most of the recently hired black teachers with white ones.[16]

Black education in the antebellum North was sparse. It was overwhelmingly segregated, and black teachers were rarely hired. Even by 1860, just over one-third of the northern black school-age population could take advantage of educational opportunities.[17] As education became gradually accessible for this fraction of black school-age youth, separate education became nearly universal.

To be clear, some blacks insisted on separate schools early on because of the harsh treatment black students experienced in racially mixed schools. This was the case in Boston, Massachusetts and in Hartford, Connecticut, in the early 1800s. However, segregation of black students was rarely by choice. In almost every community in the North, black students were in separate schools by law or custom by the 1830s. Furthermore, educational opportunities beyond primary and grammar school rarely existed for blacks in the North. Many whites believed that higher education was likely to stoke discontent among blacks, making them dissatisfied with their position in society. Others insisted that blacks were unable to thrive beyond basic academic levels. As one historian noted, "In addition to sub-standard teaching conditions, Negro schools generally provided only the most elementary curriculum. To a large extent, this limitation reflected the exclusion of Negroes from most professional pursuits and the prevailing belief that the average Negro's intellectual capacity debarred him from advance studies."[18]

Consistent with broader trends in northern black education, Alexander Crummell reported that no opportunities for higher education existed for him and his schoolmates until a group of black men established a high school for colored youth in 1831. While some states provided public funding for black education, many of their educational efforts resulted from private support and black people double-taxing themselves to create such opportunities. Yet "this school only whet our youthful appetite for larger facilities of training and culture," Crummell explained. "But alas! in those days the doors of all academies and colleges were closed to colored youth."[19]

Crummell and his peers took their education into their own hands. Led by Garnet, who had taken on a rather serious demeanor after his physical injury and his family's encounter with white slave hunters, Crummell and his peers organized themselves into a literary society. Their educational activities became quite political in nature. "We resolved," described Crummell, "while slavery existed we would not celebrate the Fourth of July."[20] For years, these teenage students gathered on the anniversary of US independence and devoted their

Alexander Crummell

Henry Highland Garnet

time to "planning schemes for the freeing and upbuilding of our race." Crummell recalled that "the other resolve which was made" amounted to a sworn commitment that when "we had educated ourselves we would go South, start an insurrection and free our brethren in bondage."

The students took great delight in their collective dreaming and fugitive planning. Crummell recalled, "Garnet was a leader in these rash and noble resolves." He looked up to Garnet, who was his senior in age but also commanding and inspiring in presence. Garnet had a soberness about him that grew out of his pain; it was, as Crummell described, a "seriousness which is the fruit of affliction, the melancholy and the reflection which spring from pain and suffering." And though Garnet was living with injury, his nimble mind and stubborn commitment to social action made him a role model among his peers.

In 1835, Crummell and Garnet finally got an opportunity to act on the plot they accepted as their collective mission. A school called Noyes Academy opened in Canaan, New Hampshire, where "youth of all races, and of both sexes, were to be received in it." They were joined by another of their classmates, Thomas S. Sidney. The students likely had a grand and memorable send-off, joined by their families as well as their schoolmates who stayed behind, all of whom understood these students' striving to be bound up in the shared destiny of their race.[21]

They traveled four hundred miles, a wearisome and unforgettable journey. "Rarely would an inn or a hotel give us food," Crummell recalled. They were denied shelter at every stop on the trip. The three students traveled from New York City to Providence, Rhode Island, by steamboat, where blacks were prohibited from passing through the cabins. They were "exposed all night, bedless and food-less, to the cold and storm." The circumstances of the journey were extremely damning for Garnet, whose injured leg made him most vulnerable to the harsh conditions. Despite his visible disability, white conductors of ships and coaches refused to make any accommodations. Such inhospitable travel conditions anticipate those of other black students going to school in the years to come, such as Booker T. Washington being forced to ride on the outside of a coach when traveling to Hampton Institute in Virginia in 1872.[22] Their student recollections are strikingly similar.

There were no railroads, so the young men traveled by coach from Providence to Boston, then stopped at two other cities before reaching Canaan, New Hampshire. The conductors of the horse-drawn coaches required the three young men to ride on top of the wagon. Crummell described the journey as humiliating in general, but the threat to Garnet's life while having to ride on top of the coach day and night was particularly terrifying. The young men met "taunt and insult at every village and town, and ofttimes at every farmhouse, as [they] rode, mounted upon the top of the coach, through all this long journey." Crummell explained, "The sight of three black youths, in gentlemanly garb, traveling through New England was, in *those days, a most unusual sight;* started not only surprise, but brought out universal sneers and ridicule."[23]

When they finally arrived in Canaan to attend Noyes Academy, they were welcomed by a group of forty white students who were also enrolled at the school. Crummell described the reception by the white students as warm. There were about fourteen black students enrolled, one of whom was a Miss Julia Williams from Charleston, South Carolina.

Julia Williams attended a school in Canterbury, New Hampshire, before arriving at Noyes. The previous school was run by a white Quaker woman named Prudence Crandall. Whites removed their students from Crandall's school after a black girl enrolled. The departure of all the white students prompted the teacher to invite other black girls to attend, which angered the white townspeople even more. Local whites regularly attacked the school as well as the students. Crandall was jailed and eventually closed the institution for safety reasons. The story of Williams's previous school foreshadowed what was to come at Noyes. Williams and Garnet would eventually marry, though their time at Noyes was short-lived because it was forced to abruptly shut down. Like what Williams experienced in New Hampshire, the school's closure was due to violent white opposition.

Such aggressive campaigns to restrict and suppress black education intensified as campaigns for white common schooling as a right of citizenship grew stronger in the antebellum North. And this was no coincidence. Such parallel developments "were part and parcel of a larger impulse to expel black people from the polity in the early nineteenth century," explains historian Hilary Moss.[24] Furthermore, the question of separate or mixed schools, when opportunities did exist for black education, would be an ongoing battle in the North

Noyes Academy Removal, Mikel Wells (1999)

through the nineteenth century. In many ways, the battles over segregated schooling in the North anticipated the de jure segregation that became enshrined in the South during Jim Crow.[25] The controversy surrounding Noyes Academy reflected this embattled educational context.

According to Crummell's recollection, "On the 4th of July, with the wonderful taste and felicity, the farmers, from a wide region around, assembled at Canaan and resolved to remove the academy as a public nuisance!" Subsequently, on August 10, "they gathered together from the neighboring towns, seized the building, and with ninety yoke of oxen carried it off into a swamp about half a mile from its site." Crummell recalled the sight of these men literally dragging the school building into the swamp. Motivated by their hatred, they labored for two days to make their point clear: the white townspeople refused to tolerate the presence of "what they called a 'Nigger School' on the soil of New Hampshire."[26]

Suspecting that they might be attacked if the mob returned, the students began "moulding bullets" under Garnet's leadership. That night the students heard the tramp of horses approaching before "one rapid rider passed the house and fired at it." Crummell recalled how "Garnet quickly replied by a discharge from a double-barreled shotgun which blazed away through the window." The shot likely scared off the men approaching the students' residence, possibly saving their lives. Local officials demanded that the black students leave the school and the state within fourteen days after the shooting incident. When the black students departed Canaan, "the mob assembled on the outskirts of the village and fired a field piece, charged with powder," at their wagon.[27]

Crummell, Garnet, and Sidney experienced the same indignities on their journey back to New York as they encountered on their trip to New Hampshire. Crummell explained, "We returned home over the Green Mountains of Vermont, along the valley of the Connecticut, through Troy, down the Hudson to New York," and "all through the route Garnet was a great sufferer." Crummell and Sidney did their best to comfort their friend and schoolmate during the journey, but at certain moments they were unsure if he would make it. They used their clothes to create a bed for him to lie on while on the river as he tried to regain strength, and they attempted to shade Garnet by holding their umbrellas over him when the sun was too harsh. Despite the indignities they suffered, these young men did all that they could to care for one another, modeling a vision of friendship equally as commendable as their educational strivings.

They had returned home for a few months before learning of a new opportunity. A manual labor seminary, Oneida Institute, in the village of Whitesboro, New York, run by a white abolitionist minister named Beriah Green, "opened its doors to colored boys." The three schoolmates geared up again and made the journey together. They attended the school for approximately three years, graduating in 1839.[28]

THE RIDDLED NATURE OF BLACK EDUCATION IN THE FREE STATES

Embedded in the stories of Alexander Crummell, Henry Highland Garnet, and their classmates is a sobering fact: slavery and antiblackness continued to intrude on the lives of black people living in free states. North of slavery black students continued to experience severely limited educational opportunities—if any at all—and they routinely witnessed the precarity of their people in American society. These factors greatly contributed to their development as scholars. It marked their individual and collective strivings.

Before she became a poet, educator, and abolitionist activist, Charlotte Forten was a young African American student in the antebellum North. Forten moved to Salem, Massachusetts, from Philadelphia at sixteen years old in late May 1854, and she immediately began writing in her journal. Forten expressed her intention to record her thoughts, that she might "judge correctly the growth and improvement of [her] mind from year to year."[29] Forten's family sent her to Salem to attend a racially mixed school. She had previously been tutored at home in Philadelphia after being denied admission to the city's white schools. This was a privilege very few black Americans could afford. Forten came from a wealthy and very active abolitionist family. James Forten preferred to keep his daughter home than have her attend Philadelphia's segregated schools. But he eventually realized her need for companionship. In Salem, Forten could attend a racially mixed school while staying with the family of Charles Lenox Remond, an abolitionist and friend of her father's.[30]

Forten's battle was not unique. Desegregation efforts in the North were an ongoing struggle. In 1849, writer and abolitionist Benjamin F. Roberts filed a lawsuit against the city of Boston because his daughter had to pass multiple schools on her journey to attend the city's black school. Roberts followed in the tradition of his maternal grandfather, who also protested segregation in Boston in 1800.[31] "It is with feelings of amazement," Roberts expressed, "that we witness Englishmen, Frenchmen, Irishmen, Germans, Scotchmen, and others, in our community, who enjoy all the local privileges, and are not ignorant of the fact that we are shut out from the institutions of learning in the land of our nativity."[32] Roberts identified how school policies helped make citizenship synonymous with whiteness in their collapsing of ethnic differences among European Americans while excluding the city's black students. Schools, more than any other social institution, were a critical site in establishing this line of distinction. During the 1849 case, Benjamin Roberts shared his own experience of attending segregated schools in Boston. He recalled he and his peers traveling from their parents' homes and passing "the doors of several schools," and witnessing white students "enjoying the blessings of the nearest schools to their homes." Roberts explained, "The pupils of the several schools, as we passed, took particular notice of our situation; and we were looked upon by them, as unworthy to be instructed in common with others."[33] Such experiences reinforced the idea that black people were not equal citizens, nor were they deemed legitimate students.

In 1850 the court ruled on *Roberts v. Boston*, establishing the controversial precedent of "separate but equal" in American law. Despite the ruling, black Bostonians succeeded in desegregating the schools a few years later through state legislation. The fact remained, however, that the overwhelming majority of black children receiving education in the North did so in segregated schools. As one historian noted, "By 1860, some small and scattered communities agreed to integration, but the larger cities, including New York, Philadelphia, Cincinnati, Providence, and New Haven, hoped to stem increasing agitation by correcting existing abuses and making the Negro schools equal to those of the whites."[34]

Few opportunities existed for mixed education. Some African Americans, like Charlotte Forten's family, advocated for desegregated schools on the grounds of equal citizenship, and often as an expression of their abolitionist dreams. Despite the vision of justice motivating the calls for educational equality, however, "black children in racially mixed settings frequently suffered harassment from white peers and low expectations from white teachers" in the antebellum North. After Boston schools desegregated in the mid-1850s, some of the city's teachers routinely placed misbehaving white children in "the nigger seat" next to black students as punishment.[35] In other instances, white teachers threatened black students with punishment if they spoke to them in public. Fugitive slave and abolitionist Frederick Douglass was a fierce advocate of mixed schooling. Yet even he removed his daughter, Rosetta Douglass, from a school in Rochester, New York, because of such hostilities. The school admitted his daughter but prohibited her from boarding with the other students. They also hired a teacher to instruct her separately at the school.[36] Access to white educational institutions rarely, if ever, translated to equal treatment. While separate schools emphasized black people's marginalization in society, the treatment of black students in mixed schools caused great concern for black parents, even the staunchest supporters of desegregation.

Consistent with such trends, Charlotte Forten found opportunity for academic training in a mixed school setting in Salem, but she would also experience a great deal of alienation as a black student. Her diary tracked more than her intellectual development. Impressed upon its pages were her internal struggles as a black student in a white society. The entries reveal her perceptive eye for matters of racial injustice in its egregious and mundane forms. At key moments, Forten expressed frustration with her classmates' lack of outrage over slavery, and their selective tolerance of black students frequently occupied her thoughts. She also espoused sharp critiques of northern states, indicting them for their collusion with the peculiar institution by jailing and returning runaway slaves.

Forten's development at Salem's Higginson Grammar School went beyond lessons she recited with her white classmates. She learned a great deal from the racial politics shaping nearly all her social interactions, in and outside of school. While race was not explicitly named by her teacher in the classroom, it shaped every aspect of Forten's world. She bore witness to this in her journal. There could be nothing outside of race in a world built and sustained by the ongoing violent extraction of labor from enslaved black people, and where black Americans, free and enslaved, continued to experience antiblack persecution in both physical and symbolic form.

The first major event recorded in Forten's diary was about Mr. Anthony Burns, a fugitive slave from Virginia. Similar to Alexander

Charlotte Forten

Crummell and his classmates in the 1820s, Forten witnessed the ongoing hunt of fugitive slaves in the North during the 1850s. However, this was not her first time witnessing or hearing of fugitives being captured in "free" states. Such controversies were often the subject of conversation and events just outside her family's home in Philadelphia.

On the evening of Thursday, May 25, 1854, Forten was tired from a long day at school and did not intend to write in her journal.

However, the news she'd learned that evening about Mr. Burns compelled her to do so.

> Another fugitive from bondage has been arrested; a poor man, who for two short months has trod the soil and breathed the air of the "Old Bay State," was arrested like a criminal in the streets of her capital, and is now kept strictly guarded,—a double police force is required, the military are in readiness; and all this done to prevent a man, whom God created in his own image, from regaining that freedom which, he, in common with every other human being, is endowed.[37]

Mr. Burns's trial appeared in the pages of Forten's journal and therefore the inner chambers of her mind for the next few months—and likely much longer.

Forten, a young aspiring anti-slavery lecturer, discussed Mr. Burns's capture and subsequent trial with her classmates and teachers. While opposed to slavery, her friends at school did not share her outrage. The teacher spoke against slavery but objected to Forten's view that ministers and churches aided "the infamous system," that they were complicit in their general silence and failure to take a collective stand against slavery.

Mr. Burns's trial began on Monday of the following week, May 29, 1854. Forten followed its developments closely. During these days, she expressed her struggle to accept the teachings of abolitionists like William Lloyd Garrison, who encouraged "non-resistant principles." While Forten believed these to be of "the very highest Christian spirit," they seemed out of reach for her. "I believe in 'resistance to tyrants,'" she confessed, and "would fight for liberty until death."[38] Like many black abolitionists, she channeled a militant commitment to freedom that rivaled the widely celebrated white American patriot Patrick Henry.

Friday, June 2, 1854: Mr. Burns's fate was announced. "Our worst fears are realized," wrote Forten. "The decision was against poor

Burns, and he has been sent back to a bondage worse, a thousand times worse than death." The news caused the cloud above Charlotte's head to hang even lower. Slavery was the source of her hurt, but she also named the state of Massachusetts and the federal government as equal adversaries. The nation colluded with slave owners in stripping Mr. Burns of his freedom. They all had a hand in exacerbating the suffering of black people. "To-day Massachusetts has again been disgraced," Forten declared. "Again has she shewed her submission to Slave Power."[39]

Burns's arrest was abetted by the presence of federal troops in Boston and its surrounding areas. According to Forten, this federal military presence was shameful. They occupied the city in the interest of slaveholders. It bespoke a "cowardly" government. "And if resistance is offered to this outrage, these soldiers are to shoot down American citizens without mercy." The irony: these "express orders of a government which proudly boasts of being the freest in the world; this on the very soil where the Revolution of 1776 began; in sight of the battle-field, where thousands of brave men fought and died in opposing British tyranny, which was nothing compared with the American oppression of to-day."

The fate of the fugitive slave was inextricably linked to that of all black people in the nation. Forten understood the difference in her material circumstances from that of fugitives like Mr. Burns and other blacks in bondage, but she also understood her social alienation as a young black woman to be bound up with this man's fate. "A cloud seems hanging over me," wrote Forten. Indeed, it hung "over all our persecuted race, which nothing can dispel." This was a burdened way of seeing oneself and the world, a vision her white classmates did not share. This kind of veil hung over the lives of black people, giving a distinct texture and color to their perspective. Forten was frustrated by the very thought of returning to school the following week. "Would that those with whom I shall recite tomorrow could sympathize with me in this," she wrote. "Would that they could look upon all God's creatures without respect for color, feeling that it is character alone which makes the true man or woman!"[40]

At school, Forten's teacher encouraged her to "cultivate a Christian spirit in thinking of [her] enemies." But like Garrison's principles, such an endeavor seemed like a hill too high to climb. The wound was too fresh. She found the idea of showing kindness toward those who advocated for slavery or who were ambivalent toward it to be incomprehensible. The recent events filled her with anger. They deepened her conviction and mission. Seeing this crisis up close provided "a fresh incentive to more earnest study, to aid me in fitting myself for laboring in a holy cause, for enabling me to do much towards changing the condition of my oppressed and suffering people."

Events like the trial of Mr. Burns but also the ongoing indignities Forten suffered and the hostilities she witnessed other black Americans experience all contributed to her feelings of "civic estrangement," to borrow a term from black literary theorist Salamishah Tillet.[41] Forten recalled, "Girls in the schoolroom" were cordial one day and the next "feared to recognize me" on the street. Other students gave her "the most distant recognition possible." But she refused such pitiful forms of recognition. "These are but trifles, certainly, to the great, public wrongs which we as a people are obliged to endure. But to those who experience them, these apparent trifles are most wearing and discouraging; even to the child's mind they reveal volumes of deceit and heartlessness, and early teach a lesson of suspicion and distrust." Such experiences, Forten confessed, made many blacks fearful, "with too good reason to love and trust hardly any whose skin is white,—however lovable, attractive, and congenial in seeming."[42]

On one occasion Forten's friends were refused entrance to a museum and insulted with foul language because they were black. They were called everything but a child of God. These were the kinds of "trifles," or antiblack rituals, that sustained the civic estrangement Forten expressed in her personal writings. She grew weary of such cruel wrongs, insisting they could not be "much longer endured." "A day of retribution must come," Forten quietly wrote to herself. "God grant that it may come very soon!"[43] Such conflicts between black students and white citizens were part and parcel of African American schooling experiences, even when such assaults occurred in public spaces.

Black students also encountered racially motivated physical and verbal attacks at and around school. In Forten's hometown of Philadelphia, black students at the Nineteenth and Spring Garden Street School were regularly harassed by white boys from a nearby school. The white students waited outside to harass the black students on their way home. Routes to and from school have always been part and parcel of educational experiences, and, for black students, they were not always a walk in the park. On one occasion, in 1862, a student named Taylor threw a rock at one of the white boys, hitting him in the head and causing a severe injury. The police arrived at the scene and demanded that the teacher provide Taylor's home address. After she obliged, the teacher insisted that Taylor should not be the only one held responsible for the incident. "The white boys ought to be arrested," she explained, "as they often wait till [the children] are out of school and then attack them."[44] Taylor's experience reflected the vulnerability shared by black students, but also the reality that black students found ways to resist and fight back.

Charlotte Forten's resistance took the form of political protest, actively refusing to celebrate the nation's hypocrisy. Forten expressed her righteous discontent most fervently on the anniversary of American independence. This protest she shared with her predecessors, Alexander Crummell and Henry Highland Garnet, who also critiqued the holiday as students in the 1830s. In routine fashion, she protested the celebration of July 4.

Saturday, July 4, 1857: "The celebration of this day! What a mockery it is! My soul sickens of it," Forten proclaimed. On another such occasion, Monday, July 5, 1858, Forten reported spending "the afternoon and eve in *trying* to rest, but in vain. *Patriotic* young

America kept up such a din in celebrating their glorious *Fourth*, that *rest* was impossible. My very soul is sick of such a mockery." As historian Benjamin Quarles famously wrote, black abolitionists were "a different drummer," and their visions often departed from the white abolitionist movement. They had no qualms about calling out the obvious contradictions of American freedom when placed alongside American slavery. In fact, such critiques could be traced back to the ambivalence witnessed among many blacks during the American Revolution. Freedom was the first priority of black people living in a society ordered by racial chattel slavery, not the independence of any particular nation. In Quarles's own words:

> The Negro's role in the [American] Revolution can best be understood by realizing that his major loyalty was not to a place nor to a people, but to a principle. Insofar as he had freedom of choice, he was likely to join the side that made him the quickest and best offer in terms of those "unalienable rights" of which Mr. Jefferson had spoken. Whoever evoked the image of liberty, be he American or British, could count on a ready response.[45]

This is to say, critiques of July 4, as represented by Forten's diary entry but also blacks who were loyal to the British Crown during the American Revolution, reflect a key strand in black social and political thought. It was a prominent intellectual tradition among black abolitionists. Such sentiments are most widely associated with Frederick Douglass's speech, "What to the Slave Is the Fourth of July," rendered on July 5, 1852. But as evidenced by Crummell, Garnet, and Forten, black students were also compelled to take on such a critical civic posture, even before Douglass's searing indictment of the nation's mockery of freedom.

Black students' alienation in the American polity directly shaped their educational experiences, the latter having always mirrored black people's structural location in a social order stratified by the logics of race.[46] Black students bore witness to this across the generations, as evidenced by the witness of black students living and learning in the antebellum North.

North of slavery, black educational strivings long met fierce opposition. While popular historical understandings often rely on firm divides between North and South when recalling the realities of black social and political life, black students' recollections suggest that as it pertains to educational opportunity, such boundaries were faint and, at times, synthetic at best. Three decades into the twentieth century, W. E. B. Du Bois declared, "There are many public school systems in the North where Negroes are admitted and tolerated, but they are not educated; they are crucified." Du Bois's experience as a student in mixed New England schools during the 1870s and 1880s provided critical context for his future assessment. His striving and his persecution were bound up with a much longer history of black students, like Alexander Crummell, Henry Highland Garnet, and Charlotte Forten.

Learning and striving behind the veil caused black students like Forten, and her predecessors and successors, to live an embattled life. They saw themselves and their mission in tension with the greater society, precisely because they witnessed the ongoing precarity of black life and how it was exacerbated by the actions of individual persons but also facilitated and sanctioned by American institutions. Such tensions engendered a distinct way of seeing as black learners. Black students' identities took shape within the American educational landscape, but they were generally at odds with such sociocultural contexts. By their own assessments, black students were in, but not of, the American school.

Chapter 2

Becoming Fugitive Learners

. . . for hiding was a tradition not just of the body but of the mind. As the folk saying has it, "Got one mind for me and another for the master to see."

—KEVIN YOUNG, *The Grey Album: On the Blackness of Blackness*

We had to conceal our real feelings, because of our situation and only in stolen meetings or hushed tones were we able to express our hopes and fears.

—WILLIAMS SANDERS SCARBOROUGH, *The Autobiography of William Sanders Scarborough*

SUBTERRANEOUS. That was the nature of black learning. Its concealment was both a physical and psychic phenomenon. Richard Parker provides a particularly lucid example.

Born enslaved in Virginia in 1806, Parker routinely carried a book—on his head—concealed *under a hat*.[1] This clandestine curriculum was part of the education Parker pieced together through a combination of subversive acts—all of which were legally forbidden. Beneath Parker's hat was an inner world of desire and striving. The hat symbolized both the barrier to his learning as part and parcel of his social alienation as an enslaved person, and simultaneously his armor of dissemblance—an accessory to the traditions that clothed him as a fugitive learner.

Virginia established laws aimed at disrupting black education and gatherings as early as 1804, though a refined and more direct anti-literacy law would be passed in 1819. The latter outlined "that all meetings or assemblages of slaves, or free negroes or mulattos mixing and associating with such slaves at any meeting house or houses . . . for teaching them READING OR WRITING, either in the day or night, under whatsoever pretext, shall be deemed and considered an UNLAWFUL ASSEMBLY." The code then authorized whippings "at the discretion of any justice of the peace, not exceeding twenty lashes."[2] On at least one occasion, Parker met this gruesome fate. His master's daughter stealthily provided him with lessons. According to his account, the young mistress did this each day at about three o'clock after arriving home from school because Parker "was a favorite of hers." But when the master discovered the enslaved boy secretly meeting with his daughter and playing school, Parker was punished with fifteen blows.

Former slaves cited physical punishment and dismemberment when recounting white opposition to black learning. The list of punishments was extensive: the cutting off of a forefinger; the whipping of children, nearly to death, and demanding that they forget what they had learned; rubbing acid in the eyes of the fugitive learner as an attempt to plunder their sight. The violence that showed itself against enslaved people's educational strivings knew no bounds.[3] Anti-literacy laws reflected the idea that blacks were outside the social contract of the American citizenry. They were not recognized as fully human or citizen, and certainly not student. Parker represents one of many enslaved people who subverted ambient anti-literacy laws and ideology. Mandy Jones was another. Jones recalled how enslaved people on her Mississippi plantation stole away at night to climb into a pit in the ground—*under the earth*—"an some niggah dat had some learning would have a school."[4] In 1848 Charity Bowery, a sixty-five-year-old freedwoman from North Carolina, recalled: "On Sundays, I have seen the negroes up in the country going away *under large oaks, and in secret places*, sitting in the woods with spelling books."[5]

Under a hat, under the earth, under the radar of white surveillance—the fundamental politics of black education emerged. Fugitive learning was constituted by the secret and subtle forms of educational resistance that black students enacted, even as they performed staged acts of compliance in the coercive presence of white authoritative power. Black learners' choreographed dance between coerced compliance and subterfuge formed a core aspect of their disposition and academic identities. This was a distinct political orientation to education derived from enslaved people's theft of literacy and opportunities for learning that defied the will of their masters.

Such protocols of study formed a key part of the architecture of black people's psychic world behind the veil. Contemporary scholars like Kevin Young identify this tradition as central to black political and cultural life. "Hiding was a tradition not just of the body but of the mind," Young writes, or "As the folk saying has it, 'Got one mind for me and another for the master to see.'"[6] Black students had always been in on the plot. They were more than passive learners, having been well informed of the politics surrounding their educational lives.

In Savannah, Georgia, Susie King Taylor operated in the same tradition recalled by Parker, Jones, Bowery, and Young. Taylor received marching orders from her grandmother. Before arriving at the residence of Mrs. Woodhouse—a widow and free woman—Taylor and her brother were to separate, leaving some gap in time before they individually approached the teacher's home. Arriving together, or with other students, might cause unwanted suspicion. Books were to be concealed, covered in paper. Their steps were to be calculated. It was drilled into Taylor and her brother that they must follow these instructions closely. It was necessary that they avoid unwanted attention from prying white eyes, especially the police, in Savannah.

Having been "born under slave law," Taylor began this daily ritual of fugitive learning before she reached the age of ten in the 1850s.[7] Taylor's theft of learning was a formative part of her childhood (if such a thing existed for enslaved youth).[8] Like many other black children, such recurrent, choreographed acts of subversion were an integral part of her development. The violence of slavery required the hiding of one's inner life and intellectual strivings.

Black children as *fugitive learners* had embedded meaning. Whether free or enslaved, African American children were barred from education by law in most southern states, and they universally experienced violent exclusion in education across the nation, as evidenced by black students' experiences in northern "free" states outlined in chapter 1. Yet some of them learned despite violent white opposition. Thus, the language of "fugitive" denotes the competing narratives of black students' lives, emphasizing how they operated in a tradition that defined their purpose and status as human beings on terms outside of the nation's laws and dominant racial ideology. On one level, black students' learning was a communal fugitive project in that it defied anti-literacy laws and ideology. On another level, their identity as fugitive learners was one that individual black students knowingly took on, asserting their own self-possession. It is their conscious awareness of what they were doing, and their feelings as to why it was worth the risk, that speaks to the intentionality of their fugitive disposition.

Black learners knew that they were breaking laws and social customs established by a white power structure. They knowingly located themselves in a countervailing tradition, choosing to see themselves through narrative scripts other than those imposed on them by people with "legal" claims to their life, or those invested in a social order sustained by such laws. As such, students like Susie Taylor pursued their learning covertly. Black students' development across generations has entailed coming to terms with a relationship to the American school that has a history of violent exclusion and

Susie King Taylor

neglect and, simultaneously, that their education is part and parcel of a larger plot against the world as they knew it. A chorus of black student voices bear witness to this tradition.

Susie King Taylor's stealing away to Mrs. Woodhouse's residence was more than a daily practice of resistance. Indexed by this routine was an entire system of knowledge about power, education, and the political plight of black people. Taylor's actions betray an interior world among the enslaved people and, particularly, a clandestine educational politics.

Taylor and her brother attended the makeshift school run by Mrs. Woodhouse and her daughter, along with twenty-five to thirty other children. These students, their parents, and their teachers were aware that the law prohibited teaching black children to read and write. Black education was criminal activity in the antebellum South.

Unlike Virginia, Georgia's earliest anti-literacy law was established in 1770 during the colonial era. However, the state passed the following law in 1829, unifying black codes already existing across the state regarding education:

> *And be it further enacted*, that if any slave, negro, or free person of colour or any white person shall teach any slave, negro, or free person of colour, to read or write either written or printed characters, the said free person of colour, or slave, shall be punished by fine and whipping, or fine or shipping at the discretion of the court; and if a white person so offending, he, she or they shall be punished with fine, not exceeding five hundred dollars, and imprisonment, in the common jail at the discretion of the court before whom said offender is tried.[9]

Recognizing such laws as illegitimate, black Americans conceived of, and operated on, alternative visions of justice, what literary theorists Steven Best and Saidiya Hartman have called "fugitive justice."[10] Given these circumstances—the ubiquitous violence that circumscribed black students' ability to live free and dignified lives—critical parts of their learning were to be kept away from the public eye. Their educational strivings amounted to collectively conspiring against the order of things. Taylor's daily ritual was an initiation into a kind of "freemasonry of the race," to borrow from the twentieth-century writer and activist James Weldon Johnson.[11]

Some general lessons might be gleaned from Taylor's particular account. The procession of learners into their teacher's home, one at a time, underscores a core politics of black education. It expressed a defiance of white supremacist protocols and, simultaneously, black students' collective striving for a world where human flourishing was also the right of black people. And yet the choreographed ritual of fugitive learning *as a repeated act*, a routine performed day after day, must also be unpacked for its layered implications.

Knowledge transmits through more than spoken or written words. Of this, we are certain. It passes through taken-for-granted acts and gestures, as well as isolated events that leave an impression on the individual person as part of the collective. These rituals and events become inscribed in one's mind—in the flesh, even. They have the power to shape how one makes sense of the world.[12] So it begs the question: what impression did such a ritual leave on the student body, those scholars who gathered in a kitchen to steal the chance at pursuing their highest potential in mind, body, and spirit? The feelings associated with such an experience are as important as the procedural details of its occurrence.

Irrespective of the content knowledge learned under the direction of Mrs. Woodhouse and her daughter—the functional skills of reading, writing, and arithmetic—Taylor and her classmates also learned to *embody* important lessons through the repetition of their fugitive literacy acts. I am referring here to what they embodied in physical form: the procedure of discretion disciplining their bodies as they worked to execute their secret mission. The method of transmission was just as important, if not more, than the content of students' written lessons. In fact, the method, or form, was itself a political lesson about survival and struggle as it pertained to their education.

What did it mean to be a black student in an antiblack world? The form of Susie's education taught her that she and her classmates were of a persecuted people, but that they might also aspire to be bodies in dissent.[13] The *form* of their learning—books wrapped in newspaper, walking one at a time to the forbidden site—was itself *content*, lessons to be studied for deeper conceptual meaning about their lives.[14] It was part of a distinctly black curriculum. Going underground to learn, operating within their veiled existence, was part of their modus operandi. Recognition of their alienation as black children "born under slave law," coupled with their participation in an active negation of this imposed status, was central to their education. There was at least a double meaning to the literacy being acquired in Mrs. Woodhouse's kitchen. It went beyond reading the words in books. In a particular way, Susie King Taylor and her schoolmates were learning to read the world.

Some tested the boundaries of what could and could not be public knowledge pertaining to their education. As they knew, these boundaries were a moving target. But pushing against their limits was always a risk. Martin Delany and his parents learned this in the 1820s.

Martin Delany was born free in Virginia, having inherited the status of his mother as opposed to his enslaved father. Yet when it came to his education his status as a free black child was riddled with contradictions. Virginia law made it illegal for any black person, free or enslaved, to read and write. So when white neighbors caught wind of Delany and his siblings' literacy, rumors circulated, and their lives were threatened. Delany, his mother, and his siblings fled to Pennsylvania as a result, leaving his enslaved father behind.[15]

The Delany family had intimate knowledge of what cruel meaning "justice" could have for black people. A deep scar on Delany's father's face served as a daily reminder. His father got this scar when being punished by his master. It symbolized the tools of torture used to teach black people a lesson when they stepped too far out of bounds.[16] It also represented the arbitrary power white people had over the lives of black people in antebellum Virginia. This hieroglyph carved in his father's flesh was a reminder of their positionality "under slave law," whether they were free or legally owned by some other person. The scar gave meaning to the threats targeting his mother, who was accused of being an uppity free colored woman, and his siblings when their literacy was found out. Delany and his siblings' playful, public displays of their literacy could cause them physical harm and quite possibly cost them their lives.

Black students became fugitive learners, not just by definition but also through active forms of self-identification. For students like Taylor and Delany, choosing to pursue a life of learning required living outside of laws and customs they understood to be illegitimate. Black children continued to be active participants in developing these subversive politics of black education as they developed in the antebellum era. The stories they left behind stand in stark contrast to what the world said about them. The black student was a witness and participant in the fugitive project of black education from its inception. And African American students were not the only ones aware of this protest tradition in education—white people knew it too, as evidenced by their continued fear and proactive efforts to restrain it.

ANTI-LITERACY LAWS AND THE THREAT OF BLACK REBELLION

Black students were not alone in understanding their education as a political imperative. Indeed, white citizens understood the surveillance and repression of black education in political terms. By the 1830s, black literacy became increasingly associated with black rebellion, particularly violent armed resistance by enslaved black people. Such anxieties framed black educational strivings in the political imagination of white southerners, as well as some northerners. To be clear, these assessments were not unwarranted. Given black people's desire to no longer be the property of others, some went to great lengths to gain their freedom and strike a blow at the institution of slavery. Many whites observed that insurrections were often led by literate slaves.

In September 1831, the townspeople of New Haven held a meeting and blocked efforts to establish a black college by a vote of 700 to 4. To express their frustrations, some directed their aggression at a black-owned hotel, a black-owned home, and the home of a known abolitionist. Quite revealing was a local newspaper's coverage of the town's refusal to welcome this new educational venture. The paper framed this issue in relationship to the story about a slave insurrection in Southampton, Virginia, in August, led by an enslaved man named Nat Turner. The newspaper described Turner as "a shrewd fellow" who "reads and writes, [and] preaches." The story of this slave revolt was followed by another column, titled "Gabriel's Defeat." The latter chronicled the story of Gabriel Prosser, another literate black man who conspired, though unsuccessfully, to lead a slave revolt in 1800. The idea of black education continued to be linked with black rebellion in the white imagination.[17]

Radical abolitionist literature increased in circulation during the decades leading up to the Civil War. The circulation of such literary content also motivated stricter anti-literacy measures. David Walker's *Appeal to the Coloured Citizens of the World*, which encouraged blacks to take up arms and rebel against slavery, was published in 1829. Walker lived in Boston and worked as a tailor. His pamphlet was banned in many southern states, and even white abolitionists viewed the text as extremist.

On occasions, Walker stitched pamphlets into the jackets and trousers of his clients, many of whom traveled by ship to various places. Walker's subversive means of distribution resonates with the embodied practices taken up by black students as fugitive learners, indexing the core politics of black education: a subterraneous curriculum tucked beneath the surface—hidden, as they say, in plain sight.

Contemporary poet Rita Dove commemorates the secrecy of black literary life, and David Walker's heroism, as follows:

> *On the faith of an eye-wink, pamphlets were stuffed*
> *into trouser pockets. Pamphlets transported*
> *in the coat linings of itinerant seamen, jackets*
> *ringwormed with salt traded drunkenly to pursers*
> *in the Carolinas, pamphlets ripped out, read aloud:*
> Men of colour, who are also of sense.
> *Outrage. Incredulity. Uproar in state legislatures.*[18]

One might imagine—"pamphlets ripped out, read aloud"—some person reading the audacious words of Walker in the presence of others on arrival in the Carolinas or Georgia. A similar scene of such communal literacy was recalled a few years earlier, in 1822, related to an organized insurrection in Charleston—though the revolt was squashed before it could be executed. One of Denmark Vesey's co-conspirators explained that Vesey "had the habit of reading to me all the passages in the newspaper that related to Santo Domingo." Vesey also shared that he had been communicating through black cooks who worked on ships traveling between Charleston and Haiti, and that Haitians would join in black Charlestonians' fight for freedom if they would just strike the first blow.[19]

The thought of Walker's *Appeal*—a colored person not only writing a book and it being published, but the words written on the page being an unapologetic plea for colored people to rise up and demand their freedom at all costs, even if it meant killing white people who stood in their way—was simply unprecedented and unthinkable for many, until they were forced to encounter it; until they had to carry the weight of these words now printed and living in the world, forever. Surely, they stirred hearts and minds when falling on the ears of black folks. The truth of such words and freedom dreams could not be unheard. Walker proclaimed, "For colored people to acquire learning in this country, makes tyrants quake and tremble on their sandy foundation. . . . They know that their infernal deeds of cruelty will be made known to the world."[20] Such a mandate placed on the education of black people threatened to upset the entire system of white mythology structuring the known world.

Despite efforts to suppress its circulation, the text found its audience. The first documented account of the police confiscating Walker's *Appeal* was in Savannah, Georgia, before Christmas of 1829. And the text continued to appear.

> 20 more copies appeared in Georgia's capital, then another 30 in Virginia. More materialized in New Orleans and Charleston two months later. Before the end of the year, more than 200 had breached the Carolinas. Police scrambled but failed to confiscate most copies, despite in some instances sending undercover agents into black communities. In certain parts of the South, evidence emerged that the book was in fact spreading via networks of runaways. Whites began to panic.[21]

The backlash to David Walker was not without precedent. White suspicion of black education took root in the Americas well before the nineteenth-century slave revolts listed above. For instance, the 1740 Negro Act in South Carolina prohibited teaching slaves to write as a response to the Stono Slave Rebellion of 1739, the largest slave uprising during the colonial era.[22] The suppression of black literacy, as a matter of law, preceded US independence. The intentional underdevelopment of black educational life on North American soil is older than the United States itself.

The outcome of the Haitian Revolution, which spanned 1791 to 1804, only heightened this panic. This combination of events all came to inform the surveillance practices surrounding black education. Prior to black emancipation, nearly every southern state passed laws barring or severely restricting black people's access to education.[23] Such laws impacted the lives of the overwhelming majority of black people, as 95 percent of African Americans resided in the South in 1860.

Frederick Douglass drew an astute conclusion about the entwined nature of black rebellion and black literacy as an enslaved boy. He recalled assisting with a Sabbath school run out of the home of a free black man in St. Michael's, Maryland, which taught about twenty students in the early 1830s. Sabbath schools operated on Sundays and usually focused on religious education, but many African Americans, during slavery and after, used these spaces for traditional academic instruction. As Booker T. Washington explained in his postbellum slave narrative, "The principal book studied in the Sunday-school was the spelling-book."[24] This experience would be a definitive moment in Douglass's coming of age. On one occasion, Douglass's master rushed into the school, along with several other white men, threatening to kill him if these activities continued. Douglass recalled, "One of this pious crew told me, that as for my part, I wanted to be another Nat Turner; and if I did not look out, I should get as many balls into me, as Nat did into him."[25] His efforts to educate other black youth became linked with the threat of armed black resistance.

This scenario was one of many in Douglass's life where anti-blackness manifested distinctly in the form of black educational suppression. While Douglass was living in Baltimore as an enslaved child, his mistress began teaching him to read. On learning of his wife's actions, Master Hugh Auld was infuriated. Auld proceeded to lay out "the true philosophy of slavery," explaining how the written word was one of the most important axes between slavery and freedom. He declared that learning would make a slave "unhappy and disconsolate." It would incite a desire for self-determination incompatible with bondage. "If you learn him now to read," Auld explained, "he'll want to know how to write; and, this accomplished, *he'll be running away with himself*."[26] Black students learning in the time of slavery was akin to stealing oneself. As Master Auld suspected, theft of mind and theft of body often went hand in hand. The enslaved person's pursuit of education and independent thought disrupted the very political economic foundations of chattel slavery.

African American learners were partners in the subversive project of black education, which extended from desires among the enslaved to seek out opportunities to assert control over their lives as human beings and to attend to their own intellectual and spiritual desires. The subversive activities of black students took on different forms across time and space, but they continued to be expressions of this singular vision.

LEARNING UNDERGROUND

William Sanders Scarborough, often remembered as the first African American classical scholar and as a black man who published a widely used Greek textbook, documented the secret educational world of his youth. He insisted that this concealed aspect of his life was a core component of his development in the 1850s. Fugitive learning was a disposition he inherited from his mother. This accompanied, of course, her status as a hybrid of property and person, which she also bequeathed him. While Scarborough's father was a free man, his mother was enslaved, and therefore the "chattel principle" also marked the son, as the status of enslavement was passed matrilineally.[27] This was an economic reasoning that turned black women's wombs into an extension of the Middle Passage.[28] Scarborough's mother learned to read and write in the clandestine schools run by free blacks in Savannah, Georgia. She raised her son up in the same tradition.

After learning some fundamentals in reading and writing from his parents, Scarborough became a student of a "peculiar" white man who offered him private lessons on a daily basis. Mr. J. C. Thomas was "intensely southern." According to Scarborough, Thomas "opposed anything that meant progress to the Negro, yet for some

Photo of W. S. Scarborough in Daniel Wallace Culp, Twentieth Century Negro Literature: or, A Cyclopedia of Thought on the Vital Topics Relating to the American Negro *(Atlanta: J. L. Nichols & Co, 1902)*

reason he took an interest in me and taught me to read and write, though my parents first put me in the path of knowledge by teaching me my letters." Scarborough advanced in his studies, all the while learning to maneuver through the world in ways that circumvented white supremacy. He understood that part of his world needed to be cut off from the view of most white people, likely even those with somewhat liberal leanings like Mr. Thomas. Scarborough put into words a lesson all black students learned when he wrote, "As a people . . . we had to conceal our real feelings, because of our situation and *only in stolen meetings or hushed tones* were we able to express our hopes and fears."[29]

While Scarborough's family experienced personal liberties that were out of reach for most enslaved people—for instance, his enslaved mother was allowed to live with his father, a free man—this did not shield Scarborough from the reality that he was a slave and could be subjected to the will of a white master at any time. He heard stories of the violent fates black people met when they stepped too far out of line. He had witnessed "slaves sold on the auction block."[30] This context informed his understanding of what was at stake and why his education had to be kept a secret. Scarborough was keenly aware that he could not give any indication whatsoever that he thought himself equal to whites. A gesture, a word, a look could have grave consequences.

Scarborough learned to walk the tightrope—subverting the illegitimate power of white supremacy while simultaneously being cautious not to press his luck too far at the wrong time. His existence was a calculated one—a life lived on the pulse of a nerve. Like all black learners, he carried a hyperawareness of his body, his gestures, and the injury thrust on him.

Yet the fugitive learning of Scarborough's childhood exposed him to broader atmospheres and allowed him to be of great use to his people. He wrote the following of his secret scholastic endeavors:

> I did not parade my efforts, however, as I daily went out ostensibly to play with my book concealed, but really, as time went on, to receive further instruction from free colored friends who helped me on, and living by themselves, my parents had unusual freedom for such opportunities to further my education. This learning was soon put to practical use.

> I was often called upon by friends and family to write "permits." Without these a colored man would have been punished for the misdemeanor of visiting his family. My conscience has never troubled me for rendering this assistance, though I would not recommend as good ethical training such continued practice by a boy for any length of time. However, *all of us then felt justified in it because of the system under which we were forced to live.*[31]

Not only did Scarborough knowingly break the law to continue his education, but he also used his literacy to forge passes for enslaved men in what contemporary scholars have termed "abroad marriages." These men were owned by one master and their wives and children by another, or a wife may have been free and her husband enslaved (or vice versa).[32]

Aware that his literacy acts were illegal, Scarborough explained that his conscience never troubled him. He and his family operated from a different set of ethics. Their vision of justice was one beyond the bounds of the law, especially given how the same laws made it permissible for them to be the property of another. The lesson here is not only about the act of secretly reading and writing. Of even greater import, perhaps, is the alternative set of ethics by which Scarborough lived in the world, ethics he understood to be decidedly against those imposed by the dominant society. Again, fugitive justice was a competing vision of righteousness and fairness engendered among those who have been systematically unprotected and violated by the laws of the land. Black students understood their identity as fugitive learners to carry a dual image. Theirs was a split, double consciousness: one imposed from without and accountable to white laws, the other being the countervailing narratives that grew out of their dreams and desires as a persecuted people.[33]

Fugitive learning not only meant secretly learning to read and write; it also meant developing a lens of critical literacy, counter-readings of what was good and true in the world, even if doing so was at odds with dominant "legal" procedure. Scarborough, Susie King Taylor, Frederick Douglass, and many other black youths who became literate used their skill to write passes. They were never passive in the struggles for black freedom. Given how intertwined children's vulnerability was with that of their parents and community members, it often meant they had to be active participants in their shared struggle for justice.

When the Civil War broke out, it became difficult and more unsafe for Scarborough to move about. His secretive educational pursuits were disrupted. "As the war went on," he wrote, "colored boys were always in danger when found on the streets. As a rule they were seized and made to do duty in the hospitals where the Confederate soldiers lay sick and dying." Scarborough's parents had transparent conversations with him about the stakes of the war. They all had a feeling that their freedom was on the line. When blacks whispered about the success among southern whites, who celebrated any advance made by the Confederate army, it caused him to feel sad and cry. Nonetheless, he "still read and studied privately, feeling that [he] must be prepared whatever might be the outcome."[34]

Scarborough understood the layered significance of his education. It was an individual pursuit of intellectual development, and yet a collective resource for writing passes and reading to those who were illiterate. It was also about preparing one's mind for a world that did not exist. As the war continued, the young man studied that he might be useful to his people in whatever world was to come after.

At about twelve years old, Scarborough witnessed the gains made during Sherman's "March to the Sea" near the end of 1864. Union troops advanced from the city of Atlanta, which they had taken over, and moved farther into enemy territory to take the port of Savannah. He specifically recalled how Union troops destroyed goods and property in the city, taking what they found useful from the inventory of local stores and shops. Scarborough and other blacks participated in the looting once the Union army took all that they wanted. He took special liberties to replenish his school supplies. "The Union forces broke open the rest of the commissariat stores and allowed the Negro people to carry away what was not used by themselves," wrote Scarborough. "Many useful and needed things were thus gained by my family. I recall that my own share of the spoils consisted of an abundance of boxes of penpoints, pencils, envelopes, and paper."[35]

There was a feeling in the air, a hope and a prayer that a new day was coming. Anticipating freedom, Scarborough took it on himself to prepare for the new life ahead. Studying and refining his academic skills was his way of readying himself. His education proved to be an asset to his people while still in bondage. Surely it would be useful for whatever was to come after, if black people gained the chance to work at building a new world for themselves—if, and when, freedom arrived.

Dreams of freedom had long been fugitive desires shared among black people. As generations of African American students would continue to learn and attest, their educational strivings were to be beautiful experiments with such dreams.[36]

Chapter 3

Learning and Striving in the Afterlife of Slavery

For the first time I was free to read and study and go to a real school in a real schoolhouse, and be taught by a real teacher without any further subterfuge to gain an education.

—WILLIAM SANDERS SCARBOROUGH, *The Autobiography of William Sanders Scarborough*

The landlord wanted us all to stop school and pick cotton. But Mother wanted me to remain in school, so, when the landlord came to the quarters early in the morning to stir up the cotton pickers, she used to outgeneral him by hiding me behind the skillets, ovens, and pots, throwing some old rags over me until he was gone.

—WILLIAM HOLTZCLAW, *The Black Man's Burden*

MANY PEOPLE UNDERSTAND freedom as an event. But it wasn't. It was an ongoing process. Both before and after the Emancipation Proclamation and the passage of the Thirteenth Amendment, black people snatched their freedom any way they could. Some ran and crossed over into the camps of the Union army. Others became "contraband of war" as Union soldiers took over their cities and towns. Some heard the news they had been praying for by word of mouth. As evidenced by the Juneteenth holiday, some enslaved people learned of their freedom after a delay of several months;

and to be clear, there were those who continued to be beaten and illegally forced to work for several years following the Civil War.[1] But irrespective of how it arrived, when the news reached the ears of black people eager to be free, the celebration turned religious experience was in a class of its own. It was jubilee, as the formerly enslaved called the biblical time of freedom.

"The effect upon the people cannot be described," William Sanders Scarborough wrote, "only imagined. There was that rejoicing with cries and tears by which only a long enslaved and suffering people could voice their emotions as they realized that the day of freedom, so long prayed for, had at last dawned." Black people immediately picked up and ran on to see what freedom could be. They intended to "begin a new life under a new regime," Scarborough explained.[2]

Susie King Taylor was in the number of those enslaved people who took actions into their own hands. She sought out the camps of the Union army in 1862, well before the war ended. Accompanying her uncle and his family of seven, Taylor ran to St. Catherines Island, off the coast of Georgia, where they would be shielded by the Union army. They soon moved to St. Simons Island, also off the Georgia coast, by boat.

While in transit, one of the captains learned that Taylor could read and write. He asked her to prove it by producing written words and reading them aloud. For some, Taylor's literary abilities were unthinkable, absent proof. An enslaved black person who could read and write was generally understood to be an oxymoron, "a contradiction in terms," to borrow from novelist Toni Morrison.[3] After expressing their amazement at this little black girl who seemed "so different from the other colored people," the white military men asked if she wanted to lead a school. Taylor immediately accepted the opportunity, asking for books right away. She recalled, "In a week or two I received two large boxes of books and testaments from the North. I had about forty children to teach, beside a number of adults who came to me nights, all of them so eager to learn to read, to read above anything else." In addition to her lessons, "Chaplain French, of Boston, would come to the school, sometimes, and lecture to the pupils on Boston and the North."[4]

Before the age of ten, Taylor was stealing away into the kitchen of a free black woman to learn how to read and write. By the age of fourteen she was heading up her own school under the flag of the Union army. A runaway turned contraband of war, Taylor was now putting the education she acquired by theft to some practical use. She set her pedagogical vision against the chattel principle: she insisted on reimagining how black people could be part of the social order as fully endowed citizens and human beings.

Schools like Taylor's took form across the Union camps as more and more enslaved people fled plantations and crossed the lines of war in pursuit of freedom. Agents of the Bureau for Refugees, Freedmen, and Abandoned Land (commonly known as the Freedmen's Bureau) called them "native schools," having noticed them springing up across the South. After traveling across the southern states with the intent of organizing an educational program to prepare freedmen for citizenship, inspector John W. Alvord reported that the former slaves had already begun this work on their own. Many of the leaders in such native schools were fugitive learners like Susie King Taylor who acquired their education in secrecy before the war.

Black educational life was an autodidactic phenomenon in the United States from the beginning. Such self-directed study continued even as black education came to rely on resources of white allies, particularly those from the North. Northern missionaries and Freedmen's Bureau agents absorbed and centralized the educational efforts already taking place among black people themselves. As previously discussed, white northerners—even the most supportive of the abolitionist cause—could, and often did, hold strong anti-black sentiments. African Americans knew that white northerners were not necessarily the solution and therefore did not rely on them exclusively. As was the case in slavery, during the first days of Emancipation African Americans were self-taught.[5]

African American southerners built schools and created educational opportunities in places where black literacy had long been violently prohibited. Such actions were part of their labor to make freedom a real thing, and this was more than a practical matter. It was spiritual work. "So universal is the feeling I am describing," wrote one Freedmen's Bureau agent, "that it seems as if some unseen influence was inspiriting them to that intelligence which they now so immediately need." He then described the native schools as follows:

> Not only are individuals seen at study, and under the most untoward circumstances, but in very many places I have found what I will call "native schools," often rude and very imperfect, but *there they are*, a group, perhaps, of all ages, *trying to learn.* Some young man, some woman, or old preacher, in cellar, or shed, or corner of a Negro meeting-house, with the alphabet in hand, or a torn spelling-book, is their teacher. All are full of enthusiasm with the new knowledge THE BOOK is imparting to them.[6]

Black people developed a subversive political vision of education during slavery, and that politics of education achieved heightened significance now that the day of jubilee had come. Going to school was one of the first acts performed by black people as they strived to initiate themselves into a new realm of human existence. Historian Vincent Harding described how the freedpeople put their dreams into practice:

> Before their freedom from slavery had been officially recognized by the nation . . . the black community was moving forward . . . seeking out their own way, defining their own freedom, taking the initiative to build their own institutions and speak their own convictions. . . . Freedom at best required significant levels of political autonomy. It meant the right to protect themselves, and the guarantee of federal aid . . . to assist in maintaining their liberty against the still lively spirit of slavery and white domination. *Freedom meant education.* Freedom meant land.[7]

Black people's education had always been bound up within a broader plot for self-determination and their struggle for human dignity.[8]

For many African Americans, open immersion into the written word without having to conceal the pursuit of their highest potential was like a baptism marking their new life as freedpeople. Scarborough described this as "the first great event" in his life as a young man. "For the first time I was free to read and study and go to a real school in a real schoolhouse, and be *taught by a real teacher without any further subterfuge to gain an education*."[9] Freedom meant that blacks no longer had to hide their efforts to study, at least not in the ways they had previously.

Black education became generally permissible in the South after the Civil War, and once it happened there was no turning back. Black southern education began to formalize in the Union camps where former slaves organized themselves into schools. Missionaries from the North helped advance these educational activities, motivated by a passion to teach the formerly enslaved how to lead civilized Christian lives. This was often done in the most paternalistic of fashions, steeped in a belief that the freedpeople were indebted to their northern white saviors and that they were morally damaged resulting from generations of bondage.[10] Black missionaries also went south to teach the freedpeople, largely motivated by a sense of racial solidarity, seeing their fate deeply intertwined with that of their brethren who were recently emancipated. Their labor reflected the autodidacticism of black education, and their mission was distinct from that of white northern missionaries who did not see their fate as linked with that of the formerly enslaved. As previously mentioned, African Americans often viewed white missionaries as paternalistic and untrustworthy.

What was done in the dark could now come into the light. The educational strivings of the formerly enslaved led to the first public school system in the South. This transformation had great implications for black educational life. As historian James Anderson described, "Ex-slaves used their resources first in a grass-roots movement to build, fund, and staff schools as a practical right; then they joined the Republicans to incorporate the idea into southern state constitutional law. With these actions they revolutionized the South's position regarding the role of universal public education in society."[11] This change also benefited poor whites, who now had access to tax-funded public schooling.

But new laws could not change white public sentiment. Southern whites maintained a strong sense of hostility and repulsion toward the idea of blacks receiving an education. One Louisiana senator had a visceral reaction to the sight of black students playing on the grounds of a school during recess. After stopping to look and take in the scene, he turned to Inspector Alvord of the Freedmen's Bureau, "looked intently," and asked:

"Is this a school?"

"Yes," Alvord replied.

"What! Of niggers?"

"These are colored children, evidently," Alvord stated.

"Well! Well!," he said, throwing his hands up, "I have seen many an absurdity in my lifetime, but *this is the climax of absurdities!*"[12]

White resentment also manifested through physical violence. One white dissenter fired a shotgun into the schoolyard where black students and their teacher played in Kentucky; some broke into the homes of black teachers and beat them; whites who taught black students were socially alienated; others tormented black students on their way to school.[13] A Freedmen's Bureau agent reported multiple instances in Mississippi in 1865 where black communities raised money to build a school for their children, only to have white men forbid them from using it then seize the school and use it for white children instead.[14]

Burning schools was one of the most common practices of suppressing black education. A conservative estimate suggests that at least 631 black schools were burned down in the South between the years of 1864 and 1876.[15] Given this context, caution continued to be important for African American education. Even still, many of them risked their own lives to protect the interest of their communities, especially the teachers who were targeted by white vigilantes.[16] Black education was a violently contested privilege.

Even as it became more formalized within the apparatus of American schooling, critical aspects of black people's educational endeavors—their motivations, and the political goals undergirding their visions of schooling—had to be kept to themselves. White disdain for the idea of black equality and freedom structured feelings in the South. These sentiments were expressed through acts of physical and economic interference. African Americans wanted to use education, and not simply for modest acceptance into the societal structure premised on white supremacy. They dreamed of using education as a vehicle to transform the social context of their lived reality entirely. This meant a remaking of the world as everyone knew it. Extending from fugitive learning, black education was an expression of freedom dreams: visions of a world beyond the strictures of white rule, a world not premised on the debasement of black life, labor, and identities. These dreams could not be expressed freely. This vision would be seen and treated as an offense to white southern life and, in many respects, American life more generally. Such thoughts were simply unwelcome in the open air.

Even after slavery was abolished, black people's educational visions continued to be patterned by fugitive learning, because they continued to be met by violent white opposition and northern paternalism. Black educational life continued to be riddled in this way. It was intimately situated in the afterlife of slavery, "imperiled and devalued by a racial calculus and a political arithmetic" that had been shot through the national culture centuries before the first freedmen's school had ever been built.[17]

One might ask: Did white southerners recognize that black advocacy for universal public education also benefited their interests? This seems not to have been the case. Perhaps some recognized the benefit but valued their claims to whiteness more than equitable educational opportunity. There are scattered instances where poor rural white families sent their children to schools established by the freedpeople because there were no white common schools.[18] However, more often than not, the white response was violence and disruption: "ashes, insults, and blood," to borrow from Du Bois.

Black education was not opposed simply because it represented African Americans' attempts at mental development and citizenship. Their educational strivings also posed a threat to the cheap labor they were expected to supply to the elite white South and its agricultural economy. But, to be clear, poor whites developed a vested interest in the exploitation of African Americans as well, even as they reaped few material rewards. As one white southerner explained, the subjugation of black people "gives independence and dignity to the poor man of the South . . . for however poor the [white] man in the South may be, he can stand erect when he looks down and knows . . . the negro is below, and will remain so."[19] This conflict between black people striving for their highest potential and the demands placed on their labor to fill backbreaking agricultural work and roles as domestic laborers for white families was at the heart of the matter. And their abjection was codified by a symbolic investment in black inferiority to maintain myths of white supremacy. This was a kind of whiteness that could be owned even by the poorest of white people, for blacks were made to be the most despised class of the human species, a people *useful only when made hewers of wood and drawers of water*.[20] They were at once indispensable to the economy of the nation, even as they were hated and generally recognized as a problem. Writing of the development of racial capitalism in the United States, black studies scholar Charisse Burden-Stelly effectively argues that African Americans have factored into the mode of production as "*value* minus worth," this being the ongoing contradiction of blackness in our modern reality.[21]

The racialized demands placed on African American labor post-Emancipation had direct implications for their education. This meant school schedules were forced to accommodate the crop calendars so as not to interfere with black students' work as field hands. Historian Walter Johnson points out that black labor was part of an algebraic equation that determined crop projections. When planters solved for pounds of cotton to be sold, they calculated "bales per hand per acre." Planters multiplied "the number of hands times the number of acres each hand could be expected—would be forced—to tend," and they planned their sowing based on these calculations. Healthy adults were "full-hands." Women who were breastfeeding were "half-hands." Young kids just starting out were "quarter-hands."[22] Such political economic dynamics also found expression through "practical" educational models emphasized by white philanthropists—an ideological orientation that emphasized a commitment to agricultural and domestic labor. This also meant the lack of development of black high schools: farmers and unskilled laborers, many insisted, did not need access to what increasingly became known as "the people's college." Time and again, black students witnessed this political economic conflict between their educational pursuits and the super-exploitation of black labor in the decades following slavery.

William Holtzclaw was born in 1876 in Alabama. Both of his parents were formerly enslaved. Their family worked as sharecroppers on the land of a white man who "had his fortune, consisting largely of slaves, swept away by the ravages of the Civil War."[23] Holtzclaw was allowed to attend school freely as a small boy. During his early years the local school was run by southern white teachers. However, these teachers were eventually phased out and replaced with black teachers, often having nothing more than a fourth-grade education.[24] As Holtzclaw grew older, he became more valuable as a field hand, and their white landlord demanded his presence in the field. His mother objected and instead helped him devise schemes to circumvent their landlord's insistence that he miss school to pick cotton. Holtzclaw recalled,

> As I grew older it became more and more difficult for me to go to school. When cotton first began to open,—early in the fall,—it brought a higher price than at any other time of the year. At this time the landlord wanted us all to stop school and pick cotton. But Mother wanted me to remain in school, so, when the landlord came to the quarters early in the morning to stir up the cotton pickers, she used to outgeneral him by hiding me behind the skillets, ovens, and pots, throwing some old rags over me until he was gone. Then she would slip me off to school through the back way.[25]

Holtzclaw learned that his education was in direct conflict with the demands placed on his body as a field hand—hence the rags his mother threw over him as cover when the landlord came looking. At a fundamental level, black education disrupted the norms of racial capitalism, a longstanding tension that can be traced back to the literate slave who embodied a direct challenge to the political economy of chattel slavery. Hiding behind pots and beneath rags carried meaning about the significance of Holtzclaw's learning in the years to come. Though he was living after the Civil War and Reconstruction, a time when black education was legally permissible, Holtzclaw's desire to learn was not a priority for the white landlord. Once again, he and his family, like many other African Americans, resorted to fugitive practices of learning to pursue education.

Holtzclaw hid behind pots and under rags. Susie King Taylor wrapped her schoolbook in paper. These were the postures of fugitive learning, a continuum of experience passed on to black students because they continued to live and strive in an antiblack world. African Americans' access to education continued to be manipulated to serve the interests of white people, who continued to wield power over them, and whose political and economic interests were prioritized in the American social order.[26] These dynamics conditioned Holtzclaw's world as a young student, as well as other African American learners of his generation and after.

Holtzclaw's mother had a deep awareness of this reality. Therefore, she guided him in her own manner of subversive pedagogy. Perhaps it was a carryover from her witnessing of fugitive learning as an enslaved woman. Old means of circumventing white power continued to be a necessary posture amid the travestied emancipation African Americans witnessed in the afterlife of slavery. She ushered her son into an educational tradition that was a characteristic extension of black social life, a critical rejection of the imposed boundaries meant to appease white accumulation of power and wealth.

"I can see her now," recalled Holtzclaw,

> with her hands upon my shoulder, shoving me along through the woods and underbrush, in a roundabout way, keeping me all the time *out of sight of the great plantation* until we reached the point, a mile away from home, where we came to the public road. There my mother would bid me good-bye, whereupon she would return to the plantation and try to make up to the landlord for the work of us both in the field as cotton pickers.[27]

Holtzclaw's going to school—his and his mother's pursuit of a life *out of sight of the great plantation*—was a continuation of the general strike: black people's ongoing protest against the conditions of work under a racialized labor economy, where they were perpetually situated at the base of the social hierarchy. This tradition was most evident in those blacks who fled plantations during the Civil War, transferring their labor to the Union army, helping achieve their freedom. But the spirit of this protest both preceded and continued beyond the general strike of the Civil War.

Holtzclaw's words should be taken both literally and figuratively when he states that his mother was working to keep him "out of sight of the great plantation" as she smuggled him to school through the woods. African American parents wanted their children to get an education so that they could escape the limitation of agricultural and domestic labor in the South, where they were controlled by white people. In many ways, living under these conditions looked and felt too similar to the years of slavery, a recent past they were constantly working to transcend.

Going to school to get out of the sight of the plantation was a core tenet of black educational heritage in the afterlife of slavery. Black Americans emphasized the importance of education for "getting their girls out of white people's kitchens." This was the kind of talk Richard Robert Wright Jr. overheard among adults in his life while growing up in Georgia at the turn of the twentieth century. For these families, education was about more than reading, writing, and arithmetic. "They wanted for [their children] emancipation from ditch digging, the washtub, the domestic service and menial labor in general. They felt that education would bring higher pay for their labor and make them more respected in their communities, and help them to do better things than they had ever done for themselves."[28] As black studies scholar Saidiya Hartman observed, domestic work for black girls continued to carry the stain of slavery, in both the South and the North. "The kitchen was the field and the brothel . . . still in the house of bondage." She continued, "The kitchen contained a 'whole social history,' not only of racism and servility, but sexual use and violation."[29] Wright observed black parents articulating an educational politics concerned with circumventing the threat of sexual violence endemic to black women's and girls' experiences as a distinct group of laborers in a society that was fundamentally antiblack and patriarchal.

Robert Spencer, born in 1913 in Tunica County, Mississippi, recalled how many children were prevented from going to school, even after the turn of the twentieth century. "Many of them didn't have that opportunity 'cause the white man," he explained, "you had to be in that field, 'cause they'd tell your parents, say, where that boy at or that girl or something or another, you know. They had to pick cotton and everything." Spencer described how white supervisors kept tabs on the black farmers and their children. "They had a white man that, you know, go around, rode a horse all the time see who was working and who wadn't working."[30] African American youth across southern states, and well into the twentieth century, witnessed white planters and supervisors interfering with their education, advocating that their role as field hands be prioritized over going to school. For instance, Benjamin E. Mays, born in 1894, recalled that his ungraded one-room school in Ninety Six, South Carolina, operated for a maximum of four months, while the white school usually ran for six months, even though African Americans were over 66 percent of the population in Greenwood County. He explained, "Discrimination and farm work accounted for the shorter term for Negroes. Most of the cotton was picked in September and October; and early in March work on the farm began. It would never have occurred to the white people in charge of the schools that they should allow school to interfere with the work on the farms."[31]

Even though blacks were greater in number, white citizens continued to have an outsized influence, as was customary under Jim Crow. Mays was nineteen years old before he ever attended school for a full term. Like many African American youth in these first generations after slavery, Mays interpreted his educational struggles as bound up with those of their predecessors. His father, who was born enslaved, learned to read because his owner's son would take him "down in the woods to a secluded spot and there teach him," even though it was "unlawful to teach a slave to read."[32]

Novelist Ralph Ellison recalled how many of his classmates were forced to miss school to work in the cotton field in Oklahoma City during the 1920s, even as many of their parents moved west to give their children better opportunities. "But during the fall cotton-picking season certain kids left school and went with their parents to work in the cotton fields," he recalled. "Now, most parents wished their children to have no contact with the cotton patch, it was part of an experience which they wanted to put behind them. It was part of the Old South which they had come west to forget."[33] This conflict between the labor demands placed on the bodies of African American children and black educational strivings persisted, and black communities continued to strategize around education as a tool for challenging such limitations imposed on their lives.

Black students learned that their education maintained an antagonistic relationship with the economic interests of white benefactors and employers. This lesson was expressed in *the black interior*—at kitchen tables, between black students and teachers, among parents and community members.[34] Even as this was not openly expressed to white people, it was generally understood within African American communities. Students came to know this as part of their educational mission. It was common knowledge, reflecting the "real feelings" Black people could only express in the "stolen meetings" and "hushed tones" referenced by William Sanders Scarborough.

"THEY ALWAYS CAME IN GROUPS": THE WHITE GAZE IN THE BLACK SCHOOLHOUSE

Paradoxically, the educational campaigns and reforms that helped black education develop institutionally into the twentieth century were, by and large, a packaged version of industrial and agricultural—what was called "practical education"—bundled with basic academic skills in reading, writing, arithmetic, and geography. The white reformers and self-appointed champions of black education believed that this model of education was best suited for black people's role in society. It was their intent to prepare African Americans for the jobs carved out for them based on the raced and gendered hierarchies of American society. This was done even as black people wanted to move away from the racialized labor economy of the South, which in no uncertain terms was a carryover from slavery.

Given the controlling nature of the white architects of black education—a group of philanthropists and education reformers who dictated the development, scope, and structure of black education (at least from a top-down perspective)—African American students continued to experience part of their educational life in secret, or in a veiled context.[35] They constantly calculated what could and could not be revealed to the outside world. African Americans continued to be marked as second-class citizens, and as violence continued to circumscribe their world in the broader political sphere, they were cautious and strategic about how much of their inner thoughts and feelings could be made public. Employing this kind of restraint and self-fashioning became second nature. This, in and of itself, was a critical aspect of black political strategy: an intentional masking of one's thoughts and feelings while navigating a hostile environment, and simultaneously angling to obtain resources necessary for individual and collective progress while assuming the least amount of risk or trouble. It was a tortured calculus to be sure, but one necessary for ongoing struggle.

Concealment and subterfuge continued to be a lesson in black school life. African Americans developed a long-term political strategy that became embedded into the cultural context of the educational spaces they created and maintained. They wore the mask of compliance toward systems of authority when there was no meaningful alternative. Yet they transgressed this system when left to their own devices, when away from the eyes of white surveillance. This sort of doublespeak is akin to what Zora Neale Hurston, the cultural anthropologist and literary giant of the Black Renaissance, called a "featherbed resistance."[36]

Hurston came to know this aspect of black political life through her own educational experience in Eatonville, Florida, in the late nineteenth and early twentieth centuries. This shines through in her recollections of white visitors observing black schools. "A Negro school was something strange to them," she wrote, "and while they were always sympathetic and kind, curiosity must have been present, also." While not something that happened every week, these kinds of visits were far from uncommon. And they were part of the rituals of Jim Crow schooling, through which white officials routinely exercised their power over African American educators and students. When visitors gave black teachers advance notice, Hurston described how "the room was hurriedly put in order, and we were threatened with a prompt and bloody death if we cut one caper while the visitors were present." While obviously hyperbolic, Hurston emphasized the level of caution black schools took when having to entertain white visitors. On other occasions, however, these visitors showed up unannounced. One visit left a lasting impression on her. One afternoon, "two young ladies just popped in." Hurston recalled how the visit flustered her teacher, Mr. Calhoun. "But he put on *the best show* that he could. He dismissed the class that he was teaching up at the front of the room, then called the fifth grade in reading. That was my class," Hurston recalled.[37]

If not handled with care, these kinds of visits could have grave consequences for black schools, depending on who the white visitors were and to whom they were connected. On this occasion, the students read "the story of Pluto and Persephone" from their readers. Hurston recalled Mr. Calhoun's uneasiness as some of the students stumbled over words or spelled words out when unclear of their pronunciation. She was the fifth or sixth student in line to read. Knowing where she fell in line, Hurston located her place in the text and immediately began to "work out" the paragraph she would be responsible for reading aloud. Hurston confidently read her paragraph and was sure she had done a good job.

"The two women looked at each other and then back at me," she wrote. "Mr. Calhoun broke out with a proud smile beneath his bristly moustache, and instead of the next child taking up where I had ended, he nodded to me to go on. So I read the story to the end." The visitors spoke with Mr. Calhoun once he dismissed the class, and he proceeded to call Hurston over to meet the guests. The two ladies took a liking to her. "They asked me if I loved school, and I lied that I did," she wrote. While there were certain things about school she didn't like, Hurston explained, "I knew better than to bring that up right there, so I said yes, I *loved* school." The two white ladies patted Hurston's head and invited her to visit them while they were in town. When she visited, they gave her gifts and would later send more packages to her after they returned to their home in Minnesota.[38]

Now, what appears to be pride and cleverness in Hurston's account is, in fact, a complicated performance that has subversion embedded within it. The subtlety is important here. Hurston's scenario reveals a *shared understanding* among her classmates and teacher about partitioning off part of their inner thoughts from the white guests visiting their school. Black students had to look the part when these white ladies came into their classrooms, to indulge their paternalism for the purposes of not compromising potential support for the school or to not give any opportunity for some deeply held stereotypes about black people's intelligence or hygiene to be reinforced by their account. The fifth-grade Zora Neale Hurston understood that these white women, impressed by her ability to read so clearly and passionately, were likely some extension of a broader part of white surveillance over black life. They were visitors *in* her community, not *of* her community. Most importantly, any offense caused to these women could potentially end in severe repercussions for the school, its leaders, or potentially the students themselves. Such was the precariousness of black life under Jim Crow.

The intrusion of white surveillance into black school life was a characteristic that spanned time and space. The principal of the Greensboro Colored School in Georgia recounted that he had to stop his work more than 130 times within the first six months of the school's opening in 1949 to escort groups of white visitors through the newly erected facility. Local white officials were eager to show "what [they] had constructed for [their] Negroes."[39] Furthermore, as Angela Davis recalled from her school years in Birmingham, Alabama, in the 1940s and 1950s, these encounters were not always pleasant. White visitors often belittled teachers in the presence of their students.

The racial etiquette of Jim Crow, which demanded deference to any and all white people, could be dragged into their black schoolhouse when a white official entered the room. Angela Davis remembered, "Only on special occasions did we see [the white school board's] representatives face to face—during inspections or when they were showing off their 'Negro schools' to some visitors from out of town." She continued, "Whenever the white folks visited the school we were expected to 'be on our P's and Q's,' as our teachers put it." These encounters puzzled Davis. She wondered why she and her classmates had to behave better for white visitors than they did when it was just black people, if they truly did not believe that whites were superior. At the same time, she witnessed the power and control these white visitors seemed to hold over her school and teachers.

"They always came in groups," Davis emphasized.

> Groups of three or four white men who acted like they owned the place. Overseers. Sometimes if the leader of the group wanted to flaunt his authority he looked us over like a herd of cattle and said to the teacher, "Susie, this is a nice class you have here." *We all knew* that when a white person called a Black adult by his or her first name it was a euphemism for "Nigger, stay in your place."[40]

Representing power in such ritualized fashion was central to reproducing antiblack domination. The fact that students "all knew" how to interpret this moment is of importance in this scenario. This knowledge was informed by other interactions students witnessed between parents and white people or by conversations they heard among adults discussing racist slights by whites that black people encountered in public. Whatever the case, students were clear about where they stood in relation to their teachers and white visitors during these interactions.

It is worth noting the subversive sleight of hand even as black teachers and students had to lean into their alienation in these moments. It is not one or the other. These staged moments of compliance and performances of manners and learnedness for the white guests were at once a performance of refusal, even if for the moment only within the black interior. As Hurston explained on a separate occasion, white people might have been able to read her writing and hear the words she spoke, but they could never read her thoughts. "All right," proclaimed Hurston, "I'll set something outside the door of my mind for him to play with and handle. . . . I'll put this play toy in his hand, and he will seize it and go away. Then I'll say my say and sing my song."[41] The same applied to the inner worlds of black teachers and students recalled in the scenarios above. Even in these small moments, we see black teachers and students enacting Hurston's "featherbed resistance," their smiles and pleasantries often masking their critiques and refusal.

Pursuing school to get beyond the sight of the plantation—to borrow from William Holtzclaw—was about striving for an education that was accountable to black desires for freedom. Such desires were often at odds with the projection of oneself shown to white people who held influence over black students and their communities. Black students living in the afterlife of slavery learned that their mission was at odds with the roles carved out for them by powerful white elites and school officials. This informed how they moved through the violent landscape of Jim Crow schooling, an institutional and ideological context that was always at odds with the interests of black teachers and students. Such awareness was a key part of their education as African American learners. What's more, these keen, perceptive practices became vital interpretive resources for black students' reading of the world around them and the words that structured it.

Chapter 4

Reading in the Dark: Becoming Black Literate Subjects

I don't read such small stuff as words,
I read men and nations.

—SOJOURNER TRUTH

Instead I teach you to read well. I teach you second sight—the word and also the meaning. The testament and the content.

—IMANI PERRY, *Breathe: A Letter to My Sons*

TONEA STEWART AND her grandfather sat on the garret of their home as he told her the story. Papa Dallas recalled how the overseer found him trying to read and write under the big oak tree on the Mississippi plantation where he was enslaved. He desired to read the Bible on his own, but such righteous motives did little to lessen the offense. Mississippi law made black literacy and criminality equal transgressions. For many, it was a fundamental act of black rebellion. The overseer made an example out of the young boy, whipping him in front of the other slaves. As if beating him was not enough, the overseer then put acid in his eyes, to permanently fix him. Papa Dallas recalled this story to his granddaughter while living in the Mississippi delta during the 1950s in the final season of his life.

From Papa Dallas's mouth to Stewart's ears, the words of the overseer are remembered and passed on: "Let this be a lesson to all of you darkies. You ain't got no right to learn to read!" The old man insisted that his granddaughter remember. He asked that she carry the story with her and pass it on. Stewart was to bear witness and live life in defiance of the overseer's proclamation. She was to live a life in refusal of this lie. These were her marching orders.[1]

How is literacy registered in a context where reading and writing could end with one's sight being physically burned out? This is a practical matter. It is also a matter of the intimate history literacy shares with physical violence. Tonea Stewart wrestled with this conundrum as her grandfather responded to her inquiry about "the ugly scars around his eyes." No more than six years old at the time, Stewart was about the same age Papa Dallas had been when his attempts at literacy cost him his sight.

Punishment for black literacy acts varied during slavery. Some dissident learners were killed. Some were sold as "damaged goods." One child was terribly beaten and instructed to forget what he had learned.[2] But the marks left by this violence often achieved the opposite of forgetting. They forged a shared countermemory. Black people's reading of their history with literacy, and the marks it left on them, shaped a distinct political disposition toward education. It left a distinct and distinguishable impression on black students as a particular group of learners in American society.

Stewart's witnessing invites us to think more deeply about the relationship between sight and reading. We might linger with Du Bois's provocation that black folks possess a gift of "second sight" in their life behind the veil. This multitude of sights implies a plurality of reading practices. While Papa Dallas could no longer read words on a page, we might still think of him as "properly literate," as he communicated deeper meaning about the education his granddaughter set out to acquire.[3] His reading was one in the tradition of abolitionist and fugitive slave Sojourner Truth. While technically illiterate, Truth was usually the most gifted reader in the room, and insisted, "I don't read such small stuff as words, I read men and nations."[4]

These multiple registers of sight converged in the lives of black students. Their journey to literacy meant learning to read the written word and the antiblack world in which literary texts were always embedded. The word and the world: both were texts, and they informed one another. Proper literacy for black students meant reading with this second sight. What students read on the page and what they bore witness to in the world were deeply intertwined. A proper reading of words on the page demanded an incisive social analysis of the world of power surrounding them. Deep learning, critical literacies—however one phrases it—were contextual in this way.

One generation of black students after another learned that there was a relationship between race and reading. What's more, failure to read properly, beyond the superficial level, could have grave consequences. Second sight was a tool for survival, even while it was derivative of Afro-alienation. Such literacy was high stakes. It compounded the significance of conventional, technical literacy—by which I mean the ability to produce, decipher, and comprehend words on the page.

ORIGINS OF A BLACK LITERARY TRADITION

In a modern world ushered in by the transatlantic slave trade and the vast global project of racial chattel slavery, can black people's literacy be anything but complex? Black Americans' earliest efforts to read and write were attempts to transgress the widely held belief that they were some subgenre of the human species. They weaponized their reading and writing to contest dominant white beliefs that black people were at the lowest point in the chain of being. Literary historian and theorist Henry Louis Gates Jr. identified the trope of "the talking book" in the earliest slave narratives written in the English language. The enslaved encountered white people reading books—or what appeared to be a process of books talking through white subjects, but not the African captives. Literacy, in such contexts, operated as a notable distinction between free and enslaved. In their freedom narratives, formerly enslaved people narrated themselves moving from being an object whom books did not speak to or through, to subjects writing their own stories. Such narratives, written after the authors purchased their freedom or escaped, literally chronicled the enslaved person's journey to literacy and liberation. This trope in black slave narratives—as well as the physical books written by formerly enslaved people—constitute the first formalized African American literary tradition: black people reading and writing themselves into being, into freedom.[5]

Books and written texts have long been understood to be visible symbols of reason and human culture. "At least since 1600, Europeans had wondered aloud whether or not the African 'species of men,' as they most commonly put it, could create formal literature, could ever master the arts and sciences," observed Gates. "If not, then it seemed clear that they were destined by nature to be a slave."[6] The slave narrative as a genre refuted this notion that black people were intellectually inferior and destined to be enslaved by whites. Put succinctly by black literary theorist Joshua Bennett, these narratives were to "serve as black humanity's literary proof."[7] Yet black learners continued to encounter suspicions regarding their intellectual abilities, throughout slavery and its afterlives—and there is no use in acting as though such wonderings have ceased to occupy the public imagination.

There were layers to the violence constraining black literary realities. Perhaps the first layer was the imposition of English, and other European languages, over and against the mother tongues of enslaved Africans. Such actions were motivated by pragmatic concerns of conquest, certainly, but the story is more complicated than this. We might look to African scholars, such as the Kenyan writer Ngũgĩ wa Thiong'o and Malawian linguistic scholar Sam Mchombo, for context here. Entangled with the suppression of African languages was also the insistence that African people, and their ways of speaking and knowing, lacked reason and the capacity to hold complex, sophisticated ideas.[8] If the plundering of African languages (and cultures) is understood as a first wave of aggression, then black students' violent exclusion from opportunities of literary expression—a circular logic using ideas of black inferiority to justify treating blacks as inferior—might be thought of as a second wave of aggression as it pertains to black literacy. The land of the literary has been riddled territory for black students as a result. Their journey as readers has been a central site of conflict in their educational heritage.

READING THE WORD AND THE WORLD

Before reading words on a page, Jerry Moore sat on a blanket, in the corner of the one-room schoolhouse where his mother taught during the early 1920s in Webster Parish, Louisiana. As Moore put it, he was raised up in the classroom. His mother was a teacher, and his father was a minister and parish supervisor for black schools. He watched his father organize the local black farming community as they raised money to build new schools. Together they cultivated cotton on designated patches of land in their neighborhoods. They did this to raise funds to offset the lack of resources received from the white school board. Despite being taxpayers, black families found the provisions made for their children's education to be much lower than those provided for white children. So they raised cotton and appealed to a white philanthropist in Chicago, Julius Rosenwald, to match their contributions. Before Moore became a fully capable reader of words, the actions taken by his community to make black education possible passed before his eyes. He witnessed black people "double tax" themselves to educate the children of their race.[9]

Jerry Moore encountered many tensions in the literature and social phenomena that passed before him, leading to his distrust of master narratives. Books provided to the Webster Parish Training School, like *Red Bean Row*—a novel written by a white folklorist in 1929, about a small black community outside of New Orleans—seemed to depict black people in the most flattened ways possible. Such books reduced them to one-dimensional stereotypes. It was not just that the book portrayed black people speaking only in the most caricature-like dialect, but more that the content of their spoken words did not match the depth of black life as he knew it. Such literature portrayed them to be a simple people—a people with no purpose, no quarrel in life. Some of his teachers openly criticized the content of books placed in their schools. They taught him that black reading required discernment, at times a skepticism of literature he encountered.[10]

In the early 1930s, Moore had Miss McGee as his history teacher. On one occasion she placed two books side by side—the book she was required to teach from by the Louisiana Board of Education and a book by Carter G. Woodson, the famous black educator and Harvard-trained historian who founded Negro History Week in 1926. She explained that there were lies in the required curriculum and that Woodson's "book on the Negro" offered necessary corrections. Some days, she secretly read passages to her class from Woodson's text, making clear that this was not something she was supposed to be doing, but something that needed to be done nonetheless. Moore learned what it meant to be a vigilant reader by witnessing Miss McGee's fugitive pedagogy. A spirit of correction was necessary when engaging in the realm of words—words that, in fact, structured the very world in which Moore lived, and *how* he could live in it.

Students at Webster Parish eventually learned of the differences between their school and the nearby white schools. Jerry Moore learned that while the formal curriculum of the black schools emphasized the importance of students becoming farmers and domestic workers, the curriculum in white schools encouraged students to become leaders and active citizens. There was a relationship between this reality and the stories depicted in books like *Red Bean Row* and the required textbook, *Modern Times and the Living Past*, where the author proclaimed to students, "Not only are almost all the civilized nations of to-day of the white race, but throughout all the historic ages this race has taken the lead and has been foremost in the world's progress."[11] Moore's initiation into the realm of literate subjects forced him to encounter the reality that he was not just a student but that he was a black student. There was a difference.

BARRIERS TO ENTERING THE LITERARY WORLD

As revealed in Jerry Moore's narrative, black students experienced a double bind in their literary journeys. There were barriers to accessing the written world, and at the same time, black people's lives were often condemned in the literature when they did gain access to it. Neither of these facts were totalizing for black learners, but they were significant. As we have seen previously, Jerry Moore's experience was not unique but part of a historical continuum, stretching back to the antebellum period and through to Jim Crow.

Mary McLeod Bethune learned of her exclusion from the literary world at a very young age as well, even as someone who became a college president, advisor to multiple US presidents, and the only woman of color present at the founding of the United Nations. Bethune was born after Emancipation, in 1875, but her family continued to work as laborers for the Wilsons, the white family that previously owned her mother and older siblings in South Carolina. So, while she was a child of Emancipation, the memories and relational dynamics of slavery touched Bethune's life in intimate ways. On one occasion Bethune accompanied her mother to the Wilson plantation, where she had an early literary encounter. She played with the young white children of the Wilson family as her mother handled matters of work. When Bethune attempted to pick up a book, a young white girl took it from her. Though a child herself, the young girl had been thoroughly educated in the codes of power in the post-Reconstruction South. She lectured Bethune, declaring, "You can't read that—put that down." This event left a deep impression on Bethune, who later described it as "the first hurt" she remembered from her childhood.[12] "It just did something to my pride and to my heart," she recalled. "*I could see* little white boys and girls going to school every day, learning to read and write . . . all types of opportunities for growth and service." At the time, Bethune was no more than ten years old. A school for black children eventually opened in her community, but this early experience remained vivid in her mind as she embarked on her educational journey. "You can't read that—put that down" was carved into her memory. Early on Bethune came to know that the literary world was not an open-access affair, especially for black students.

Public libraries were not common in southern states until the early 1900s. Even then, however, black students learned that they were prohibited from using public libraries or checking out books. While the twentieth century is generally thought of as the period of "open access" to knowledge because of public libraries, and the twenty-first century as the "information age," the reality of black readers challenges such periodization. Libraries were civic spaces paid for by tax dollars, but the racial politics of such spaces reflected the ongoing assault on black citizenship. Black students' exclusion from these repositories of literature represented their broader realities as estranged citizens.[13]

The novelist Richard Wright found a way around this barrier while working in Memphis, Tennessee, during the 1920s. By this time, he had dropped out of high school in Mississippi, having only completed a few weeks of his coursework. Wright left school to work and help support his family. The white men on his job occasionally sent him to pick up books from the library on their behalf. "There was a huge library near the riverfront," Wright explained, "but I knew that Negroes were not allowed to patronize its shelves any more than they were the parks and playgrounds of the city." Yet he was allowed "to get books for the white men on the job" as he had done several times. Wright described his own desire to check out books, as well as his hesitance to share this desire with his coworkers.

After making multiple trips to the library on their behalf, he began to develop a scheme: "Which of them would now help me to get books? And how could I read them without causing concern to the white men with whom I worked? I had so far been successful in hiding my thoughts and feelings from them, but I knew that I would create hostility if I went about this business of reading in a clumsy way."[14]

Like most black Americans during Jim Crow, Wright was socialized to conceal parts of his thoughts and desires in the presence of white people. He learned this from reading the world around him over the course of his life. Events like the killing of Uncle Hoskins in Arkansas because he ran a successful saloon taught Wright that many whites viewed black aspiration as a threat. Indeed, as black thinkers like Ida B. Wells teach us, the source of white hostility leading to lynchings was often economic jealousy. There was also the time Wright's junior high school principal demanded that he revise his graduation speech, removing content that might be offensive to the white school leaders in attendance. Such experiences conditioned Wright's suspicion of his white coworkers.[15]

Wright decided to approach the man he least suspected of being a "Kluxer" to help him check out books. He tried to scope out someone who did not seem to fit into "an anti-Negro category." He settled on Mr. Falk because he was a Catholic Irishman. Falk's religion and ethnicity made him unpopular among the other southern whites, positioning him as a potential ally. This need for a white sponsor to access library books was something like a Virginia Woolf moment, except Woolf was excluded from the library in England on the basis of her sex as opposed to her race.[16] Wright's reliance on Mr. Falk is especially tied to the long legacy of white sponsorship and paternalism in black literary history: Phillis Wheatley's white mistress speaking on her behalf to authenticate that Wheatley indeed wrote the poems to be published under her name; white abolitionists writing forewords to slave narratives as a means of legitimizing the words of the fugitive men and women who decided to put their experiences down on paper, to speak for themselves; white Union generals granting Susie King Taylor permission to lead a school only after she proved—to their amazement—that she could in fact read; white women choosing to shower a young Zora Neale Hurston with gifts after visiting her class and being impressed by her performance of literacy. This list can go on, up and through the Black Renaissance era, where many black writers and scholars had to rely on white patrons (who held particular views about what constituted meaningful black literature) to fund and publish their work. The commonality between such scenarios is that power is endemic in the literary realm in more than one way. This lesson presented itself to black students in multiple forms.

After some initial hesitation, Wright convinced Mr. Falk that he could be trusted and had a reliable plan. Wright would forge a letter and present it to the librarian, the same way he always did, only the books listed would be for him to read as opposed to the white man whose name was on the note. Wright would use Mr. Falk's library card, and Mr. Falk would borrow books using his wife's membership card. This was the plot Wright came up with before penning a "fool-proof note" for the librarian. "*Dear Madam: Will you please let this nigger boy . . . have some books by H. L. Mencken?*" Then he ended the note by forging Falk's name. He explained, "I used the word 'nigger' to make the librarian feel that I could not possibly be the author of the note." The scheme hinged on Wright's keen reading of racial politics. He had to understand the perception of his own place—that is, how his own body was read by whites around him. His informed reading of the social world aided him even as Wright worked to circumvent said readings of himself and his race. Wright's description of the encounter with the librarian further elucidates this point.

He entered the library, just as he had done on previous trips, though this time he was concerned that his nerves would betray his motives. Wright explained, "I doffed my hat, stood a respectful distance from the desk, looked as unbookish as possible, and waited for the white patrons to be taken care of. When the desk was clear of people, I still waited." He waited for the librarian to acknowledge him, not wanting to come across as an entitled Negro.

> "What do you want, boy?"
>
> As though I did not possess the power of speech, I stepped forward and simply handed her the forged note, not parting my lips.
>
> "What books by Mencken does he want?" she asked.
>
> "I don't know, ma'am," I said, avoiding her eyes.
>
> "Who gave you this card?"
>
> "Mr. Falk," I said.
>
> "Where is he?"
>
> "He's at work, at the M------ Optical Company," I said. "I've been in here for him before."
>
> "I remember," the woman said. "But he never wrote notes like this."
>
> Oh, God, she's suspicious. Perhaps she would not let me have the books? If she had turned her back at that moment, I would have ducked out the door and never gone back. Then I thought of a bold idea.
>
> "You can call him up, ma'am," I said, my heart pounding.
>
> "You're not using these books, are you?" she asked pointedly.
>
> "Oh, no, ma'am. I can't read."[17]

Wright continued this routine going forward. His forged note, referring to himself as "this nigger boy," the embodied act of looking "unbookish," as well as his false proclamation of "I can't read," all signaled things he knew about the world in which he lived. He played into racial scripts about himself that would make the encounter believable. He also performed scripts that would make himself less threatening or suspicious to the white woman he needed to fool. Wright was a high school dropout, an identity that might lead people to believe him to be less intelligent. But, as this event clearly demonstrates, Wright developed an incisive reading of the world and how to navigate it as a fugitive learner.

When Wright did get the books, he kept them concealed, wrapped in newspaper as he carried them around. This way he would not attract unnecessary attention. How poetic that this same practice of concealment—covering one's books—was the exact method employed by enslaved children like Susie King Taylor and William Sanders Scarborough as discussed in chapter 2. While much had changed, there continued to be deep currents that blurred the boundaries of time and space. Black readers continued to self-censor their literary strivings out of necessity. What's more, they continued to employ subversive practices as they navigated their lives as literate subjects.

The barriers experienced by students like Bethune and Wright were a distinguishable part of black students' shared literary heritage. And it was an ongoing phenomenon. In the late 1930s, "about 21.4 percent of southern African Americans had public library service, about half the white level of 42.7 percent," and this figure was even lower for the majority of African Americans living in rural communities. Indeed, in 1956, Congressman John Lewis began his civil rights organizing in his hometown of Troy, Alabama, at the age of sixteen, rallying his siblings and cousins to register for library cards, knowing they would be turned away.[18] This was before his active involvement in the Student Nonviolent Coordinating Committee (SNCC), founded in 1960. In the 1960s, African Americans were still pushing for greater access to public libraries. As observed by historian Michael Fultz, "The brutal beatings of two black ministers in Anniston, Alabama, in 1963 for attempting to desegregate the city's library represented one point along the continuum."[19] Accounts by black students documenting their exclusion from libraries are plentiful, representing an important (though rarely recognized) part of black educational history, both in terms of antiblack persecution and the story of African Americans organizing to demand equitable learning opportunities.

Ralph Ellison, born in Oklahoma City in 1915, recalled the uproar when a black preacher forced his way into the public library in protest. "There was no library for Negroes in our city," Ellison explained, "and not until a Negro minister invaded the main library did we get one. For it was discovered that there was no law, only custom, which held that we could not use the public facilities." Local officials quickly responded by building a small library for black residents. "The result was the quick renting of two large rooms in a Negro office building . . . , the hiring of a young Negro librarian, the installment of shelves and a hurried stocking of the walls with any and every book possible. It was, in those first days, something of a literary chaos." The rebellious act of the local minister led to black readers in Oklahoma City having a room of their own.[20] This was at least a start. Despite the apartheid conditions, the young Ellison took full advantage of this makeshift library, helping set him on the path to becoming author of the classic American novel *Invisible Man*.

This matter of libraries and black literacy is important not only for the question of access to literature and information but also when one considers the racial politics of knowledge production. The story of heroic historian John Hope Franklin illuminates this point. Like Ralph Ellison, Franklin was also from Oklahoma and born in 1915. He was "reading well at six years of age, but there was no library except that provided by [his] parents' limited resources." What few books he could access in the town of Rentiesville, Franklin read and reread, so much so that he damaged his eyes. Franklin confessed, "I had, indeed, suffered from eyestrain due to reading in poor light." Fearing the loss of his sight altogether, Franklin's mother took him to see an optometrist in Muskogee in 1921. The doctor disabused the family of their fears, prescribing medication and eyeglasses to correct the issue. But reading in the dark was not the only external factor impacting Franklin's sight as an avid reader. The trouble antiblackness caused for his vision and literacy was not so easily corrected. Ironically, on that same trip to the optometrist,

Franklin's mother took him to feast his eyes on Muskogee's Manual Training High School. The school's modern structure was rare for an African American community.[21] I say the visit was ironic, because just four years later Muskogee's white school board punished the black teachers and fired the principal for teaching students from Carter G. Woodson's textbook, *The Negro in Our History*.[22] That the young boy walked the grounds of this very school as he sought to correct his troubled vision in my mind foreshadows the historian he would become. And to be clear, the antagonism represented by the banning of Woodson's textbook appeared in Franklin's education and career as a historian in much more intimate ways.

Franklin graduated from Fisk University then began graduate studies in Harvard University's history department—the same department where W. E. B. Du Bois and Carter G. Woodson earned their degrees, in 1895 and 1912, respectively. Like these scholars before him, Franklin encountered the depths of antiblackness in the academic world. This he encountered not only in the content of knowledge itself—in the curricula and books assigned to him—but also in the very structures of institutions where knowledge was created and preserved. Franklin learned that segregated research libraries reflected the system through which antiblack ideas were manufactured. During his dissertation year, in 1939, Franklin went to Raleigh, North Carolina, to conduct research on free African Americans during the antebellum era. When he arrived, the director of the State Department of Archives and History assured him that "the archives had relevant materials but admitted quite frankly that in planning the building the architects had never anticipated that any African American would ever do research there." Pitying Franklin, the director agreed that he had a right to conduct research then devised a plan and asked the young scholar to return in a few days. Franklin arrived the following week and "was escorted to a small room across from the large whites-only research room. It had been outfitted with a table, chair, and wastebasket and was to be my private office for an indefinite period of time."[23]

Refusing to be deterred by such encounters of epistemic violence, Franklin chose to read such experiences through the frame of an early lesson learned from his mother. Along with his mother and sister, Franklin was ejected from a railroad car in 1921 because they sat in a white section of the train. Angry and embarrassed by the incident, Franklin began crying when they returned home, prompting his mother to help him see the experience in a new light. As he told it, "She admonished me not to waste my energy fretting but to save it in order to prove that I was as good as any of them." Scholarship would be his weapon of choice. He told new stories that reflected black life as nuanced and full of lessons about the human experience. Franklin recounted, "I became a student and eventually a scholar. And it was armed with the tools of scholarship that I strove to dismantle those laws, level those obstacles and disadvantages, and replace superstitions with humane dignity."[24]

Other black learners told their stories about the Jim Crow library. For instance, Ida Mae Holland of Greenwood, Mississippi, recalled her excitement anytime her mother (a washerwoman) received used Perry Mason novels from her white women clients. Holland, a child of the 1950s and 1960s, explained, "I was glad to have them because we couldn't afford to buy books from Chaney's drugstore, and black people weren't allowed inside the county library."[25]

Another example: David Bradley had just graduated high school in Pennsylvania when Martin Luther King Jr. was assassinated in April 1968. He vividly recalled listening to his father that summer, as he told the story of his exclusion from the public library as a student at Livingstone College in North Carolina.

> A book he'd needed had been unavailable in the college library. He had not been in the South long—was not attuned to the pervasiveness of southern racism—and so he had walked in the front door of the town's public library and asked for what he wanted.
>
> The librarian had regarded him, he said, with shock, but with, he thought, a little pity; she had told him to go to the back door

> and knock and she would hand the book out to him. Embarrassed both by the insult and by his lack of savoir faire but holding the knowledge contained in that book more dear than dignity or pride, he had gone around to the back and, after waiting a few moments to give her time to get there, knocked. It had been, he said, half an hour before he had admitted to himself that that door was never going to be opened.[26]

Though Bradley did not personally experience this degrading encounter, it was part of his own inheritance as a black learner. He went on to the University of Pennsylvania in the fall of 1968 and experienced varying degrees of marginalization in higher education, experiences that were surely an extension of this longer history of antiblackness in the literary world. His father's story made black marginalization in education more than just a historical phenomenon. It was deeply personal and bound up in his own family lineage.

Another black student's narrative underscores how an awareness of antiblackness shaped even the smallest moments in her educational journey. There existed a white perception that black people would not care for books, or that they were unworthy of fresh, unused books. Katie Cannon learned that there were aspects of black literary practices that were about proving to the world that black people were "decent human beings." Whether or not they were effective or prudent strategies, some literacy acts by African Americans sought to represent the race in a respectable light, to disprove what the world said about them. Katie Cannon came of age in North Carolina during the 1960s. She explained, "You couldn't go to the library in my town. . . . We couldn't go roller-skating, couldn't go to the pool." However, a bookmobile occasionally traveled through communities, giving black students the opportunity to borrow reading material. Even the bookmobile emphasized the racial hierarchy of American society in that it had a black side and a white side. The books on the black side were of a noticeably different quality. They were older books that were previously used by white students.

Cannon remembered how her "grandmother always insisted that we return the books in the same condition that we received them. This was her effort to *prove* to the white community that we were decent human beings."[27]

There is more than one way to read and assess Cannon's grandmother's strategy of protest. Black literacy manifests at multiple levels in this scenario when we account for Cannon's striving to engage with the literary world of books alongside her grandmother naming the social text to be read—the politics of Jim Crow structuring the encounter. There was much to be inferred and negotiated on the black side of the bookmobile. It was a physical manifestation of the color line and thus of her and her granddaughter's veiled existence. The arrangement of the mobile library suggested something about Cannon as a literate subject: that she was not a decent human being. Cannon's grandmother insisted that she be aware of this lie, and that she refuse to be reduced to it. Taking the bookmobile as an object—or a text even—we might read the meaning it carried about the value (or lack thereof) associated with one group of readers over the other. And, like Cannon's grandmother, black learners used their own second sight and the plurality of reading practices it engendered to refuse this meaning.

Proper literacy for black students—from Mary McLeod Bethune to Jerry Moore to John Hope Franklin to Katie Cannon—meant achieving a mature appreciation of the relationship between race and reading and how such relations were embedded in the canons of knowledge and educational structures. Black students were disavowed as readers and experienced restricted access, at best, to the literary world. What's more, they developed an awareness of the antiblack sentiments shaping the content of books and knowledge systems housed in libraries. They learned of, but were taught not to absorb, widely held beliefs that blacks were subpar readers and lacking literary culture. Becoming black literate subjects meant developing counterreadings of these presumptions and social phenomenon. These were lies they had to refuse as part of their reading practice. To be properly literate required the honing of one's inner eyes as black readers. From behind the veil, black students had to learn to read in a way that accounted for their double consciousness. Their second sight required a distinct kind of engagement with the word and the world.

BLACK READING IN CONTEXT

Reading is contextual. This context extends beyond schoolhouses and libraries or bookmobiles. The political and economic forces shaping an environment always have some relationship to structures of schooling embedded within it and the experiences people have within those institutions of learning. Jerry Moore witnessed his community coming together to cultivate cotton in an effort to build the school in which he would be taught. Mary McLeod Bethune encountered resistance to her literacy by the children of her mother's former masters. John Hope Franklin recognized a kinship between academic culture and the violent debasement he and his family experienced in Jim Crow Oklahoma. As mentioned before, some African American students detected relationships between the southern agricultural economy and restrictions imposed on black education. They noted that some children were unable to attend school during harvest season, and in many instances school boards shortened the black academic calendar to ensure that the hands of black children were free and available for work in the field.

The phenomenon of white planters working coercively to keep black children in the fields (and sometimes the homes of white people) as opposed to going to school began in the nineteenth century and persisted well into the twentieth century. William Holtzclaw, whose mother helped him sneak off to school against the wishes of their white landlord in the 1880s, provides an early account of how the demands of cotton impacted the educational lives of black children. Around the age of six he noticed the white landlord demanding that his mother send him and his brother to the field instead of school. To work around this demand, Holtzclaw and his brother attended school on alternate days. On the days Holtzclaw went to school, his brother stayed home to work, and they exchanged lessons at night; the following day they switched roles.[28] Responding to the persistence of this threat, African Americans continued to find ways of subverting the power of white planters.

Dorothy Robinson, born in central Texas during the first decade of the twentieth century, recalled conversations between her father, a tenant farmer, and local white officials who found black education to be an inconvenience. On one occasion their landlord demanded that her father "take those kids out of school and have them help gather this crop." But her family routinely defied such orders. On another occasion, the local school superintendent attempted to interfere with her father's efforts to send his sons outside of the community for high school. Speaking to Robinson's father, the superintendent asserted, "Caleb, niggers don't need any education."[29]

The white school official believed the idea that Robinson's brothers should move to another district for high school to be absurd. They were two young men that could be of great help by using their hands in the field. Why should they aspire to anything beyond this? The exchange recounted by Robinson took place in the 1920s, a time when many southern cities had no high schools for black students, especially small rural communities like the one in which Robinson and her family lived.[30] Sending her brothers away was the only opportunity for them to further their education. Most, if not all, black parents preferred that their children attend school—like Holtzclaw's and Robinson's parents. However, black economic precarity made it difficult to excuse children as field hands given the demands of the southern agricultural economy and the forceful hand of white elites who benefited from it the most.

Even by the 1950s and 1960s, black education continued to be undermined by the racialized labor economy of the Jim Crow South. Ida Mae Holland recalled not only how King Cotton shortened her school year but also that many young black girls were forced to be domestic laborers during their teenage years in the Mississippi delta. She was keenly aware that "Leflore County's black schools usually opened a couple of months after the white schools to ensure that enough hands were available in the fields." Holland and many of her friends exchanged stories in the school hallways and bathroom about things they witnessed while working in the homes of white people. Some stories revealed the extreme gap in wealth between blacks and whites, as evidenced by the material differences these girls observed between the two communities. Other stories exposed their sexual vulnerability to white men and women in these homes, where they cooked, cleaned, and cared for other people's children.[31] There was a disjuncture between the educational desires their communities cultivated within them and the limitations externally imposed by the society in which they lived. They read—both in the world at large and the words that passed before them—the contradiction of being a learner while also being defined as valuable only for their unskilled labor as exploitable workers, infinitely available, and fungible, as field hands and domestic servants.

Despite and perhaps because of efforts to undermine their educational striving, many students developed a sophisticated reading of power. They had resources in their parents, black teachers, and at times their peers to help them make sense of these matters. Recall that Holtzclaw's mother helped him devise plans to circumvent their landlord's insistence that he report to the field as opposed to the classroom in the late nineteenth century. Susie King Taylor's enslaved grandmother taught her how and why she must conceal her books on the way to her teacher's home in Savannah, Georgia. Katie Cannon's grandmother cultivated her granddaughter's awareness of the racial politics of the segregated bookmobile. Ralph Ellison recalled the many parents in Oklahoma City who expressed a desire for their children to get an education because they "wished their children to have no contact with the cotton patch."[32] Black communities expressed their discontent with the efforts to stifle black education at dinner tables, in family conversations, during community gatherings, and, at times, to white people directly. Their discontent indexed a set of counterreading practices that were informed by a critique of the social order.

Dorothy Robinson echoed these sentiments, describing the pride her family took in her education over the years, as she worked toward becoming a teacher. Her educational striving made her a symbol of progress for her family. "Through me the families were pushing the boundaries," she wrote. They were pressing "farther from the field work and domestic chores, which to my parents' generation still held deep connotations of slavery."[33] This desire to distance oneself from the kind of work that carried the stain of slavery added important meaning to black literacy. The demand to read and write and get a good education was closely linked to a desire to gain employment beyond unskilled agricultural and domestic work—not because these jobs were not important but as a desire to escape the abjection black people continued to experience in such roles. What's more, the Industrial Age was burgeoning by the end of the nineteenth century. Black laborers, especially those in the twentieth century, understood the dwindling import of the agriculture business at the level of the worker. The signs were all around them.

Obtaining an education to escape oppressive labor conditions had to do with achieving a new way of being in the world as black people. Students encountered this mission in explicit terms, and it shaped their outlook on the world around them. Such critiques empowered students to read the disjuncture between the devaluing of their lives by the outside world and the high value their families and communities placed on them. In order to be capable readers, black students had to learn to read between the color lines. This was particularly the case for black students in the South. But to be clear, limitations imposed on the opportunities for black literacy transcended regional boundaries.

BLACK READERS BEYOND THE SOUTH

Northern libraries did not formally exclude black readers, but neither did they extend a warm welcome. As one scholar observed, "Racially restricted library access existed in the North, but much of it was perpetrated under cover." While libraries did not hang signs that read "No Colored Allowed," there were other ways to discourage black readers from coming in. This often took the form of "a stern expression on a white librarian's face, an all-white staff and clients, the request that a black library user sit at a table where white users wouldn't sit."[34] Students in northern cities were also less likely to encounter books by black authors or counternarratives about black people in their schools. An engagement with alternative, black scripts of knowledge could help students challenge stereotypical narratives about black life found in ordinary schoolbooks and the broader political sphere. Black teachers were often responsible for exposing students to such counterreading practices, but African American educators were far less common in northern cities than in the South.

Political thinker and civil rights activist Malcolm X attended junior high school near Lansing, Michigan, in 1940 when his white English teacher urged him to limit his aspirations. His dream of becoming a lawyer was deemed unreasonable, despite his rank as the top student of his class. "A lawyer—that's not a realistic goal for a nigger," his teacher Mr. Ostrowski explained. Instead, he insisted that Malcolm become a carpenter. "You need to think about something you *can* be. You're good with your hands—making things. Everybody admires your carpentry shop work. Why don't you plan on carpentry? People like you as a person—you'd get all kinds of work."[35] For similar reasons, Huey P. Newton, founder of the Black Panther Party, described his education in the public schools of Oakland, California, as demotivating and disruptive to his aspirations as a black student during the 1950s. Not only was the education he received irrelevant to his life and experiences, but as he explained, these schools "nearly killed [his] urge to inquire" and "explore the worlds of literature, science, and history."[36]

Few opportunities existed for Malcolm X to acquire counternarratives to ward off the antiblack ideas he encountered in the racially mixed schools he attended in the North. He eventually dropped out, and it was not until prison that he learned of books and ideas that supported new ways of looking at the world—new ways of reading and interpreting his reality. "*Souls of Black Folk* by W. E. B. Du Bois gave me a glimpse into the black people's history before they came to this country," Malcolm X recalled. He continued, "Carter G. Woodson's *Negro History* opened my eyes about black empires before the black slave was brought to the United States, and the early Negro struggles for freedom."[37] Like Jerry Moore, Malcolm X encountered Woodson's writings as a resource that helped shape a new mode of interpretation. But they encountered Woodson's literature on starkly different terms: one in a segregated classroom, the other in prison.

African Americans in northern states repeatedly emphasized that they rarely encountered black history and literature in formal school settings. And despite this reality, some encountered alternative curricula in community spaces and in their homes. Sara Lawrence-Lightfoot was a student in New York City during the 1940s and 1950s, but her parents were educated in southern black schools and had strong ties to historically black colleges. Recognizing what their daughter would and would not get in New York City's schools, the Lawrences worked to fill in the gap. Sara remembered her father writing to her school in protest because of the racially hostile language found in her textbook. Even though her father was the vice president of the local school board and a strong advocate of "Negro history" and culture, very little of this made its way into her classrooms. Sara recalled encountering just one poem by a black person in all of her twelve years in the city's schools, and she was often the only black student in her classes, especially the college preparatory courses.

Two particular moments left a deep impression on Sara, proving to her the need to be vigilant of the knowledge and words that passed before her as a black student. The first occurred in her eighth-grade citizenship class.

> Miss Shopper—her pale face caked with powder, her eyebrows drawn on with black pencil, wisps of white hair escaping from underneath her red wig—taught us that Abraham Lincoln led the country in the War between the States and that the battle had nothing to do with slavery. Her eyes rested on me—the only Negro child in the class—daring me to challenge her interpretation of history.

Sara discussed this encounter with her parents that evening, and they promptly made the correction, leaving no question that her teacher was misinformed. "It was 'the Civil War,' and the institution of slavery was at its very center," they explained. Sara also recalled her "father's rage at discovering the word 'barbarian' used to describe the Mayan Indians of Central America" in her social studies book. "He could not resist lecturing us on the 'extraordinary' Mayan civilization—its creativity, organization, and resilience—and then immediately sat down at his typewriter to bang out a restrained but angry letter to my teacher."[38]

Her father's counternarratives about history reinforced other lessons Sara acquired at home, often around her family's dinner table. She referred to this as "the family curriculum": a set of values, knowledge, and ways of being transmitted in the home, which interacted with lessons learned in school. This family curriculum was steeped in literature and culture by black people not covered in the official school curriculum, knowledge her parents gained from their education in the South.

This migration narrative of black pedagogy is one that reappears in other student accounts. Herb Boyd was a Detroit high school student in 1951 when he encountered a new southern migrant named

Willie. There was a distinction in the education Boyd received and the one Willie experienced before he reached Michigan from Georgia. Willie had a southern accent and a gold tooth, which made him the target of many jokes. Yet Boyd and other kids were taken aback by the ease with which Willie told them stories about people like Booker T. Washington and George Washington Carver. On one particular occasion, Boyd and a group of students were joking with one another—reciting poetry and playing the dozens—when Willie shocked them again. He recited the words to "Lift Every Voice and Sing" from memory. He then sang the song for all to hear. This song, known then as the Negro national anthem, was a core part of the educational culture handed to Willie by his black teachers in Georgia. Boyd came to consider these experiences with Willie as his "first lesson in 'black studies' long before the designation was embraced."[39]

Sonia Sanchez and Angela Davis, both activists and intellectuals, migrated from Birmingham, Alabama, to New York City. They moved north having already been exposed to the counterreading practices in black southern education. Sanchez, who would eventually become a leading figure in the Black Arts Movement and black studies, moved to Harlem in 1943 and found the literary landscape of the city's schools to be a new world entirely. Not only was it shocking to learn that there was no space at her new school for "Lift Every Voice and Sing," which schools routinely sang during assemblies in Birmingham, but there were also no black narratives or poetry in the curriculum. Sanchez explained,

> The only time we came across black folks was . . . during slavery in a history book where you saw pictures of them, you know, probably looking very sullen and very helpless in those books. That was the only time, so the New York education was one that was interesting. Well, it was interesting in looking at the two, in the segregated schools you learned about black folks. You got some black history. You got, I mean, some black poetry at least, you know. You got

> some black books. You know, that black folks did write. When you came to the North for freedom, you came into these schools that were "desegregated" in a sense, right? And you never ever read anything that was black.

Migrating to New York in the 1950s, and during her junior year of high school, Angela Davis realized that she knew a great deal more than students in the North about black America's history and tradition of resistance. She too learned this from her black teachers in Birmingham, Alabama, where her mother worked as an educator.[40]

The circumstances surrounding black students' literary lives varied and were particular to place. Yet the demand for a proper black literacy was consistent. The need to read with second sight transcended place. It was never just a southern phenomenon, even as a majority of black people continued to reside in the southern states. In fact, when writing of what he called "the Negro's gift of second sight," it is important to note that Du Bois couches this theorization in a personal experience of marginalization in a New England classroom during the 1870s. Irrespective of place, the antiblack color line cast a shadow over the lives of black students. Their shared vulnerability prompted shared demands in their lives as literate subjects. The importance of reading with second sight was a general lesson black students learned across time and place, across the particular circumstances that varied from one context to the next.

THE COMMUNAL VALUE OF BLACK LITERACY

While reading might typically be thought of as an individual act, black students' literary heritage emerged in community, as a collective endeavor. As previously discussed, many enslaved learners—such as Frederick Douglass, Susie King Taylor, and William Sanders Scarborough—recalled forging written passes for other enslaved people to visit family members on nearby plantations or to make attempts at escape. These underlying values of communal literacy continued to shape the lives of black children post-Emancipation. Carter G. Woodson recalled reading newspapers for his formerly enslaved father in Virginia during the 1880s. A group of West Virginia coal miners recruited him to do the same in the 1890s. These men, who were also Civil War veterans, relied on Woodson to read books and newspapers aloud after long hours in the mines.[41] These after-work literary sessions, which took place while Woodson was still a student himself, were in many respects his first assignment as an educator.

As was the case for Woodson in the late nineteenth century, black students' literacy continued to be communally valued well into the twentieth century. Beginning in 1922, John Hope Franklin, at seven years old, "went each Saturday afternoon to the home of Mr. Nathan Bohanan, who was blind, to read to him." Franklin's mother volunteered his services, and he found the time to be quite rewarding. He explained, "I read to him from recent issues of the *Muskogee Daily Phoenix*, the *Black Dispatch*, which was published in Oklahoma City and contained good coverage of nationwide news concerning African Americans, and the Sunday school lesson."[42]

Communal literacy had many functions in African American communities. Ida Mae Holland recalled her mother being a skilled midwife in their Mississippi delta community, even as she was unable to read and write. When her mother delivered babies, she relied on Ida Mae to fill out the birth certificates, which were then filed with the county records. Ida Mae explained, "A licensed granny midwife had to be able to read and write in order to sign certificates of birth . . . [but] mama didn't know her ABC's, let alone how to read and write, but I did. She decided that when she got her permit to practice, I would be her assistant to handle the paperwork for her." While Holland's mother was not technically literate, she participated in a literate culture, pushing her daughter to get an education and relying on her to help serve their local community as a midwife. Ida Mae's mother would simply "sign her mark" in the place of a signature. Ida Mae's story is reminiscent of many African

Americans who relied on their children's literacy after slavery. Some black learners even read contracts drawn up by landlords and local stores to safeguard their families from being cheated and exploited.[43]

An engagement with black educational history requires an appreciation for how black Americans who were technically illiterate interacted with and advanced a black literary culture. Literacy was not only to be an introspective, antisocial, or individualistic endeavor. It was widely believed that the future of the race depended on students being astute literate subjects. Proper black literacy, at its core, was a shared project, and political in nature.

Relatedly, black literacy was a mode of expressing freedom and a resource in fighting against white supremacy. It was used to correct the written record, which often condemned black life. It was a means for black people to document the world as they knew it—an opportunity to record their counterreadings of the word and the world. It is worth observing that the stories in this very book were extracted from autobiographies and first-person accounts by black writers and those who chose to give an account of their educational worlds that it might be revisited and studied in the future. In reflecting on their experiences as students, black writers emphasized the historical relationship between race and reading in their lives, as well as the lives of students before them.

LOOK AT LITTLE IDA MAE HOLLAND READ: A BLACK GAZE OF THE WHITE GAZE

So far, Ida Mae Holland has surfaced as the girl who recorded the names of the black children her mother helped guide into the world, as the student who observed white people shortening the black school year calendar, as the young woman who gossiped in the bathroom with her schoolmates about things they saw while working in white people's homes. Ida Mae was also a troublemaker. Some knew her for being in places young girls weren't "supposed" to be, for ditching school, and the list goes on. So it was ironic when she of all people earned a reputation as the best reader at Stone Street School in Greenwood, Mississippi. It was an interesting turn of events, when she—the student that so many people thought of as fast and untamed, particularly because of her close affiliation with sex workers who rented rooms at her home—became the shining beacon of hope for her school and community.

During one school semester in the late 1950s, news broke that a group of important white people would be visiting the school in response to the recent *Brown v. Board of Education* decisions in 1954 and 1955, which aimed to desegregate schools. Stone Street's principal, Mr. Coleman, wanted to demonstrate how bright his students were during this visit. Like so many others, he wanted to disprove the idea that black students were less capable than white students with whom they might be going to school in the near future. Mr. Coleman also wanted to demonstrate that black teachers were capable educators, hoping that they would not be thrown by the wayside if and when schools actually desegregated.[44] Mr. Coleman announced the upcoming visit on a Friday before it took place. Everyone seemed to be on edge. At the principal's request "all able-bodied students were recruited to clean up the more neglected parts of our building: the dirty windows, moldy bathrooms, scuffed up hallways, and trash-strewn, overgrown lawns." Students, teachers, and people from the community immediately started tidying up the school.

It was a big deal anytime white visitors came to black schools. Recall Zora Neale Hurston's experience in the previous chapter, where she and her classmates were required to read and perform their literacy before an audience of two white women visitors who dropped by unannounced. These visitors usually held a great deal of influence, even if they were not official school authorities. A negative report from any respected white citizen could lead to repercussions for African American students and teachers. Such dynamics in power meant that, at times, black school leaders and students had to pander to white guests. So the pomp and circumstance of this occasion at Stone Street was in many ways a coerced performance. It was a complicated mixture of insecurity and the assertion of pride, all at the same time. To be clear, the insecurity wasn't because they believed themselves inferior but because they knew white folks thought them to be so. They were knowledgeable of the fact that their precarity had long been intimately shaped by such beliefs.

However one chooses to reach such social dynamics, the reality is that Principal Coleman wanted his school prepared to put their best foot forward. He refused to offer anything that could be used as evidence to reinforce the ideas publicly expressed by white school officials about his students. In preparation for Monday's visit, he called the school community together for a rally. Ida Mae's recollection of this event is worth quoting at length.

> When we sweaty laborers were in our places, he asked us to stand and pledge allegiance to the federal flag, sing "God Bless America," and recite the Lord's Prayer. With Abraham Lincoln, Kate Smith, and Jesus Christ now suitably paid homage to, Mr. Coleman began his oration.
>
> "Teachers, students—a *great* honor is being bestowed on us here at Stone Street School. Our superintendent called me early this morning to say that many great educators will be coming to evaluate our school—to see how we're doing. I said to him"—he stepped out from behind the beat-up podium and raised his arms dramatically—"We're ready! Yes, sir—we're *ready!* Come ahead with your visit!"
>
> The *amens* and *yessahs* began with a few adults—staff mostly, then some teachers—and cascaded quickly to the seventh graders. Everlena and I and a few other well-known malcontents joined in, just for the hell of it, raising our voices with the others. Mr. Coleman was on a roll:
>
> "Yes, I told him, come ahead with your visit. You will find that we know how to read. We know how to write. And we know how

> to do arithmetic!" Everybody hung on his words. We began to feel blessed—like a chosen people. Even old Jaybird Jackson, who was eighteen years old and had been left back in the sixth grade for more years than I had been in school, applauded wildly, tears falling around his snotty nose. Mr. Coleman paused to acknowledge the ovation. "Come ahead—we welcome your visit! Come ahead—because you will find that this school, Stone Street School, is bringing forth the Colored Leading Class of Tomorrow!" The applause was deafening.

Mr. Coleman emphasized the importance of the visit. He then instructed "each teacher [to] select the best reader from each class." From this group of finalists, he would choose one to represent Stone Street during the special program the following Monday.

Ida Mae was not selected to read for the guests. She was not even chosen as her class champion. Queen Oliphant would represent the school. This did not come as a surprise. Most students knew Queen to be a Goody Two-shoes anyway. She was often favored over her peers. Even Ida Mae had to admit, however, that Queen did a good job with her rendering of James Weldon Johnson's "The Creation." She read it as if she herself were the teacher. By the time Ida Mae got home, everyone in the neighborhood knew about the upcoming visit. The pastor even said a special prayer for Queen at church that Sunday.

Monday morning arrived and Ida Mae, about eleven years old, woke up to the smell of food cooking. Because of the occasion, Ida Mae got a Sunday breakfast on a Monday morning. Her mother also laid out her best clothes—last year's Easter dress. "I wants you t' be clean and 'spectable in front of all dem big-shot white folkses," she recalled her mother saying. Indeed, everyone came to school clean and dressed to the tee. "There were no truants from Stone Street School that day. All the students were present and accounted for and wearing their best clothes," Ida Mae recalled. And all the teachers' hair had noticeably been done the night before.

The day began in ceremonial fashion. The band played, the majorettes processed into the auditorium, the room was packed with everyone—including students from the local high school. All the welcome speeches took place. Then the time came: Queen was called on stage to deliver a reading. It was such a high-pressure moment for a child. It would be hard to blame anyone if they cracked under such force. It must have felt like the weight of the world was on her, like the fate of the entire race was being balanced on her shoulders. And that is just what happened: Queen's nerves got the best of her, and she froze. She just dropped the book and ran away.

Something took hold of Ida Mae and convinced her that it would be a good idea to go up to the microphone. Somebody had to do something, she thought. The teachers tried to stop her: "Ida Mae Holland, siddown!" she heard one of them say. Holland got to the stage and picked up the book. She settled on Ernest Lawrence Thayer's "Casey at the Bat," cleared her throat at the microphone, and "the auditorium went stone silent."

> I held the book with one hand, the way our teacher had taught us was proper. "The outlook wasn't brilliant for the Mudville nine that day; / The score stood four to two with but one inning more to play." I paused for emphasis, the way Leroy Harper had taught me. "And then, when Cooney died at first"—my hand went to my heart— "and Barrows did the same"—my hand flashed down like an umpire's "you're out" sign— "A sickly silence fell upon the patrons of the game."
>
> . . .
>
> Halfway through the poem, I had the entire assembly hanging on my every word. By the time Casey came to bat, teachers and students alike were rooting aloud for him.
>
> . . .
>
> The final pitch came on a crescendo, then I modulated into a strong, sad voice—"But there is no joy in Mudville—mighty Casey

> has Struck Out." I lowered my hands, hung my head, and let the weight of Mudville, Gee Pee, Greenwood, the Delta, the whole South sink onto my little shoulders. Then I closed the book and bowed to each person on the stage.

The response to Mr. Coleman's speech during Friday's rally was nothing compared to the response Ida Mae received from the crowd.

Mr. Coleman hugged Ida Mae as everyone cheered, and the white superintendent made his way to the podium to address the audience. He commended Ida Mae for her spectacular reading. This, he said, was evidence that black kids were learning just fine in the all-black schools. Ida Mae was evidence that schools *did not* need to integrate. "Our colored boys and girls know how to read! Well, now we can say to them [referring to advocates of integration], just look at . . . little Ida Mae Holland, if they want to know how well our colored children can read!"

READING THE STONE STREET SCHOOL SCENARIO THROUGH A BLACK GAZE

And now, a reading of the school official through the lens of second sight: an awareness of the color line and its influence in this scenario; a black gaze—to borrow from black feminist theorist Tina Campt—which demands a way of seeing that is not about *looking at* Ida Mae, but *looking with* and *alongside* Ida Mae, and through her experiences as a black female student in the Mississippi delta.[45] The superintendent twisted Ida Mae Holland's literacy act to support his efforts to undermine demands for racial justice in America's schools. The paradox here is that even if Ida Mae had not given a spectacular reading, even if the event ended with Queen running away with stage fright, this too would have been sufficient evidence for the superintendent's claim. The argument would then be that African American children were incapable of competing with white students in school and therefore that integration was a bad idea.

Many made such arguments. For the white superintendent, all roads led back to this conclusion.

Second sight also requires caution when reading the words of the superintendent alongside the words of Mr. Coleman. At first glance they seemed to be saying the same thing: black kids were learning in their schools; they were capable readers and scholars. However, their motives differed quite drastically. Mr. Coleman's desire to display his students' abilities was motivated by a vindicationist impulse. His was a desire to dispel myths about black people's intellectual inferiority and instead demonstrate that these children were on their way as "the Colored Leading Class of Tomorrow!"

The superintendent wanted to prove that everything was well and good in the South, that nothing about Jim Crow society needed to be changed. Segregation was in the best interest of children like Ida Mae Holland. *Just look at her read.* Taking the words of these two men at face value was not enough. Students like Ida Mae needed to know the meaning behind the words, even when they seemed to be saying the same thing. It required reading with second sight—having to account for the perspective of power and whiteness as well as one's own vantage point as a black person living under persecution in a Jim Crow society. In the process, students had to draw meaning that contended with the disjuncture between these competing visions.

But Ida Mae Holland was *looking back*. The vision cast from her vantage point tells quite a different story. One might take solace in Ida Mae's duplicity in this moment, as she performed her literacy act in front of her community for the enjoyment of a white superintendent committed to racial segregation. In the scenario, Ida Mae *acts* like she is reading from the book, but she is actually reciting from memory. No one in the audience was aware of this, except for her friends Everlena and Leroy Harper. Leroy taught her the poem "Casey at the Bat" during their ditch parties at Everlena's house in exchange for cigarettes. She had him say it enough times so she could "learn it by heart." Ida Mae—who would later become a theater professor—developed a skill for performing and working an audience, even under such coerced circumstances as this particular event. As Leroy put it, Ida Mae was "a nat'ral-born play-liker!"

Like so many other students, Ida Mae was forced to display and perform her intellect to be measured as an assessment of her entire race. This burden of representation had been part and parcel of black learners' experience since the time of Phillis Wheatley. Europeans and Americans, inquisitive about the intellectual capabilities of black students, "undertook experiments in which young African slaves were tutored and trained along with white children. Phillis Wheatley was merely one result of such an experiment." The writings of black scholars like Wheatley were "seized upon both by pro- and anti-slavery proponents as proof that their arguments were sound."[46] For so long, black literacy and reason have been scrutinized and surveilled at the behest of white suspicion and curiosity, manipulated and underdeveloped to support white interests. This history was in the room when Ida Mae got up to read before the skeptical white spectators.

Zora Neale Hurston observed this in her Florida community around the turn of the twentieth century, when her class was required to read aloud for the pleasure of two white women visitors. Richard Wright struggled with his school principal's attempts to tone down the rhetoric in his junior high valedictorian speech, so that he would not offend the white visitors during the graduation ceremony. And the list goes on. Through such fractured moments, black students encountered the complexity of their lives as literate subjects. Like double consciousness more broadly, black readers often found themselves having to contend with a white gaze, having to interact with the words and world constituting their literary lives through the eyes of others.

Reading is a deeply political act for black students, precisely because of the dynamics of power embedded in literature and the literary procedures recalled in this chapter. Being properly literate as black learners demands an understanding about the deep relationship between race and reading, but also the importance of reading the word and the world as co-constitutive. A literacy of both is necessary because the two shape and reinforce one another. A proper literacy is one that privileges reading between the (color) lines, one that holds words accountable to the tensions formed between power and black desires for freedom and justice.

The path to becoming literate subjects has been a shared journey for black students. Across time and space, distinct social dynamics and structures of power have cut across the range of their experiences, binding them together. Over the course of their journey, to read in the dark has required the gift of second sight. It means attending to characters of power and racial domination that are always embedded in texts, or contexts, even when such characters are not easily visible or go unnamed. While both a boon and a curse, such vigilance has long been essential to black students' development.

Chapter 5

A Singing School for Justice

This eve. heard Harry read, then the children came in, and sang for us, and had a regular "shout" in the piazza, of which, of course Prince was the leader. He is the most comical creature I ever saw. Besides the old songs they sang two new ones, so singular that I must try to note down the words—some of them. But of the tune and manner of singing it is impossible to give any idea.

—CHARLOTTE FORTEN, journal entry, November 30, 1862

THERE WAS A SONG in the black interior. Beneath the veneer of compliance and deference to white authoritative power, the black school was always a singing school of protest and fugitive planning, where black students could dream up a world more beautiful and more than just the one around them. Within their minds, their imaginations, their songs, their classrooms, they could block out the noise—at least for a little while. Abolitionist Charlotte Forten (Grimké) jumped at the opportunity to teach the freedpeople during the Civil War. She arrived at St. Helena Island, just off the coast of South Carolina, in October 1862.

In addition to lessons in reading and writing, Forten also taught the children stories about the Haitian Revolution and the John Brown song. On Monday, November 10, she wrote the following in her journal: "We taught—or rather commenced teaching the children 'John Brown,' which they entered into eagerly." She continued, "I felt the full significance of that song being sung here in S.C. by the little Negro children, by those whom he—the glorious old man—died to save." Three days later, she described "talk[ing] to the children a little while to-day about the noble Toussaint. They listened very attentively. It is well that they sh'ld know what one of their own color c'ld do for his race." The legacy of Toussaint Louverture and John Brown, Forten hoped, would "inspire them with courage and ambitions (of a noble sort,) and high purpose." Forten also recalled the students of St. Helena gifting her with songs of their own. She tried to record some of the lyrics in her journal, but the spirit that accompanied the children's singing, what it seemed to carry and transmit, could not be described in words: "the tune and manner of singing it is impossible to give any idea," she explained.[1]

Mary McLeod Bethune, born in 1875 to formerly enslaved parents in South Carolina, explained that, after Emancipation, black people cleaved to leaders among them who would organize them "into singing schools."[2] Singing was more than mere entertainment or leisurely activity. It awakened one's being, both the body and the spirit. Students sang songs together to undertake the gathering of minds. They commenced to hum a tune, together, that they might find themselves as one, seeking a shared vision for a collective future—indeed, one better than the world they knew. It wasn't just the activity of singing but the metaphor of the chorus. Black teachers and students often sang songs that resonated with the protracted struggle of their collective lives.

In 1900, a black school anthem was given as song to air when five hundred black student voices gifted it to the world. "Lift Every Voice and Sing" was written by principal (and former student) of Jacksonville's Stanton School and civil rights activist James Weldon Johnson. Johnson's brother Rosamond, also a teacher at the school, was responsible for setting the ballad to music. It became a key feature in black student life as the Negro national anthem. The song was formalized as part and parcel of black people's educational heritage. Black studies scholar Imani Perry characterized the song as a cultural artifact linked to a broader set of "practices that were primarily internal to the black community, rather than those based upon the white gaze or an aspiration for white acceptance." She called such rituals and routines a tradition of "black formalism," which consisted of ways of doing and being conditioned by internally held values, aesthetics, and cultural norms.[3]

A variety of voices recall the song's place in the cultural context of their education but also their recollection of black formalism in African American schools, as represented by black music and literature. Albert Murray referred to "Lift Every Voice and Sing" as the "school bell anthem" at the Mobile County Training School in Alabama, which he attended in the 1920s. It was "the comb your hair brush your teeth shine your shoes crease your trousers tie your tie clean your nails rub a dub stand and sit and look strait make folks proud anthem!"[4] Sonia Sanchez recalled the same of Tuggle Elementary School in Birmingham, Alabama, in the 1930s and early 1940s.[5] Reflecting on these early years, the poet insisted that this song, along with other poems and literature by black writers, planted seeds in her mind that would grow into her literary contributions during the Black Arts Movement decades later.

Al Young, the former poet laureate of California, offered similar recollections of his second-grade teacher in Laurel, Mississippi, during the 1940s. "Miz Chapman, my tireless and inspired all-day second-grade teacher," Young wrote in one of his books, "was smuggling down to me the majesty and magic of poetry and the blues." Despite the constraints imposed on black education during Jim Crow, including racist school curricula and violent surveillance by white school authorities, "Miz Chapman nevertheless forced us to memorize poems, especially works by colored writers."[6]

John Bracey, born in 1941, described how every morning students sang "Lift Every Voice and Sing" at Washington, DC's Lucretia Mott Elementary and Benjamin Banneker Junior High School.[7] The song's lyrics spoke of "the blood of the slaughtered," the bitter experience of a "chastening rod," and yet a people marching on "till victory is won." It was a song that mimicked the highs and lows of black people's odyssey in the new world. It also asserted bold and futuristic pronouncements like "May we forever stand." This anthem was built into the daily rituals of Bracey's school life, as it was for so many other students across the southern states. This song was instilled in the minds of students who would assume leadership roles in the Black Freedom Movement. The ritual of singing the song, day after day, as a formalized part of the school culture planted important seeds in the minds of students.

LIFT EVERY VOICE AND SING

James Weldon Johnson (1871–1938)

Lift every voice and sing,
Till earth and heaven ring,
Ring with the harmonies of Liberty;
Let our rejoicing rise
High as the list'ning skies,
Let it resound loud as the rolling sea.
Sing a song full of the faith that the dark past has taught us,
Sing a song full of the hope that the present has brought us;
Facing the rising sun of our new day begun,
Let us march on till victory is won.
    Stony the road we trod,
Bitter the chast'ning rod,
Felt in the days when hope unborn had died;
Yet with a steady beat,
Have not our weary feet
Come to the place for which our fathers sighed?
We have come over a way that with tears has been watered.
We have come, treading our path through the blood of the slaughtered,
Out from the gloomy past,

Till now we stand at last
Where the white gleam of our bright star is cast.
God of our weary years,
God of our silent tears,
Thou who hast brought us thus far on the way;
Thou who hast by Thy might,
Led us into the light,
Keep us forever in the path, we pray.
Lest our feet stray from the places, our God, where we met Thee,
Lest our hearts, drunk with the wine of the world, we forget Thee;
Shadowed beneath Thy hand,
May we forever stand,
True to our God,
True to our native land.

Despite the deep meaning this song held for the mission of black teachers and students, some schools were mindful not to give the impression that they were too militant or that they placed the interests of the race over those of the country. When Bracey's school had white visitors, teachers prepared the students to sing "The Star-Spangled Banner." This was a marked distinction from their ordinary routines. "But in homeroom every morning," he stressed, "you had to do as part of your culture, you sang the Negro national anthem. . . . We only sang 'The Star-Spangled Banner' when white people showed up. . . . You had to go to the assembly hall the day before and practice 'The Star-Spangled Banner' because nobody knew it."[8]

As is customary in black formalism, African American communities cultivated their own norms, rituals, and ideas about what constituted a purposeful education for students. At key moments, like the one named by Bracey, students became aware of these distinctions. Furthermore, this routine of going to the assembly hall the day before a white visitor arrived to rehearse what teachers and students understood to be a masked performance of their school's cultural norms reveals how black students witnessed the subversive pedagogy of black teachers. It demonstrates how they were required to participate in these acts as dissident learners. Students learned lessons about what it meant to navigate their confined existence in a world premised on black subjugation. Black teachers wore the mask of compliant educators who deferred to the norms of the American educational system and local white authorities, even as they subverted it daily by having their students sing the Negro national anthem, critique Jim Crow, and study lessons about black resistance. There is a relationship between Charlotte Forten's teachings and her students' singing on St. Helena Island in the 1860s and the lives of black students like Murray, Sanchez, and Bracey in the twentieth century.

Singing "Lift Every Voice and Sing" was a ritual that held embedded meaning about black America's history of oppression, resistance, and futuristic visions of freedom and equality. The anthem reflected the interiority of a black world—a set of feelings and a distinct political plight. Indeed, it was the black school bell song.[9] Angela Davis learned to associate resistance with its lyrics, as opposed to the generic language of freedom in "The Star-Spangled Banner" or "My Country, 'Tis of Thee" when growing up in Birmingham, Alabama. While she was not a gifted vocalist, Davis described how she loved to sing "the last phrases full blast: 'Facing the rising sun, till a new day is born, let us march on till victory is won!'"[10] This song's content, and the form in which it was taken up, expressed the core mission of black students.

John Bracey found humor in the confusion he and his classmates experienced in coming to terms with the fact that their national anthem was not *the* national anthem.

> If you said national anthem, we stood up and sang "Lift Every Voice and Sing," but if there was a white superintendent or somebody . . . *[makes a gesture as though he's speaking over a school intercom]*

> "Everybody report to the auditorium. We have to practice the national anthem," everybody'd say, "We already know the national anthem." They'd say, "No, the white national an–" "Oh, that national anthem, okay." Then you had to go down to, "Oh say, can you," . . . which is a horrible goddamn song. When the white person showed up, you sang both of them. You'd open up the program with "The Star-Spangled Banner," but you close with "Lift Every Voice and Sing." If you had wanted to bet money with me when I was in fourth grade, I would have told you "Lift Every Voice and Sing" was the national anthem. White people had some crap they sang, but this is the national anthem.[11]

Bracey reveals how students were called to participate in their teachers' maneuvering around the constraints of Jim Crow school structures. Their behavior was at odds with the structural neglect represented by doctrines of separate and unequal. In staging compliance at Lucretia Mott Elementary, the students and teachers emphasized to themselves that their educational vision was set apart from the demands of white school officials, and to others that they were a self-determined people working to build a new world.

Such singing was accompanied by important moral lessons and oratorical training from their teachers and community members. Black studies scholar Hortense Spillers explained that even when lessons during her youth were not explicitly about black history and culture, they often accrued distinct meaning based on contextual factors in her segregated community of Orange Mound, Tennessee, during the 1940s and 1950s. The King James Bible and poems like William Ernest Henley's "Invictus" took on distinct meaning when seen through the prism of black cultural politics. Spillers recalled that such poems and recitations of scriptures formed an important part "of our first formal training and made for fantastic oratorical development! . . . How could you beat 'I am the master of my fate, I am the captain of my soul' in the mouth of a 10- or 12-year-old black child in front of her admiring elders?"[12]

Such lessons played critical roles in the moral education of African American students and the cultivation of dignity among them, despite a world that condemned black life. What's more, the seeds of this oratorical training named by Spillers bloomed into the stentorian rhetoric one hears when reflecting on the sounds and voices of the Black Freedom Movement. The black phonetics and cadences we often associate with speakers like Martin Luther King Jr., Maya Angelou, and so many others were cultivated in these environments. These traditions were put to work in the struggle for civil rights, helping stir and sustain resistance among African American people standing up to a world wicked and hell-bent on maintaining black abjection.

Students also used traditions of black formalism as they fended off onslaughts by white school leaders and a broader hostile world. Scenes from Maya Angelou's education in Stamps, Arkansas, reflect this reality. Angelou recalled her shock when the principal at Lafayette County Training School instructed everyone to sit down after singing the American national anthem and reciting the Pledge of Allegiance at her 1940 graduation. It was customary to sing "Lift Ev'ry Voice and Sing" after saluting the flag. The abrupt change made Angelou uneasy. "We had been ready to follow our usual assembly pattern," she explained, "the American national anthem, then the pledge of allegiance, then the song every black person I knew called the Negro National Anthem. All done in the same key, with the same passion and most often standing on the same foot."[13] She quickly realized what was happening when "not one but two white men came through the door off-stage" before the shorter of the two, Mr. Edward Donleavy, walked up to the podium.

Donleavy's speech just about ruined graduation for Angelou. His remarks degraded her and her classmates' accomplishments, and they violated the entire occasion. "Donleavy had exposed us," Angelou thought to herself. "We were maids and farmers, handymen and washerwomen, and anything higher that we aspired to was farcical and presumptuous."[14] Donleavy and his colleague left immediately after the speech, because they supposedly had another engagement that prevented them from sitting through the graduation ceremony. They arrived abruptly and left in the same manner. While the two men departed, they left an ugly feeling behind that made it difficult for Angelou to enjoy the rest of the ceremony. Before Donleavy's appearance, she was looking forward to hearing Henry Reed's valedictorian speech, which he had rehearsed for months with the help of his English teacher. The address was entitled "To Be or Not to Be," inspired by Shakespeare's *Hamlet*. Henry had worked on "the dramatic stresses for months," practicing how and where to place his emphasis, identifying the exact words and syllables he would press on to achieve the desired affect with his listeners. "The English teacher had helped him to create a sermon winging through Hamlet's soliloquy." But after Donleavy's speech, it mattered not how Reed perfected his address, how loud and strong his voice was. Angelou was over it. She rolled her eyes and refuted all of Henry Reed's words in her head: "'To Be or Not to Be.' Hadn't he heard the whitefolks? We couldn't *be*, so the question was a waste of time."[15]

But the end of Henry's speech got through to Angelou, pulling her back into the crowded auditorium. He seemed to have made a last-minute modification to his address. Angelou "looked and saw Henry Reed, the conservative, the proper, the A student, turn his back to the audience and turn to us (the proud graduating class of 1940) and sing, nearly speaking," the lyrics of the Negro national anthem. Then, out of habit, the entire class began singing. Then the parents and community members in the audience joined in. This impromptu performance was at once scripted and unscripted. Angelou recalled how in this moment she heard the song—like really heard the song—that "hymn of encouragement"—for the very first time. And "the tears that slipped down many faces were not wiped away in shame." In that moment, Angelou was not just an ordinary graduate; she "was a proud member of the wonderful, beautiful Negro race."[16]

Black students of Angelou's generation and after recalled how commencement ceremonies marked important turning points in their lives and for their families. Like Henry Reed, James D. Anderson was the valedictorian of his 1962 graduating class at George Washington Carver High School in Eutaw, Alabama.[17] The school's principal selected a speech entitled "The Brink of Change" for Anderson to deliver during the commencement. Principal Beasley made the selection because he did not want Anderson "to say something that [would] get the school in trouble." The speech needed to be sensitive to the fact that certain representatives from the school board would be present—and by representatives he meant white people, because although the county was 80 percent black, the school board was all white. Carver High School was in desperate need of new resources—a science building in particular—so this was a delicate matter. Anderson trusted Principal Beasley's judgment, having grown personally aware of the racial politics in Eutaw. As he explained, "What was happening in school in a moment like that was so consistent with what happened in everyday life." Despite the complicated racial politics, Anderson was mostly just excited for the occasion. Graduation marked an important milestone for his family. Anderson's mother had no opportunity to attend or graduate from high school. She also graduated from Carver in the early 1940s, but at the time the school only went to the ninth grade. The high school program was established after she became a wife and mother. Historically speaking, Anderson and his classmates were part of the first generation of African Americans—in Eutaw, and beyond—to have universal access to a high school education.

Anderson thoroughly rehearsed his address and learned it by heart. At Carver, students were not allowed to read from papers when delivering speeches or reciting poems at formal events. He even practiced how he would pause when the school bell rang during his oration, because Principal Beasley informed him there was no way to turn it off. Anderson knew exactly how he would continue his speech after the bell to make the transition feel seamless. He also made a mental note that he would not look his mother in the eye during his address. If he looked at his mother's face, he would likely get emotional and lose it in front of everyone. He wanted to be prepared for everything. But whatever excitement Anderson had for graduation and whatever enthusiasm he expected the audience to have in response to his speech paled in comparison to the news he received from Principal Beasley right before the ceremony. Anderson was pulled out of line as the graduates prepared to process into the auditorium, which caused him to worry. Getting pulled out of line usually meant you were in trouble or failed to meet graduation requirements. But neither was the case in this instance. Principal Beasley informed Anderson that just before his valedictorian address, it would be announced that he received a scholarship to attend Stillman College. Knowing this announcement would come as a shock, Principal Beasley gave Anderson the good news in advance so he would not forget the words to his speech.

The news about Anderson's scholarship to Stillman was completely unexpected. In fact, Anderson had been extremely anxious leading up to graduation because he was so unsure about his next steps. He had never witnessed anyone from Eutaw go away to college. Not for lack of ambition but for a lack of opportunity. Anderson's older brother was Carver's valedictorian the previous year, and he had moved to Detroit with family members to work in a factory. The detail that affected Anderson the most was learning that Principal Beasley had personally traveled to his alma mater in Tuscaloosa and explained to Stillman's dean of students, B. B. Hardy, that he had a student at Carver High School who was special and worthy of a scholarship. Anderson's life changed forever after this graduation in May 1962. In a way, this event also had a lasting impact on African American history. James Anderson's 1988 book, *The Education of Blacks in the South, 1860–1935*, is a singular work on the complex history of race, power, and education in the United States. Many of the ideas and analyses in *School Clothes* are a direct result of Anderson's contributions to historical knowledge, a labor of love intimately bound up with that moment at his high school graduation, and so many others that came before and after.

It is important to note that such cultural experiences of black formalism and the politicized care shown by educators in the narratives described above were not only a phenomenon of the black middle class or rare occurrences in African American education. In her memoir, *Sometime Farmgirls Become Revolutionaries*, Florence Tate described the cultural world of Manassas Elementary and High School in Memphis, Tennessee, in the 1940s. It was a place where rituals of singing were built into the life of the school, along with speeches by important black political leaders. While Manassas had fewer resources in comparison to Booker T. Washington High School, a school more closely associated with the black middle class, Tate described how "faculty and administrators made it a point to make us kids feel good about ourselves and recognize us for our achievements and talents." She especially recalled how her school principal, Mr. Hayes, "brought a parade of great Negroes to Manassas."

Guests included historical figures like "groundbreaking educator Mary McLeod Bethune, and heralded opera singers Roland Hayes and Dorothy Maynor." Students regularly "assembled in the school's large auditorium" and would "gather to hear these inspiring and eminent guests discuss their experiences and share their talents." Tate and her classmates always felt special because of the pride Principal Hayes took in introducing Manassas's students to these special guests. She writes, "Mr. Hayes would always present us to the guests, proudly expressing how beautiful and smart we were, and leading us—students ranging from the first through the twelfth grade—in song." The students and principal sang together to welcome their guests—these black heroes. He often led the students in a popular song, "Let Me Call You Sweetheart," while directing them "to follow his pencil baton with [their] heads as [they] sang." Tate affectionately recalled, "It was one of our favorite rituals."[18]

Subversive curricular objectives undergirded the world of black schooling. The standards and routines we see from student perspectives often contradict images that appear from the outside looking in. Student voices complicate popular narratives of decay and inequality as they pertain to black education of the past. I make such observations not to absolve the injustice of de jure segregation but to suggest that the dynamism of black life can never be confined to such narratives about separate and unequal that only emphasize lack and deficiency. The songs, the rituals, the chorus—they were metaphors for how to know and be in the world on new terms, a cadence and pace of life set apart from the current world order. Their stories were never one or the other, but instead lives lived somewhere between the realities of material neglect on the one hand and black spiritual strivings on the other.

It wasn't just singing. The small acts of fugitive learning recalled in this book extended from a larger, more expansive plot. From the one-by-one stealing away of Susie King Taylor and her brother to go to school in antebellum Georgia, to William Holtzclaw hiding behind pots to evade the cotton field for the classroom, to Zora Neale Hurston and Ida Mae Holland, in different places, at different times, batting their eyes and reading eloquently for white visitors at their schools, black students were in on the plot. They were raised up in it. This came to a head most vividly in May 1963, when students of Birmingham, Alabama, expressed their fugitive learning in spectacular fashion.

Approximately four thousand black students were arrested after marching in protest of Jim Crow's draconian customs and the ubiquitous violence shot through their everyday lives. Students protested the physical violence they knew to be an integral part of black life via lynchings, police terror, and physical abuse in the workplace, but also the aggressively unequal accommodations they received in their public schools, the economic exploitation and manipulation

African American students escorted to jail during 1963 Birmingham Children's March

of their family members as low-skilled workers, and more. The Children's March in Birmingham was a public revealing of black students as fugitive learners.

Black students had been watching and listening to people talk about marching and not "letting nobody turn them around" their whole lives. They learned about the long struggle for freedom they inherited during Negro History Week programs and off-script conversations with their teachers, things often said in hushed tones and passing moments.[19] Some learned this in a very systematic fashion. As William D. Hutchinson recalled, some of Birmingham's African American teachers secretly used alternative textbooks to "provide us Black students with a course that realistically depicted the lives lived by our ancestors under slavery." Two decades before the Birmingham Children's March, when Hutchinson attended Carrie A. Tuggle Elementary (a school named for the former slave turned educator and social activist), he received "a course in 'Negro History' taught from a textbook written by the Black historian, Dr. Carter G. Woodson." Hutchinson explained that "the history, as presented by Dr. Woodson, differed significantly from that presented in the text written by the prolific white historian, Henry Steele Commager, that was mandated for our use in the higher grades." Hutchinson insists that it was clear, to both teachers and students, that "in the Black schools in Birmingham, the text by Woodson was used surreptitiously." He maintains that in order to explore the depths of his early education in black segregated schools, one must "lift the veil on the efforts made by Black educators to teach subjects to their students in opposition to the coursework dictated for us by racist school systems and administrators."[20] Suffice it to say: black students learned they had a distinct mission.

After his release from the Birmingham jail in April 1963, Martin Luther King Jr. found African American adults hesitant to protest and risk being arrested or losing their jobs. White employers assured black workers they would be fired if they participated in the civil disobedience organized by the freedom fighters. This presented an opportunity for students to take a step forward and stand in the gap. So Black students volunteered to go to jail. Organizers desired to fill the jails to the point that there was no more room to take prisoners, eventually exhausting the city's finances, thus demonstrating that Black people's determination far exceeded the holding capacity of the city's police. The goal had been to break the back of Jim Crow in Birmingham, one of its most notorious southern cities.

As one might expect, including children was heavily debated. As a ninth-grade student, Freeman Hrabowski "listened to adults seriously questioning the idea of asking children to march as a tactic in the struggle for civil rights."[21] Seeing no one else able to step up and do the work, the children, from elementary through high school, made the decision on their own. Black students realized they were just as vulnerable to the terrorism of Jim Crow rule as the adults who wanted to protect them. "I realized that as much as our parents and elders cared for us, they could not protect us from the horrors of racism, which raged like a fire," Hrabowski explained. He and his peers witnessed "the bombing not only of churches but of the homes belonging to people like Reverend A. D. King, Dr. King's brother, and the most prominent black attorney in town, Arthur Shores."[22] Less than six months prior to the Birmingham Children's March, on December 17, 1962, someone had bombed Bethel Baptist Church for the third time in three years. At the time of the explosion, a dozen children had been rehearsing for their Christmas play. No one died in this incident; however, just months later, four girls—Addie Mae Collins (14), Carol Denise McNair (11), Carole Rosamond Robertson (14), and Cynthia Dionne Wesley (14)—would be killed in the bombing of Sixteenth Street Baptist Church in Birmingham.[23]

Black youths' vulnerability was bound up in the same precarity as their teachers and parents, who were equally susceptible to antiblack terror. Echoing this awareness, Angela Davis stated, "I remember, from the time I was very small, I remember the sounds of bombs exploding across the street, our house shaking. I remember my father having to have guns at his disposal at all times because of the fact that at any moment . . . we might expect to be attacked."[24] While Davis was not a participant in the march, or a Birmingham student in 1963, her recollections speak to students' awareness of the violence that circumscribed black life, even as they sometimes lacked the precise language to understand its root. In that their mission as learners had long been understood as part and parcel of a protracted struggle for freedom, they were often required or compelled to be active participants in the race's collective fight for justice.

Even loving adults could offer only limited protection for black students. This was made apparent every time a white school official entered their classrooms. Such visits were themselves acts of terror. The seemingly small act of a white official's disruptive surveillance of black classrooms contributed to the atmosphere of antiblack violence: recall, for instance, the purposeful interpretation of Ida Mae Holland's skillful reading as an excuse to maintain separate and unequal facilities. Black learners witnessed towering educators forced to perform an accommodating smallness in the presence of Jim Crow authority. Davis, for instance, had to make sense of the embodied reaction of her teachers as they endured belittling comments and gestures from white visitors. One recurring example was how these visitors insisted on calling black teachers by their first names—just "Susie"—even as accepted custom dictated that adults, especially teachers, be addressed with titles of respect: mister, miss, doctor, or professor. African Americans in the South were especially vigilant of such customs.[25] "When this white assault was staged," wrote Davis, "I tried to decipher the emotions on the teacher's face: acquiescence, obsequiousness, defiance, or the pain of realizing that if she did fight back, she would surely lose her job."[26] In these moments, important people in black students' worlds were told that even they needed to know their place. That place was always somewhere in the shadow of white authority, deferring to the far-reaching hand of whiteness and its calculus of power. In moments like the one Davis recalled, students witnessed their teacher, and all she represented, being taken away and returned marked by the white gaze—teacher and students, all being forced to live the meaning of this moment.[27] During such rituals of power, African Americans students witnessed the black body being transformed into a slave body.[28] Here was the social hierarchy of race, structured by the slave past, even as time purported to put distance between black people and the peculiar institution. These insults—mundane and constant—were part of sustaining and reinforcing the larger injury of antiblack domination.

Black students knew what the world said about them and what it did to them and their people. If lucky, they were given the language to talk about it and space to interrogate and plan action against it—to dream outside of it. For Susie King Taylor, this was the kitchen of a free black woman; for Richard Parker, it was the book hidden underneath his hat as an enslaved boy; for John Bracey, it was his classrooms when white administrators were not around, when they sang songs and performed reenactments of iconic historical moments of black resistance, like the Haitian Revolution; for Angela Davis, it was plotting to sit in the white part of the bus with her high school friends, having been inspired by stories like those of fifteen-year-old Claudette Colvin, who refused to give up her seat to a white woman on a Montgomery bus in March 1955, and of Rosa Parks, who followed in Colvin's footsteps exactly nine months later in December 1955. During the weeks leading up to May 1963, students attended secret meetings hosted at night and during the weekends to prepare for their march against racial terror in Birmingham.

Teachers and activists from the Southern Christian Leadership Conference (SCLC) held regular meetings to train students in the tenets of nonviolent direct action. Sometimes the meetings were on Saturdays; other times they were on weeknights. Students went with their friends, siblings, and classmates to these secret planning meetings. Carolyn King-Miller, a high school student during the 1963 Children's March, recalled the following of these gatherings: "It was nice getting out of my community, going with other community people. Let's say maybe ten or fifteen young people from my community would go to these Saturday meetings. We would learn the civil rights songs, you know, 'I'm Not Going to Let Nobody Turn Me Around,' and understanding what they mean. They would feed us, so we were happy."

Leaders like the minister James Bevel explained to students that they received secondhand athletic gear from white schools. This helped students understand why their team's uniform did not match their school colors. Carolyn recalled the movement leaders explaining that "we were fighting so that you no longer have to walk past a school to go to another school, walk past a white school to go to a black school. We were told that the books were secondhand books that the white students didn't need anymore. And we wanted that."[29]

Students understood the upcoming march to be a challenge to both the major and minor assaults constituting the persecution of black lives in the world around them. Denials of public accommodations and equal access were structural manifestations of the aggressive neglect black people experienced within the American public sphere more broadly. They also understood the march to be a challenge to the everyday, mundane slights they experienced in social interactions with white people on buses, on the streets, and, at times, in their classrooms. Black people's protests had nothing to do with getting closer to white people but everything to do with the ability to live free and dignified lives, unrestrained by degrading laws and customs. Their fight was for the full integration of opportunity in society.

At these meetings, students watched footage from other instances of nonviolent direct action and engaged in discussions about why they needed to show restraint even when they were unfairly assaulted by police or white members of mobs in the crowd. Students learned how and why they must fall on their knees as a group if they were to be taken to jail, to go limp if they were being physically detained, so that they would not be seen as aggressively resisting. They wanted to expose the ugliness of Jim Crow and its key perpetrators: police deputized to enact state-sanctioned violence on people peacefully demanding an end to white terrorism. "But, you've got to remember that all the planning was a secret," Gloria Lewis emphasized in her recollection of the march.[30] This was not something that students could speak of freely in public spaces. Once again, critical aspects of black students' worlds continued to be veiled, attended to within the black interior. The coordination of events was often routed through the local DJ, Shelly "Playboy" Stewart. Stewart had the ear of just about all the students of Birmingham. He spoke in code, using popular language and songs of the day to communicate messages. This was a modern analog to the sorrow songs of the enslaved, and of course black children of Birmingham had been taught that the slaves often used songs to communicate secret messages.

Angela Davis recalled how she and her high school classmates laughed at white textbook authors who misinterpreted the Negro spirituals. They possessed a counterknowledge that allowed them to interpret such textbook passages differently than the white authors intended. The textbooks presented these songs as examples of the slaves being happy.[31] Black teachers offered Davis and her classmates a different interpretation of these songs as early as elementary school. Like their ancestors, the students of Birmingham used their cultural life to express the messages they needed to keep concealed. As Freeman Hrabowski explained, this is what was going on in "our internal world." Hearing rumors of threats against black teachers and parents, that they "would lose their jobs if they marched," students welcomed this opportunity to fulfill their mission.[32]

D-day—as students came to know it—took place on Tuesday, May 2, 1963. At eleven o'clock students were to leave school and meet at Sixteenth Street Baptist Church, where they would receive marching orders. Some teachers tried to prevent students from leaving. Others turned their backs to write on the chalkboard as the clock struck eleven—a winking gesture that it was all right for them to leave if they chose to do so. Parents had varied responses to their children participating. Some gave their blessings; others forbade students from participating. Many students disobeyed parent and teacher orders. While they recognized the practical concerns of adults for their safety as children, many students felt compelled to do what their teachers' and parents' lessons had long taught them to understand as the right thing to do. They chose faith and the fight for freedom over fear.

Freeman Hrabowski recalled leaving the church and, as he described it, "leading my line downtown, with the goal of kneeling on the steps of City Hall and praying for our freedom":

> My heart was pounding, and my head was swimming with fear. Before we could reach the steps, however, we were stopped by the Birmingham police. Police Commissioner "Bull" Conner, himself, stopped us and asked me, "What do you want little Niggra?" and, meaning to or not, spat on me. As I replied, "We want our

freedom," my fellow demonstrators and I were shoved into the paddy wagons in a moment of confusion.

Hrabowski was in jail for five days before his parents were able to get him released. Other marchers were jailed for longer periods of time. When Hrabowski returned from jail, he heard a rumor that students who participated would face disciplinary action by the school authorities. While this action was strongly considered, students were not suspended on their release from jail.[33]

The world was watching.

President John F. Kennedy was sickened by the events in Birmingham, as the film footage of children being attacked by dogs and sprayed with water hoses circulated on television. But black children around the country also bore witness to this historic moment, and it was instructive for their lives. For example, Lisa Delpit was a sixth-grade student in Baton Rouge, Louisiana, when she learned of the Children's March on television. It became part of the discussion taking place "through the children's grapevine," as she put it. "I remember sitting in front of the family television," Delpit recalled, "mesmerized and terrified by the newscasts showing Bull Conner's snarling police dogs attacking young black teenagers, and snarling white policemen simultaneously assaulting them with clubs and powerful fire hoses." Delpit's witnessing this event was framed by her sister's involvement in student protests as a college student at Southern University.[34] Such events inspired others to act. As historian V. P. Franklin rigorously documented, "After witnessing on television the social activism of young people in Birmingham, children and teenagers in North Carolina, Louisiana, South Carolina, and other states mobilized and mounted demonstrations to challenge racial discrimination in education, employment, and public accommodations."[35]

Nearly one thousand students were jailed after the first day in Birmingham. The Children's March continued from May 2 to May 10. Some students were released from jail only to return to the march and be arrested again. Over four thousand schoolchildren participated in this coordinated act motivated by generations of fugitive learning and tradition. Some were as young as six and others as old as eighteen. Black political leaders and local city government eventually reached an agreement after the series of marches, boycotts, and public displays of dissent made their mark on the city. These events in Birmingham became an important turning point in the civil rights movement. They moved President Kennedy to pass a comprehensive civil rights bill in June 1963; the March on Washington took place in August, where Martin Luther King Jr. delivered his famous "I Have a Dream" speech, and in June of the following year the Civil Rights Act of 1964 was passed, which outlined significant measures to dismantle Jim Crow segregation. The historical record is clear: it was the action of black students that broke the back of Jim Crow in Birmingham, the most iconic segregated city in the country.[36]

The Children's March did not take place by happenstance. It was not a sporadic moment of black student dissent. Instead, I trace a through line from Susie King Taylor in the 1850s—Taylor, her brother, and other fugitive learners secretly entering the kitchen of their teacher's home to learn—and black students marching in Birmingham in 1963, having secretly prepared for their nonviolent direct action. Black students learned that they inherited a mission to transform a world that misrecognized their humanity and that propped itself up on their subjection. These "young crusaders," to borrow from historian V. P. Franklin, were part of a multigenerational tradition of black students helping galvanize the Black Freedom Movement. "When civil rights organizers came to town to recruit participants," writes Franklin, "children and teenagers were often the first ones to show up on the picket lines in large numbers, and often they were attacked, brutalized, and arrested by the police."[37]

Black school, at its best, initiated African American learners into a political life committed to remaking the world. The songs black students sang were not just about some world in the future but also about a fight in earthly places, in the here and now. The singing that commenced among Charlotte Forten and her students against the backdrop of the Civil War, or in Mary McLeod Bethune's singing schools in the late nineteenth century, migrated into the twentieth. Such songs expressed a continuum of consciousness, sounds of struggle and striving that were an essential part of black students' inheritance.

Chapter 6

Some of Them Became Schoolteachers

But the schoolchildren of Jacksonville kept singing the song; some of them went off to other schools and kept singing it; some of them became schoolteachers and taught it to their pupils.

—JAMES WELDON JOHNSON, *Along This Way*

TEACHERS WERE AMONG the first leaders of freedpeople. In the earliest days of Emancipation, African Americans who possessed some knowledge in the fundamentals of reading, writing, and arithmetic became responsible for educating the race. Many of these early black educators were arguably still students themselves—like Susie King Taylor who, at fourteen, assumed the responsibility of teaching others when she reached the camp of the Union army, after fleeing the site of her enslavement in Savannah, Georgia, during the Civil War. Some took initiative on their own, but many were elevated to this position by the people of their communities. Reflecting on her childhood in the 1870s and 1880s, Mary McLeod Bethune explained, "Those were great days when the masses needed the few who could read and write so badly. . . . There were people looking to someone who would come and lead them, to teach them, to organize them into . . . singing schools." Bethune began her education in Sumter

County, South Carolina, and quickly became one of the many who helped teach and lead others.

Bethune's educational drive made her a leader among her people, even when it came to their work in the fields. Having realized "the seriousness and usefulness" of her learning, she often became the person trusted with keeping records for weighing cotton. Surely this was labor that could be exploited and utilized by white planters, but it also became a way to safeguard black farmers against fraud. Her fellow laborers wanted to ensure that the cotton they handed in was properly weighed and accounted for. This was their way of protecting their earnings based on wages that were already pitifully low. Bethune explained, "When we went to pick cotton for white people, they said, 'Let Mary Jane put down the number of pounds.'" She continued, "I made my learning, what little it was, just from the beginning, spell service and cooperation, rather than something that would put me above the people about me."[1]

Students like Bethune and James Weldon Johnson, also born in the 1870s, represented the first generation of black students born after Emancipation. Their formative years as learners shaped the kind of educators they would become. Johnson became an educator at the Stanton School in Jacksonville, Florida, from which he had graduated. It was at this school that he was introduced to black heroes who offered frames for his future as a leader. Johnson recalled winning a copy of Frederick Douglass's autobiography during a school competition and later hearing Douglass speak in 1888, when he addressed the Sub-Tropical Exposition in Jacksonville.[2] Douglass's story and commanding oratorical abilities left an impression on the young student.

Johnson carried these memories with him into his life as an educator, and similar currents would ripple in the lives of his own students. Johnson emphasized this point when detailing how "Lift Every Voice and Sing" became the Negro national anthem. He and his brother, Rosamond Johnson, wrote and arranged the song in 1900 to be sung by five hundred students from the Stanton School.

But the song took on a life of its own. Its circulation was accelerated by students who went out into the world as teachers. "The schoolchildren of Jacksonville kept singing the song," observed Johnson. "Some of them went off to other schools and kept singing it; some of them became schoolteachers and taught it to their pupils." This song was a cultural artifact that students carried with them, and it was linked to a broader range of pedagogical and cultural knowledge that accompanied it.[3]

Teaching is the only occupation where the apprenticeship phase begins during childhood. Without knowing it, educators begin studying for their profession when they are children. Students watch their teachers and study their habits. They draw conclusions in their minds about why teachers do the things they do, what aspects of their pedagogy are effective, and how teachers' actions affect them personally. Students who become teachers carry with them their own developmental experiences in classrooms; such lived experiences become social resources that shape practice. One sociologist assessed that youth spend about twelve thousand hours observing teachers, referring to this phenomenon as "an apprenticeship of observation." Other scholars put it in simpler terms: *students are always watching*. They learn from the routines and values shaping the culture of their learning environments, which is significantly shaped by things teachers say and do.[4]

The line between black teachers and black students was blurred from the beginning. Their shared vulnerability and shared struggle are the products of history and enduring social realities in American education. Their lived proximity to antiblackness in school and the world has long codified an intersubjectivity between them. Despite this blurring of positionalities, it remains that some African American students were elevated to the professional realm of educators. And it is to this group that our attention now turns—to those black students, like Charlotte Forten, James Weldon Johnson, Mary McLeod Bethune, and so many others named in this book who became schoolteachers themselves.

Henry Ponder was a seventh-grade student in Wewoka, Oklahoma, in 1941. He was a tall, slender, fair-skinned black boy living four miles into the country, and one of fourteen children born to North Carolina migrants. Both of his parents were born in Polk County, North Carolina, but as fate would have it, they met in Oklahoma. Ponder and his siblings worked on the eighty acres of farmland his family rented. When he was not working, he attended the Johnson School—which got its name from the black man whose land it sat on, Mr. J. Coody Johnson. Johnson set aside a plot of land so that the black children in this rural community could have a school. The Johnson School consisted of two classrooms and two teachers. It was here that Ponder, a future educator and college president, was started on his way.

Word traveled that Mary McLeod Bethune would be speaking at a Methodist church in town. Ponder and his mother—a widow by 1941—got it in their minds that he should make the trip into town to hear Miss Bethune speak. The little they knew about Bethune was more than enough to justify making the four-mile journey. She was the president of a Negro college. In the early 1940s, a black college president was, as Ponder explained, on par with someone who had gone into outer space. President Bethune "was something that nobody thought you could ever become. It was like you're flying to the moon now," he recalled. So it was decided that he would go and see the impossible in the flesh.[5]

Ponder likely heard about Bethune's visit from one of his teachers at the Johnson School, where he began his studies in the first grade. He had fond memories of the Johnson School. The teachers, Charlesetta Bruner and Theodore Malone, pushed students to aspire beyond the farmland rented and worked by their families. These teachers pushed students to study hard and strive. "The only way you can be anything is that you got to know something," they would say. Miss Bruner taught Ponder in the first through fourth grades. He was then promoted to the other part of the two-room schoolhouse, where Mr. Malone taught fifth through eighth grades.

Mr. Malone required the more advanced students to help classmates in the lower levels with their lessons. "If we were in the seventh grade, we could teach the fifth and the sixth grade," Ponder explained. This helped reinforce lessons he learned in the years before. It was also the teacher's way of managing four grade levels in one classroom. For anything to get done, some students had to assume the role of teacher for their peers. In the early nineteenth century this pedagogical strategy became popularized as the Lancaster Model of Mutual Learning, or the Monitorial System. In the Jim Crow South, however, black teachers applied this strategy to make do with the limited resources available to them and to manage their overcrowded classrooms.

Miss Bruner and Mr. Malone likely walked into town to hear Mary McLeod Bethune as well. Who hadn't read this woman's name in the paper or heard about the inspiring things she was doing for the race? This was the Negro woman who sat next to President Roosevelt at a dinner table. She helped assemble his group of Negro advisors who become known as "the Black Cabinet." She once led all the black teachers around the country as president of the National Association of Teachers in Colored Schools. Miss Bethune was an example of "somebody that knew something," as the saying went at the Johnson School.

The weather was chilly, and it was cold inside the church. Ponder remembered this, because Bethune kept her mink coat on as she addressed the body assembled before her. Her address likely struck a similar chord as other speeches she gave during these years, as World War II unfolded and questions of civic duty lingered in the air. Bethune commonly spoke on the topic of Negro citizenship, democracy, and the need for these doors to be opened wider if the country was to move into the full promise of brotherhood. "We are rising out of the darkness of slavery into the light of freedom," Bethune asserted in a 1939 speech. She declared that all the while, black people have been great contributors to American culture. Bethune pointed to Paul Laurence Dunbar, Booker T. Washington, Marian Anderson, and George Washington Carver as evidence of this. When Bethune spoke these names, she assured her listeners that these historical figures represented but "the first fruits of a rich harvest." More had to be done if the harvest was to yield its highest potential. "The democratic doors of equal opportunity have not been opened wide to Negroes," Bethune urged. Being the educator that she was—having been called from the field to the classroom, first as a student, then a teacher, and eventually as a college president—Bethune understood that one of the most egregious denials of black citizenship manifested in the realm of educational opportunity.[6]

A continuum of consciousness connected Bethune and Ponder. Ponder might have heard the statistic Bethune sometimes included in her speeches: "In the deep South, Negro youth is offered only one fifteenth of the educational opportunity of the average American child." He would have understood himself as part of the collective "Negro youth" Bethune spoke of, just as she was part of that 80 percent of illiterate Negroes after slavery who became the 80 percent literate, whom she referenced with a smile. Once a student working in the cotton fields of South Carolina herself, Bethune told a story that resonated with Ponder's struggle. Theirs was a single tradition that transcended time and place.

From Bethune's mouth to the ears of this young farm boy, Ponder himself was part of that rich harvest that had yet to fully manifest. Ponder made up his mind on the four-mile walk home that he wanted to become a college president. Mary McLeod Bethune was his North Star.

Just a few years prior, Bethune addressed a group of educators and scholars in Chicago for the twentieth anniversary of the Association for the Study of Negro Life and History. At this meeting, she lectured on the importance of placing monuments of achievement before the eyes of black children—men and women of the race who stood for something and helped cultivate aspiration in Negro youth.

"The story is told," she explained, "that in the hey-day of the Roman Empire the highways of the Romans were literally studded with the statues of their illustrious men—their men of achievement. These statues were erected that the Roman youth, gazing upon their faces, might be stimulated to greater achievement and accomplishment." Negro youth were no different, she asserted. They too needed statues of their illustrious men and women to gaze upon, that they might be "pushed forward toward their destinies."[7] On that chilly afternoon in Wewoka, Bethune herself was a monument enfleshed: a statue of a woman representing ideals, vision, and character to which black people across the country deemed worthy of aspiring. She modeled a way of life that gave them confidence that the impossible could be made manifest in the flesh, in the here and now.

School photo of Henry Ponder

One might imagine Ponder and other students from the Johnson School trekking back into the country, having been warmed on this cool night by the fires Bethune stoked inside of them. Black students' anecdotes of hearing Bethune speak and having been marked by the occasion stand out in the historical record. Student testimonies echo Ponder's assessment that "Bethune was a dynamo." Some proclaimed that Bethune was the most inspiring and dynamic speaker they ever heard. Across states and years, students bore witness to the power of her voice, how she made them feel and see in new ways.

In Oklahoma City one recalled: "I used to fantasize about being an able communicator. [Bethune] was the model that I heard, long before I heard [Martin Luther] King." In Washington, DC, another shared: "I got my heart stirred. . . . And it affected me to the point that I wanted to serve my people too!" In Jacksonville, Florida, a former student recounted how Bethune made her feel as though she were "a ton of people." She was a young dark-skinned black girl who was well aware that skin complexion mattered. So when she saw Bethune pick up the darkest child at her elementary school in front of all the students, "wrapping her arms around them and [saying], 'My beautiful black child,'" the scene became seared into her memory. The moment challenged the deep-seated colorism the young student had already come to know.

Bethune and the professional class of educators whom she led were like statues studded along the highway, erected so that black

Mary McLeod Bethune with three African American male students in tattered clothing (c. 1930)

students could look to, learn from, and aspire beyond them. Ponder went on to become a college educator and served as the president of multiple historically black colleges. Bethune inspired him to become a college president, and we might linger with Ponder's gesture of looking up and seeing a future in the flesh, standing right before him. There is beauty in these moments of students bearing witness to the heritage of black education. They learned songs from their teachers, and many of them went on with these traditions, and they kept singing as a new generation of educators. This migration narrative of black pedagogy is embedded in the story of black student life. It is a general story that can be found in the particular histories of black students across the generations.

Mary McLeod Bethune with two African American male students in formal attire (1941)

Yvonne Divans Hutchinson became a lover of words and books well before she decided to become a teacher. She was born in Little Rock but spent her formative years in Hot Springs, Arkansas, before moving to Los Angeles in 1951 after the third grade. Black students were not able to check out books from the public library in Arkansas, but her teachers at the Frederick Douglass Elementary School cultivated her early desire to become an able wordsmith. They taught her that worlds could be built and destroyed using words.

Miss Hutchinson taught me for AP American literature and chaired my high school English department. I recall arriving to school in the mornings between 2002 and 2006, knowing that Miss Hutch—as we called her—was already in the building. Her green station wagon was often the first thing I saw, because it was parked in front of the school. You could not miss the rear license plate, which read "I♥WORDS." As a veteran teacher, Miss Hutch cultivated an avid reading culture at my high school. I came to know her well during my time as a student, but I never learned much about her own educational journey until we sat down for a conversation in 2018, as I prepared to write *School Clothes*. Our conversations revealed that much of what I experienced as her student was directly tied to her personal educational journey, both the beautiful and the terrible.

Miss Hutch's experiences as a student motivated her to become a teacher. She came to think of herself as some hybrid of the memorable black teachers that taught her: Miss Kay Walker Cole from the Douglass School, and Miss Gladys Haney, whom she encountered at both Markham Junior High and Jordan High School in Los Angeles. Miss Haney was just like Miss Cole, and Miss Hutch insisted that she often thought of herself as Miss Haney "reincarnated." While Hutchinson's educational roots were in the Jim Crow South, her teaching career began in 1966, at the end of the modern civil rights movement, and consisted of teaching black students in Los Angeles. During our conversation Miss Hutch pulled out a photograph from a recent trip to Arkansas. The image displayed a plaque at her old school site. "Can you read that?" she asked while pointing to an inscription in the photo. I said, "Yes," and proceeded to read: "Former site of Douglass Elementary School, established 1883 as High Street School, renamed 1904 to 1967 in honor of Frederick Douglass, a place where thousands crossed." Wearing a proud grin and nodding her head, Miss Hutch offered, "Yeah, I'm one of the thousands."[8]

Much of what Miss Hutch recalled resonated with the story of Henry Ponder recounted above. Hutchinson started in the first grade with Miss Cole, who "taught first and second grade, and a teacher named Miss Jackson taught third and fourth grade." She moved to California after the third grade. But despite her short time at Douglass, the school left a deep impression on her: "The one thing that I do know about our teachers," Miss Hutch shared, "is that they insisted on excellence and on high standards. They were adamant about that. There was no compromise. You had to strive to be your best. If you didn't, you were in trouble." Teachers at Douglass emphasized black history in the classroom. "Booker T. Washington and George Washington Carver were ingrained," she shared. "I have a sense that our culture and our history were just an integral part of any instruction that we got from our black teachers." She explained, "I don't remember a big deal being made of it," because it was part of the school culture. "It was just part of our life until we came to California," she emphasized.

When Miss Cole stepped out of the classroom, she often left Hutchinson in charge. "If somebody came and wanted to talk to her . . . she would say, 'Yvonne, take over the class.' So I would. I would teach the class while she was out of the class, and I decided, 'Oh, this is wonderful, I'm going to be a teacher.' And I never wavered from that." Since Miss Cole taught first and second grade, Hutchinson occasionally had to sit next to her brother, who was a year behind her, and help him with reading. "She would have me sit next to kids and read with them or coach them, and I had to sit next to my brother, and he wet the bed. So I didn't like sitting by him because he smelled." By the third grade, Hutchinson recalled being able to teach other students fundamentals of reading; she could also coach them on their handwriting, teach some basic math, and help them with their art projects. As recalled earlier by Henry Ponder, these kinds of peer pedagogies were commonplace in black schools, reflecting both the need for more black teachers and also the ways students who were young, gifted, and black became elevated early on to play active roles in their educational environments.

Miss Cole was not the only person to see Miss Hutch's potential. Other teachers, community members, and family encouraged

Hutchinson's love for reading. Her mother regularly bought her the Little Golden Books, which cost twenty-five cents. But most memorable was when the "neighbor next door used to hand across the fence . . . *True Confessions* mags," Miss Hutch recalled while laughing. Some of the content in these magazines was a little advanced for her age, but she devoured the reading. One story led her to wonder why women got pregnant when they kissed men. Hutchinson's grandmother, Mama Sissy, likely would not have approved of such literary content, but she could not put it down.

Hutchinson's narrative of being a student-teacher resonates so much with that of Zora Neale Hurston that it is worth invoking the words of the Black Renaissance writer and anthropologist. While enrolled in the high school program at Morgan State University in Baltimore from 1917 to 1918, Hurston was frequently placed in charge of her class whenever her English teacher, Miss Clarke, was absent. "This happened time and time again," Hurston recalled, "sometimes for a whole week at a time." The same thing happened in Hurston's history class. "Once I had the history class for nearly a month and had to be excused from my other classes," she explained. But the experience did not alienate Hurston from her peers. She explained, "At times like that, my classmates were perfectly respectful to me until the bell rang. Then how they would poke fun at my serious face while I was teaching!"[9]

Hurston's and Hutchinson's recollections also resonate with those of Evelyn Brooks Higginbotham, scholar of black women's history and the first African American chair of Harvard University's History Department. Higginbotham grew up in a family of teachers. Her father, mother, and aunt were educators in Washington, DC's segregated schools, which Higginbotham attended before enrolling at the newly integrated Theodore Roosevelt High School in the 1950s. Very few black educators taught at Roosevelt, so Higginbotham was fortunate to have Miss Helen Blackburn as a history teacher. Miss Blackburn invited Higginbotham to assist her with incorporating black history into the school. She recalled, "When black history was being introduced in the school, Ms. Blackburn asked me for help, so I gave her a lot of materials from the *Negro History Bulletin*." Ever since she was a small child, Higginbotham accompanied her father, Albert Brooks, to the office of the Association for the Study of Negro Life and History, where he edited the *Negro History Bulletin*. This was a publication for teachers and students created by Carter G. Woodson and Mary McLeod Bethune in 1937. Having long been acquainted with the early black history movement, Higginbotham welcomed the opportunity to assist with the planning of Negro History Week celebrations, and she later became a history teacher in the public schools of Milwaukee and then Washington, DC, before earning a master's in history from Howard University in 1974, then a doctorate in history from the University of Rochester in 1984. It is noteworthy that black educator and school founder Nannie Helen Burroughs would be a central figure in Higginbotham's field-shifting book, *Righteous Discontent: The Women's Movement in the Black Baptist Church, 1880–1920*.[10]

Such intergenerational narratives of black students' journeys to becoming educators and intellectual leaders is expansive and often hidden in plain sight. A similar nostalgia colored Hutchinson's recollection of being elevated from student to teacher. The mental picture of the small version of herself walking about the classroom, "accorded the same respect" as Miss Cole, caused her to smile and laugh during our conversation. "They listened to whatever I said," Miss Hutch emphasized. "They did whatever I said to do, and I didn't have to do much because they knew that while she was gone, they had better behave."[11]

After the third grade, Hutchinson's mother and stepfather sent for her and her brother to move to California, where her parents relocated for better job opportunities. Moving to California brought new opportunities for Hutchinson as well. On arrival she attended a school in San Pedro, California, where she had white and Asian students in her class. During our discussion she recalled, "My best friend was a blond-haired, blue-eyed girl named Polly, and I had a crush on a little white boy named Richard, and my other best friend was Chiko. She was Japanese, so I was just thrilled to death." But Hutchinson was most excited about being able to check out books from the library. This luxury seemed too good to be true. She recalled writing a letter to Mama Sissy in 1951 about her new experiences in the integrated schools. She contrasted the restrictions placed on her literary strivings in Arkansas with the new freedoms she experienced in California. Years later, Miss Hutch revised this letter to include additional memories from her first years in California, and she routinely assigned her "Letter Back Home" for a writing assignment with students.

October 12, 1951

Dear Mama Sissy,

How are you? Fine I hope. I miss yall, but I like California a whole lot. Here we ride on the front of the bus if we want to. I always sit in the front, right on the long seat by the bus driver. I always listen to him talk to the people who get on and sit by me. Mostly it's ladies going to do they day work. Mama Sissy, you wouldn't believe it! White people and black people are all mixed together. They have desegregation here! The bus driver is even colored. He laugh and talk with everybody, sometimes they white, sometimes they Negroes.

My school is desegregated too. My teacher is white. She's old with faded out yellow hair, but she's real nice. She told me that I don't have to say, "Yes, Ma'am, or No Ma'am" to her like we have to say to our teachers back home. She say, "Yvonne, just answer 'yes' or 'no.'" And I said, "Yes Ma'am—I mean, yes, Miss Clark."

In my class there's all different races of kids, Negro, white, Japanese, Chinese, Mexican. I like this white boy. His name is Henry. He has brown hair and blue eyes. My two best friends are Polly, she's white, and Michiko. Polly is fat, well kinda chubby, and Michiko is a little Japanese girl. She laughs a lot. Polly lives in a hotel, and we go the same way, so we walk home together every day after school.

Mama Sissy, guess what I found one day after I left Polly's house! A little bitty magazine with nothing but colored people in it. It was just laying there on the sidewalk. It had a picture of this dark skinned man on it. His name is Nat King Cole. Before I picked it up, I looked around to see if anybody had dropped it and was coming back to get it, but people just kept on walking by, so I picked it up and started reading it.

Oooh, Mama Sissy, what a good book! All the people in it are colored, and most of them are real famous, people like Nat King Cole, the singer, and Joe Louis, the boxer, and that lady with the real pretty voice, Eartha Kitt that sings the song "Santa Baby" at Christmas time. The name of the magazine is *Jet* and it has pictures of Negro people with big houses who drive around in pretty cars and are rich. Remember how you used to tell us to be proud of ourselves and our black race? I was so proud when I read this book. I started running real fast so I could show it to Mu Deah, but I had to slow down because I almost got hit by a car when I ran across the street.

Here comes the best, best part. Here in California, they let Negroes go in the library. The way I found this out was when one day my teacher said, "Boys and girls, today the book mobile is coming to our school." I didn't know what a book mobile was, and anyway I wasn't feeling too good. I had threw up my lunch. My teacher said to put my head down on the desk. Then she went to call my mother, but I told her Mu Deah was at work and that Daddy Johnson, my mother's husband, didn't have a job and he was home and could come and get me. Miss Clark said I could stay til the book mobile came because she knew how much I loved to read.

I was excited. I know you always said I was going to go blind from reading so much, but I can't help it. I have to read. I'll tell you a secret. When you turned off the lights at night, I used to sneak Big Daddy's flashlight and read under the covers til I fell asleep.

Anyway, the book mobile finally came. It was like a trailer, only instead of people living in it, it had shelves full of books. The man librarian said they brought the book mobile around to people who didn't have a regular library in their neighborhood. I told him I had never even been in a library before because in Arkansas where I was from, libraries had signs up that said, "Whites Only." He looked sad and then smiled. He told me, "Well, now you are welcome to come and get as many books as you want as long as you have a library card."

Mama Sissy, you should have seen that book mobile. It was like a little tiny room with hundreds of hundreds of books. I was so happy! I wanted to grab up all of the books and take them home. Remember how Mu Deah used to buy me those golden books for children and the little fat books with the cartoons of Goofy and Donald Duck and Mickey Mouse? Well, this library had real books, books with hard covers and lots and lots of pages; some of them didn't even have pictures. I know how to read them, too, even though they are grownup books, novels the librarian said. I know you and Mu Deah don't like me reading stuff that is too grown because I am only in the fourth grade, but I can't help it. I want to read all the books in the world. I just love to read.

So the librarian, Mr. Leonard, let me check out four books for now til I get my library card. He said I have to get my mother's signature on my application. The best book out of all was the book called *A Tree Grows in Brooklyn* about a girl who lives in Brooklyn New York who was almost the same age as me and one time a man grabbed her in the hallway and tried to do something nasty to her, but she got away.

Mr. Leonard said with my library card I could go into any regular library in any neighborhood and check out books. He said there is no discriminating in the Los Angeles libraries. He called them branches.

I like it here, Mama Sissy. Everything is desegregated. I bet if you came to California you wouldn't even have to step off the sidewalk to let white folks pass by or go to the back door when you have to go clean up their houses.

Kiss my cousins Patsy, Bo Sam, and Earl Jean for me. Tell them I wish they could come and see California. L.A. where we live is lots of fun.

Sincerely,
Yvonne[12]

Not long after writing this letter, Hutchinson's family moved into the housing projects in Los Angeles, and she attended schools with predominantly black students, though there were few, if any, black teachers. But she did encounter Miss Gladys Haney as her homeroom instructor at Markham Junior High School. Two memories stand out when it comes to Miss Haney. On one occasion, Hutchinson responded to a questionnaire Miss Haney assigned to her seventh-grade homeroom students. One question asked students to list three things they wished for. "I said one, I would like to see my dad because I hadn't seen him since I was four years old," Miss Hutch explained, "and second I think I said I would like to have complete volumes of William Shakespeare, and I forgot what the third wish was." Then at school, the next day, Miss Haney "brought me this fat, tattered volume of the complete works of William Shakespeare. It didn't have a cover on it, but you would think that she had given me a pound of gold."

The second encounter with Miss Haney took place in the tenth grade at Jordan High School. Miss Hutch shared, "I was cute and I was skinny and the girls, all the girls wore skirts . . . kind of cupped under my behind—and I had a rather fine behind." Miss Haney "took me aside . . . and said, 'Don't you wear that tight skirt back here anymore.' She said, 'You look like a prostitute, don't wear that skirt back here anymore, it's too tight.'" After listening to Miss Hutch describe this encounter, I asked if the teacher's comment offended her. To my surprise, she did not feel slighted by the encounter—or at least she didn't recall any feelings of anger or hurt. "I said, 'Okay,'" Hutchinson explained. "But that's the way she was. She was down to earth and she didn't, she was an English teacher, but she didn't rely just on academics. . . . If you had to be told about personal things, that's what she did." Such qualities made Miss Haney seem like another version of the teachers Hutchinson remembered from Douglass Elementary. Teachers cared about students and treated them as though they were their own family. This often manifested in sharp criticism, even when students did not want to hear it.[13]

However pleasant, her experiences with Miss Cole and Miss Haney were not the only motivations for Hutchinson's desire to become a teacher. There were also aggressive, unpleasant nudges that pushed her into the teaching profession. The schools in California often felt less supportive than what she recalled from her encounters with Miss Haney or the teachers in Hot Springs. While she found some of the teachers were kind to her, many were indifferent, and some were flat-out hostile to black students. This was especially the case in the predominantly black schools, which were also different from Hutchinson's earlier California encounters, where she was one of a very small number of black students.

Some teachers made no effort to hide their low expectations of Hutchinson and her classmates. Miss Hutch published an article in the *Los Angeles Times* in 1975 detailing her experiences. She wrote, "I remember in particular one little old white-haired lady who would come in early each morning and fill every board in her room with sentences containing blanks and then, when we arrived, instruct us to copy each line, filling in the blanks. To her, this was teaching—ghetto style."[14] When speaking to me about this teacher, Miss Abel Woods, Hutchinson expressed that this was the kind of "nonsensical, low-level assignments" she gave students every day. "That's what we did. I think she was scared of black people."[15] She continued, surprisingly, "It was a white male substitute teacher who drove me to make a promise to myself that I intended keeping to my dying day." Her ninth-grade speech teacher, "a gentle, soft-spoken white woman," was out sick. "Like bright children anywhere," Hutchinson explained, the students polished off their assignment quickly "and began chattering, probably too loudly for the sub's taste." Then, she continued, "I do not remember exactly what provoked this young man—we had surely done nothing violent—but this was his parting shot: 'You're lucky I came here today. Most people don't want to come to Watts.'"[16]

Never would she forget this assault on the dignity of her and her classmates. "My fourteen-year-old heart was wounded," Hutchinson explained.[17] She dreamed of being a teacher since her days in Miss Cole's class, and experiences like this only deepened her conviction. The same year as this incident, Hutchinson watched on television and read in the newspaper about what was happening back home in Little Rock. She followed the news as nine black students braved threats of bodily harm to desegregate Central High School. She told me, "I remember being indignant at the way they were being treated. It just was incomprehensible to me that . . . people would be so carried away about somebody going to school." She frowned her face at the memory of "that Governor [Orval] Faubus person standing in the doorway."[18] Miss Hutch carried the collective memory shared by many black students of her generation, before and after. While likely recalling the image of Alabama's governor, George Wallace, blocking the auditorium door as two black students attempted to enroll at the University of Alabama in 1963, Governor Faubus did block the students from entering Central High School by proxy: he ordered the Arkansas National Guard to turn the black students away on September 4, 1957.

These accumulated experiences made Hutchinson vow to become the kind of teacher she and her classmates deserved. "What we need," she told herself, "are teachers who treat us like capable human beings, who love and *understand* us, who are going to stay around and not leave at the first opportunity." Hutchinson promised herself that she would be that kind of teacher. She vowed to herself that she "would come back 'home' to teach where [she] was needed."[19]

The assaults did not end in junior high school. After graduating ninth grade, Hutchinson enrolled at Jordan High School in fall 1958, where she encountered Miss Haney again as her homeroom instructor, but this time their interaction was cut short. A few months into the semester, her family moved from the Imperial Courts housing projects to the city of Compton. Hutchinson enrolled at Compton High School in the midst of desegregation, and there was only one black teacher on the campus at the time: the shop teacher. Transferring schools caused a bit of anxiety for

Elizabeth Eckford of the Little Rock Nine denied entrance to Central High School by Arkansas National Guard.

Hutchinson. It had not been even a year since she witnessed the controversy back home, as the Little Rock Nine desegregated Central High School while being escorted by federal troops and threatened by angry white mobs.

What's more, about a month prior to her arrival, Hutchinson read about the controversy surrounding Compton High School's black homecoming queen. "I think these white boys had written in black paint, 'We don't want no nigger for queen,'" Miss Hutch recalled. Nadine Smith, a "very attractive, popular young black woman, had been elected homecoming queen in this predominantly white school." Black students devised a plan to ensure Naddy, as they called her, had a chance at winning. Black students, who were the minority, voted unanimously for Naddy, and they successfully persuaded some white students to vote for her as well. Given the crowded field of contestants, "she got to be queen and they had a fit." Some angry students wrote, "'We don't want no nigger for queen' in front of the science building." Hutchinson recalled that by the time she arrived at Compton High School, "they had scrubbed it, but you could still see the letters." She described how until this day, whenever she drives past Compton High School, she can never unsee the marks. "I know it's there," Hutchinson explained. "I still see faint marks, black marks where they had written it."[20]

After graduating from Compton High School in 1961, Hutchinson enrolled at California State University, Long Beach. The school was "almost integrated," she shared, while rolling her eyes. "There were fifty black people on the campus of nine thousand." Assured of what she wanted to do, Miss Hutch completed her bachelor's degree in 1965. She promptly began the teacher credentialing program, which required an additional year at Long Beach State. Miss Hutch's years as a student would bleed directly into her life as an educator. Just as she began her teacher training program in the summer of 1965, Watts—the neighborhood of her youth—went up in flames, like many others around the country. The Watts Uprising scared most of the white teachers half to death. Many of them quit their jobs and fled the city. Miss Hutch recalled that many of the black schools had about 50 percent of their faculty leave following the events of that summer, and it was clear those teachers had no intention of coming back. These circumstances made for an unconventional start to her teaching career.

"The recruiters from LAUSD [Los Angeles Unified School District] came to Cal State Long Beach," Hutchinson explained, "and the employment office on the campus called us in a group and sat us down in a conference room opposite these LAUSD people, and they handed us contracts right there on the spot." It wasn't even a one-on-one interview. "It was recruiters here," Hutch explained while pointing to one side of her dining room table, "and a bunch of students here," she said while pointing to the other. They said, "Do you want to work at LAUSD?" She and her peers all confirmed their interest. In unceremonious fashion, her teaching career began—or perhaps it was fortuitous or a silver lining.

Miss Hutch immediately began the hiring process, which required navigating school district bureaucracy and paperwork. She went in person to the district's downtown office, eager to get her assignment. The receptionist told Miss Hutch everything in her file was complete; she just needed to schedule interviews with prospective schools. The lady in charge of scheduling interviews was away when Hutchinson visited the office, so a staff member directed her to go back home and call at 1:00 p.m. that afternoon.

She was eager. Watching the clock, she called promptly at one. The district representative listed job vacancies in the Los Angeles region Hutchinson selected for her placement. Markham Junior High School, which she had previously attended as a student, just so happened to be among the three schools listed. Without hesitation, she requested Markham. The lady scheduling the interview seemed shocked by the certainty of Miss Hutch's decision. "Are you aware that that's a Negro school?" she asked. Sensing that the woman did not realize she was black, Hutchinson responded in her most "refined voice": "Yes, I'm quite well aware of what kind of school it is."

Hutchinson reported to Markham in September 1966, the same place where she had been wounded as a fourteen-year-old girl, where she committed her life to being an educator for the people in her community. This would be the place where she began to make her mark as a teacher. The experience was even more beautiful because of the cohort of educators who came in with her. During this time, Markham's principal "hired 50 percent of the faculty and the majority of them were black, were young, and southern born and came into that school and did some serious teaching," Hutchinson recalled. "We had some serious school . . . Markham was a real school because not only did they teach their subjects, but they taught manners . . . they taught discipline. . . . They taught caring." If you were their student, you weren't just their "math or their English student or their shop student," Miss Hutch clarified. "You were their child, so you had to be together. Your manners had to be intact as well as your academics."

The political climate of the 1960s combined with her own experiences as a student shaped how Hutchinson showed up for her students: her pedagogy was informed by not only the enriching relationships she'd had with some of her teachers but also the wounds she incurred from some white educators and from witnessing the ongoing hostility shown toward black children in schools. Such injustice "fueled my career as a teacher," she stressed, and that is "also why I have always infused social and political awareness in my instruction in the classroom." "The Panthers, Angela Davis, all of that" was on Hutchinson's mind, as well as her students, within the first few years of her career. Some days she arrived to class styled in her afro, black leather jacket, black beret, and a briefcase bearing a sticker that said, "Free Huey!" These aesthetics from the Black Power era also translated to the substance of her lessons. Hutchinson insisted on teaching black literature and texts by nonwhite authors. She recalled, "I had *Black Boy*, I had *Nigger* by Dick Gregory, I had a *Barrio Boy* . . . Maya Angelou." She integrated these texts into her syllabus because she was committed to introducing her students to the annals of black literature, texts that were typically elided in formal school curricula. "In the course of these lessons," Miss Hutch continued, "we would have discussions about the themes and the relevance. . . . When things would happen, we would talk about it. . . . We would discuss injustice," and if students wanted to understand why "the Panthers called the police pigs, we'd talk about that."[21]

And, of course, students had their own stories to tell. Hutchinson worked to "capitalize on the oral traditions of [her] African American students." She explained,

> The oral tradition is very strong in the African American culture. It comes from African tradition. . . . I have discovered that in a classroom of students there's a vast repository of knowledge. . . . They know some things that you would be surprised that they know, so because kids like to talk and they like to tell stories and

> they like to—what do you call it?—bag on each other. . . . I try to capitalize on that and get them to refine their abilities because they can go for days . . . just run off at the mouth and come up with jokes and do a whole lot of stuff. They like to talk, so I want to get them to start with that as an approach to getting them excited about learning and then to infuse them with the knowledge that they need in order to succeed in society.

So much had changed in the world since Hutchinson crossed over the threshold of the Frederick Douglass School in the 1950s. Her initiation from student to teacher began in these early years, but she was an educator forged in the fiery 1960s. That fire stayed with her through the years. She was committed to teaching black students in ways that honored their dignity as learners, exposed them to rich academic traditions of their people, and pushed them to their highest potential.

By 1975 Hutchinson was less concerned about integrating schools and more concerned with meeting the needs of her students at home in Watts. She would publicly oppose a "mandatory teacher integration plan" proposed by LAUSD. In the *Los Angeles Times* she explained that her concern was the potential loss of "that rare breed of black teacher who is sensitive to both the educational and personal needs of young blacks struggling to survive in a racist society." There were teachers who made a political decision to teach in the ghetto, and she was one of them. It would be a shame for some "random-selection system like that approved last month by the board" to arbitrarily place such a teacher in a white school. "And of course," she added, "white teachers would be transferred where they might not be needed—or wanted."[22]

Hutchinson explained that going along with such a plan would, for her, be tantamount to abandoning one's own children. Teaching was not an ordinary job for her. The classroom was no ordinary office or factory floor. She understood her work to be a struggle of lifelong learning with and for her community and family. "Personally," she explained, "if I am selected for the transfer in compliance with this plan, I would find it comparable to the board's coming into my home and announcing that I must give up my own boy and girl so that I can go and take care of some white family's children. I would no more be willing to do that than to leave my students in Watts to go teach in the Valley."[23]

Miss Hutch fought back using her words, just as she taught her students to do. Twenty years into the profession, she was still publicly advocating on behalf of students in the ghetto. In 1985 she took on a university professor in the *Los Angeles Times* who published an offensive article about "inner-city" students. The professor reflected on her *experiment* with teaching in the public schools she researched.[24] But Miss Hutchinson was tired of the impoverished language used to describe black and brown students in Watts—language that often framed them as some kind of specimen to be observed, picked, and prodded.

June 24, 1985

This is in response to the article (June 10), "Education Professor Tests Mettle in Inner-City School."

Mimi Warshaw is to be commended for descending from the ivory tower to gain practical teaching experience in a public school. But I am distressed that the article conveys a generally negative impression and seems to reinforce the stereotype of hopeless, poorly achieving blacks in the ghetto.

As a product of that very inner city school, a former inhabitant of one of the four housing projects, and now a member of Markham's faculty, I wish to offer another insight.

Warshaw mentions her "surprise" at learning that parents cared about how their children were doing in school. Our parents may be short of money, but they have plenty of pride. My mother, a divorcee, struggled to support three children, first as a domestic worker and later as a low-paid, unskilled factory worker, yet she provided us with a set of encyclopedias, an unabridged dictionary, an inexpensive set of the classics, and a second-hand typewriter to help us with our school work. Often exhausted from working as many as 12 hours a day, she wasn't able to take us to museums or other places, but she encouraged my weekly trips to the library and bragged to her friends about my high grades and "all the books" that I read.

Warshaw speaks of being "exhausted." I, too, am exhausted after a day of teaching and tending to my family and other tasks. Teaching adolescents is a demanding and often totally exhausting chore, but many nights, as tired as I am, I lie awake marveling over the intelligent, ridiculous, funny, sad, terrible, and wonderful things that have happened during the day. She says that our kids are "noisier, boisterous, and aggressive." I find them to be stimulating, bright, perceptive (no matter their so-called ability level), and proud. The low scores on standardized tests do not reflect those magic moments between teacher and student.

I am gratified by the brilliant—and sometimes not so brilliant—poems, stories, letters, compositions, speeches, project, newspapers, and school yearbooks produced by my students. I am amazed by the large storehouse of general knowledge exhibited in class discussion, not just by my college-capable types, but by my so-called "low" classes as well. I am delighted that my students continuously challenge me and each other, that some of them become moved by a poem or delighted by a book or enthralled by a play.

Yes, our kids are sometimes rowdy, sometimes hostile, sometimes lazy, sometimes downright obstreperous, but then so are kids everywhere. The wonder of it is that our kids lack the advantages, suffer racial prejudice, and still manage to prevail.

We don't graduate as many from our inner-city neighborhood, as do middle-class schools, but we do produce college professors, doctors, lawyers, writers, and other successful members of society. That this is so can be attributed to the strength of the children and the strength, pride and dignity of their parents, who struggle under often adverse circumstances to raise their children as best they can. And to the fact that at school they have teachers who believe they can achieve and who insist on high standards.

This last factor is key to those who wish to succeed as inner-city teachers.

Yvonne Hutchinson
Los Angeles
Hutchinson is a mentor teacher at Markham Junior High School

As fate would have it, Miss Hutch became the subject of study by UCLA professor Mike Rose nearly ten years later. Only this time the portrayal of her classroom and students would not be one of deficiency but one of promise and possibility. Rose profiled Miss Hutch in his 1995 book, *Possible Lives: The Promise of Public Education in America*, where he documented cases of excellent teaching around the country. Over the course of four years Rose observed educators who were locally perceived as "good teachers"—those identified by community members as models of what was possible in education—as "occasions to think about the future of public schools." Rose's portrait of Miss Hutch revealed much of what I learned a decade later as her student: that she taught young people not just about reading words on the page but about reading the world and pursuing a more expansive, more humane vision of it. In the words of Professor Rose: "Yvonne Divans Hutchinson demonstrated, encouraged, celebrated, and guided students through an active and critical reading process that undercut the common perception that reading simply involved the decoding of words, that print had single, basic meanings that students had to decipher quietly and store away." He recorded vignettes of Miss Hutch's ninth graders at Edwin Markham Middle School interacting with texts like Malcolm X's autobiography and Maya Angelou's poetry to make sense of their own lives in Watts, California. One assignment asked students to "select a passage that grabbed them, draw it as best they could in pencil or pen, and comment on it."[25] Another asked students to do what Miss Hutch called a Quaker reading of Maya Angelou's poem, "On the Pulse of Morning," which Angelou read at President Bill Clinton's 1993 inauguration—the poem in which Angelou professed so eloquently before the nation that "history despite its wrenching pain, cannot be unlived, but if faced with courage, need not be lived again."[26] Miss Hutch instructed each student to select "some lines that spoke to him or her and read them, in sequence, into a tape recorder, creating a class reading, a new rendering."[27]

In her professional disposition Miss Hutch modeled the same critical literacy she taught her students. This is evident in a speech she routinely gave to new teachers on the importance of maintaining high expectations for black students. Miss Hutch explained to Professor Rose, "I began by enumerating all the adjectives used to describe our kids: *slow, poor, impoverished, deprived, oppressed.* We get so busy looking at children in terms of labels that we fail to look for the *potential*—and to demand that kids live up to that potential." She continued, "I tell these teachers, 'Don't think that because a child cannot read a text, he cannot read *you.*'"[28]

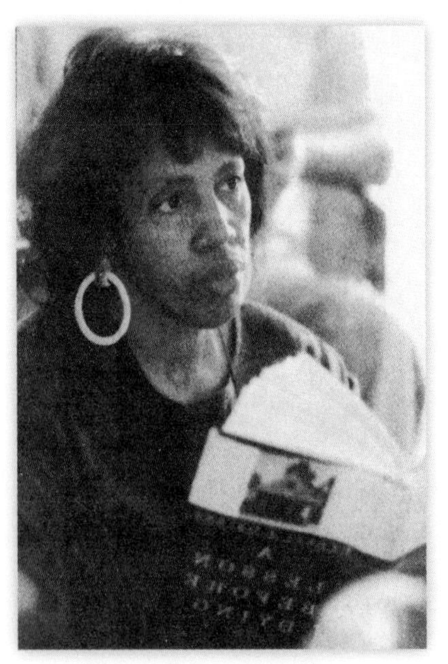

Yvonne Divans Hutchinson

Miss Hutch continued to see her classroom as an extension of her home, and as a site of possibility and for cultivating critical black literacy. This is most evident in her annual "Reading Marathon," which she began hosting at her residence during the winter holiday. During these events, Hutchinson's current and former students stayed overnight reading a book aloud together,

From a Los Angeles Times *(January 3, 1995) article profiling Miss Hutch's Reaching Marathon*

discussing the text, eating food, and going for a midnight jog. Miss Hutch began this tradition in 1989 while teaching at Markham, and she kept it going after joining the faculty of King/Drew Magnet High School in 1999. Markham was a feeder school for King/Drew, so it never felt like leaving home at all. She simply followed her students.

I attended Miss Hutch's Reading Marathon before having her as a teacher. We read Delores Phillips's *The Darkest Child* during my first year. She would tell students, "If you're not in love with reading, don't come." But the marathon always seemed to attract twenty to forty students and "guest readers." We all piled into her Leimert Park home in late December to commemorate the arrival of a new year.[29] We gathered around some text she had chosen, usually by a black author. We read and we debated. We picked apart the worlds reflected in the words of Toni Morrison, Dwight McBride, Ernest Gaines, or Edward P. Jones, and we were ultimately tasked with trying to use some piece of them to sustain and build our own worlds. The Reading Marathon was akin to religious watchnight services, a way of anticipating the new year and setting our intentions. Hutchinson modeled for students that our shared love for words, and worlding, did not have to be limited to the classroom.

School—real school—was always connected to the most intimate parts of our lives, the beautiful and the terrible. Miss Hutch insisted that this was necessary if we were to live full and dignified lives. Our studying—and teaching—is essential for how we care for ourselves until we join "the classroom in the sky," as she put it. This was especially true for black students.

Conclusion

Hieroglyphics of the Black Student Body

In this here place, we flesh; flesh that weeps, laughs; flesh that dances on bare feet in grass. Love it. Love it hard. Yonder they do not love your flesh.

—BABY SUGGS IN TONI MORRISON'S *Beloved*

These undecipherable markings on the captive body render a kind of hieroglyphics of the flesh.

—HORTENSE SPILLERS, "Mama's Baby, Papa's Maybe: An American Grammar Book"

We have worked on ourselves as canvases of representation.

—STUART HALL, "What Is This 'Black' in Black Popular Culture?"

WE ARE BOTH STORY AND FLESH.[1] Therefore, it is essential we take time and care with the stories that frame our lives and give form to our consciousness as a historically situated people. What are the distinguishable marks we wear as we move through the world? What stories are we handed to help (re)frame our mission and reality as we navigate structures and social systems created well before our time? Such questions are relevant for all humanity. These questions undergird all of the stories in *School Clothes*. Yet there is one thread we've yet to unravel: adornment. What does self-fashioning do in the lives of black students? And how is their styling woven into their narrative? For the moment, I'd like to return to William Holtzclaw.

William Holtzclaw and his family sat around in a slight panic one evening at the end of the two-month school season that lasted from July to August. This would have been sometime in the early 1880s in Randolph County, Alabama. The children had a performance to close out the term, an exhibition to display what they had learned. The teacher asked students to wear white, but Holtzclaw and his siblings did not have white clothes, "nor many of any other sort, for that matter." His father thought it unwise to buy white clothes for just one occasion, given the sparse resources they had and knowing they would not get much use out of them. The Holtzclaws lived in a pinewood cabin on the plantation of a white man for whom they worked. The meager home amounted to a single room that was fourteen by sixteen feet. Given the intimacy of the space, the entire family was drawn in to figure out a solution to the problem. Holtzclaw's mother was determined. "Her children should look as well on this important occasion as any of [their] neighbors." The house went to sleep that night with no clear solution.

The next morning, Holtzclaw and his two siblings woke up to white suits for all of them. He was in disbelief at his mother's resourcefulness. She cut up and repurposed the fabric from her only petticoat—a kind of layered undergarment worn beneath Victorian-style dresses to make them flare out at the bottom. She had to be meticulous, cutting the fabric just right to ensure there was enough to cover all three of her children. The petticoat was quite worn, so the fabric was loose. The children would have to be mindful of any big movements, lest they overextend the fabric and cause it to tear. Holtzclaw and his siblings had to adjust to these constraints. Recalling his anxiety about the clothes splitting, he shared that during the performance "we had to be very careful how we stooped in moving about the stage, lest there should be a general splitting and tearing, with consequences we were afraid to imagine." Knowing this, they carried on with a kind of carefulness. Despite their fears, the clothes held up.

It was a proud moment for their family. Holtzclaw's mother and father, both born under slave law, were not permitted to learn. For them, reading and writing would have literally been deemed criminal activity. Seeing their children stand on a platform and perform speeches they learned in school was something like watching a prayer come to life right before their eyes. Holtzclaw recalled, "We said our little pieces, and I suppose we looked about as well as the others; at least, we thought so, and that was sufficient."[2]

In adorning their bodies with the white suits made by their mother in a pinch, these students were being covered by more than makeshift school clothes. The clothes represented their collective striving to bear new marks. This was a *will to adorn* that carried embedded meaning.[3] The clothes Mrs. Holtzclaw stitched together, from scraps of her undergarment, were part and parcel of an act of covering her children in prayer, not just for the performative aspects of their culminating school event but also to commemorate what was, for her, a new day begun. Her children's going to school was part of a broader quest for a ceremony to remake black life in ways that defied or refused any remnants of the slave past. The proceedings of this school event were situated in the larger span of these students' and their families' shared genealogy as black people striving to live free and dignified lives. Going to school for these children—the first in their family to be born *on the other side* of slavery—was a part of black people's experimentation with their dreams of freedom in the first decades after Emancipation.

Narratives about school clothes in the lives of black students are rich in metaphor, but they also speak to African Americans' material reality. This seemingly mundane aspect of their stories, as in the case of William Holtzclaw, hints at deeper conceptual aspects of their social life as learners. Historical narratives of black students and school clothes from the nineteenth and twentieth centuries are varied and complex. Thinking of them as part of the experience of second sight, the clothing adds important texture to the story, a human touch; they add a decorative element to the story of black students and their journey for justice, beauty, truth, and the good in education.[4]

Families struggled to acquire shoes for young students, to protect their feet from the natural elements of the earth, and the weather, as they walked miles to school.[5] One boy and his sister shared a single pair of shoes. The brother stayed home three days of the week, allowing his sister to attend their school, which was four miles away.[6] Across time and space, we see black students dressing themselves up for a new life, and a new world, one in which all God's children have shoes, and a robe, and wings, as the African American spiritual goes. Black education was about striving for new marks and a new semantics for reading the black (student) body, a new system of meaning and value that could challenge and replace centuries of violent debasement.

The sartorial metaphor of school clothes is about the stories that cover black students, and how these coverings become resources as black students come to know who they are. Black students' school clothes were more than attire demarcating some imitative performance of dominant society and its sartorial norms. Black students were covered by dreams, and stories, and promises of a world that had yet to exist, all of which could be taken up as resources in the journey toward building the new world they were searching for.

As this book has shown, the strivings of black learners were always entangled with competing stories in black students' lives, narrative forces that undermined black people's attempts to live freely, with dignity and respect. Such conflicting interests left indelible marks on the subjectivity of African American learners. And these warring ideals constitute part of a past that is not dead, but one that continues to mark black students in the twenty-first-century present.

Black students continue to be a reminder that, for centuries, hostile white opposition to African American education "showed itself in ashes, insult, and blood."[7] Their bodies continue to represent this history, just as they are a reminder that even in the face of such violent acts of suppression, the first acts by the freedpeople were to occupy the classroom, that the formerly enslaved identified the schoolhouse as a critical battleground in their war to abolish the color line that partitioned black life on one side and the rest of the world on the other. Whether acknowledged or obscured in contemporary discourse, memories of this alienation and black students' protracted struggle against it continue to draw breath. They animate the world and the schools we navigate, even as they are all too often muted, unnamed, unattended.

The black (student) body reminds the world of what the American school has never been, and yet what it must be if justice is ever to be achieved. It is for these reasons that, in a world set on forgetting and clinging to hasty narratives of forward progress, black skin and black students invite a shared antipathy for many. They are enfleshed reminders of this living history.

The black (student) body bears its own distinct *hieroglyphics of the flesh*, for black students are the progeny of the wounded captive body of which Hortense Spillers has written. Yet some would prefer to forget such markings of the Middle Passage, where "altered human tissue, take on the objective description of laboratory prose—eyes beaten out, arms, backs, skulls branded, a left jaw, a right ankle, punctured; teeth missing, as the calculated work of iron, whips, chains, knives, the canine patrol, the bullet."[8] They find them too grotesque and discomforting, this story of scars etched by tools of torture, past and present. But acting as though they do not exist is helpful to no one.

These hieroglyphics read of "the nigger seat" in the back of Boston classrooms in the 1850s, after the city ended segregation (for the first time).[9] This designated seat near black students was employed by white teachers as a method of correction for students who behaved poorly, perhaps to suggest that they were "acting like a nigger." This tie between African American students' physical location in the classroom and that which was deemed the zone of punishment, or those in need of punishment, might be thought of as an early manifestation of the interplay between the condemnation of black life and what would become highly racialized school disciplinary practices in the twentieth and twenty-first centuries.

The black (student) body carries memories like those of an angry white man shooting into a Kentucky schoolyard during Reconstruction, as formerly enslaved Elijah Marrs and his students played during recess while taking a break from their studies. This body bears traces of the more than 630 black schools burned down in the South between 1864 and 1876. Some of these schools were burned during race riots, while others fell victim to the ongoing acts of wanton antiblack violence and terror. The black (student) body reminds the world that in the 1870s Detroit's white superintendent replaced all double desks with single desks after learning that black and white students would share a classroom. The idea of black and white students' legs touching was, perhaps, an unconscionable thought to bear.[10]

The black (student) body is a reminder that the nation allowed black education to be criminalized across the South during a time when over 90 percent of black Americans (free and enslaved) populated this region. Such precedent set the stage for generation after generation of black people being systematically barred from education. It reminds us that the nation then generally conceded that if blacks were to receive an education after Emancipation, it must be one that fit them to be a servant class of people. This student body reminds us of how African Americans' civic estrangement has always been bound up with how they have been enlisted in the nation's schools and the system of knowledge at its foundation. As Noah Webster, architect of America's chosen orthography and contributor to the Merriam-Webster dictionary, declared in 1843: as for "the woolly haired Africans, who constitute the principal part of the inhabitants of Africa," and from whom black students descended, "there is no history and there can be none."[11]

Nonetheless, the black (student) body also carries marks of a counterhistorical tradition, a fugitive tradition of learning, where fugitive slaves like James W. C. Pennington, a schoolteacher and abolitionist, challenged such narrative distortions of black life. He offered instead what he deemed "a just view of our historical origin" in his 1841 *Text Book of the Origin and History of the Colored People.* His view, from within the veil, was one that challenged what he termed "the chattel principle": all of the narratives, laws, and economic logics that justified reducing black people to property and that structured the modern world.[12]

The black (student) body is a reminder that pupils in Jacksonville, Florida, watched their school burn to the ground in 1901 during a town fire, while firefighters prioritized the homes of white citizens over their place of learning. It is marked by the memory of the fire chief's exclamation that "it will be a good thing for some of these damned niggers to get burnt out."[13] And yet, black students stood in a place of knowing and heroic resistance that refused such fiery hatred. For from this same school—the Stanton School—the black national anthem was birthed just a year prior. It was ushered into the world by five hundred black students singing the song in commemoration of Lincoln's birthday and as tribute to Booker T. Washington, all under the direction of their teachers who wrote and arranged it, brothers James and Rosamond Johnson. They sang a song filled with faith and hope, and that expressed a culture passed on to them by their predecessors, those who had journeyed through the darkest days of the past.

The black (student) body is marked by the memories of segregation laws passed in Arizona in 1909 as a response to the state's growing black population. It carries the memory of a teacher in Phoenix who set up "a screen around the desk of a Negro child" to protect the honor of white students' education when a separate black school was not feasible, thus ensuring that the law was upheld.[14] It is marked by memories like those of Madeline Stratton Morris and her peers in the 1920s, having to ritually enter Englewood High School in Chicago through its back doors, only to routinely receive failing grades by white teachers who held them in contempt.[15]

The black (student) body bears witness to the fact that by 1930, the overwhelming majority of black students in southern cities had no access to publicly funded high schools, even as all of these cities maintained at least one high school for white students, and despite the fact that "public education for all at public expense was, in the South, a Negro idea," as Du Bois reminded us.[16] It mattered not that the freedpeople were responsible for introducing universal education to the region. The public education system they created would be used to reinforce the very racial domination they hoped it could be used to dismantle.

Their black skin is a reminder that generations of children witnessed, and continue to witness, the image of Emmett Till's mutilated body in 1955. The black (student) body carries the memory of those Negro youth, who in the wake of Till's murder peeked through the mortician's window in the Mississippi delta, having heard what happened to the boy from Chicago, only to be accosted by a white man who took it on himself to lecture them about "what kin happen when you sass-out white women."[17] Choosing not to be debilitated by the trauma, black students used such witnessing to propel them into greater social activism, where they used their learning to curse such darkness and evil, all while lighting candles to illuminate new ways of being in the world.[18]

The time line inscribed on the black (student) body bears notations that between 1959 and 1963 all the black students in Prince Edward County, Virginia, had no schools to attend. Rather than integrate, the county's white officials closed public schools and established private academies for white students.[19] It reminds us that in 1960, US marshals had to escort a first-grade black girl named Ruby Bridges to school in New Orleans, while white mobs screamed obscenities, some going as far as to kill her in effigy. They proudly carried around a small coffin, holding it up to the cameras for all to see the toy doll visibly lying within it. The prop warned of the lengths to which they would go to protect their privileges and way of life.[20]

The time line is marked by black students witnessing the firing of their teachers because they were members of the National Association for the Advancement of Colored People, some educators having refused to denounce or conceal their affiliation when surveilled by white school authorities.[21] This time line etched in black student flesh reminds us of those children in Grenada, Mississippi, who suffered injuries and broken bones at the hands of white mobs in September 1966, as they attempted to integrate a school they were legally permitted to attend.[22] Such stories index the shared vulnerability of black adults and black children, demonstrating the limited protection adults have been able to offer the youth, no matter how much they tried and sacrificed; and at the same time, these stories emphasize that no matter how much they fell short, such sacrifice continued to be a radical act of love and an assertion of human dignity.

The black (student) body is a reminder that all of this has happened, and yet black students can and have always inhabited a tradition that teaches them to be aware and vigilant of these forces—and more importantly, to refuse such arrangements in this world we know. Theirs is a tradition that transmitted a sense of self-worth and respect to generations of black students, compelling them to always strive for new marks, new ways of being, new clothes to wear in a world that continues to present skewed life chances and ongoing condemnation for black people, a stratification conditioned by slavery and its afterlives.[23]

And, again, black students' witness reminds us that this past is no past at all. It is living history that continues to structure the world we inhabit. We might pass their stories on as covering for current and future generations, who must continue to do battle against miseducation and aggressive neglect. Like the students in this book, they might do so while also seeking out beauty, joy, and right relationship, and while striving to catch the likeness of a world they might build. Indeed, a world better—more beautiful and less terrible—than the one we have known.

Black students are not without history. Their educational heritage is one of persecution and ongoing resistance. It is rich and vast, and it provides necessary cultural armor for navigating the educational landscapes we inhabit today. Black students have been looking back, documenting their worlds across the generations.

Their witness deserves an audience.

Acknowledgments

THIS BOOK BEGAN as a conversation with Dr. Theresa Perry at Frugal Bookstore in Roxbury, Massachusetts. A group of educators and organizers affiliated with the Boston Network for Black Student Achievement gathered in December 2017 to discuss plans for cultivating an affirming literacy culture in Boston schools for African American learners. The meeting's theme was "Book Clubs for Black Kids." We had a lively conversation about James Baldwin's *The Fire Next Time* and different ways of teaching Baldwin's letter to his nephew to African American students. The meeting concluded, and Dr. Perry pulled me aside to ask if I had any interest in writing something that translated my research to a wider audience, "because most people don't know anything about the history of black education," she explained. Then she asked, "Don't you think that's a good idea?" But the question didn't really seem like a question at all—more like polite instruction. I agreed and was grateful she'd taken an interest in my work. Before I knew it, I was on an email thread with editors at Beacon Press. A meeting was scheduled for March 9, 2018, at Henrietta's Table in Cambridge, Massachusetts, where Dr. Perry introduced me to Rachael Marks and Helene Atwan. From that day forward, Rachael has been an outstanding supporter and editor. I am grateful to Dr. Perry for believing in my work and for the team at Beacon Press for giving me the space to figure out what needed to be said and how I wanted to say it.

My friend and colleague Ernest Mitchell helped cultivate the idea for *School Clothes* without knowing it. During a practice job talk based on my first book, *Fugitive Pedagogy*, in fall 2017, Ernest suggested that I remove a section about black student voice and the archival record. He encouraged me to save it for a separate project. He explained (and I remember the words exactly), "You can write a whole book on the black student as witness, if you wanted to." In my mind, this event was the call and Dr. Theresa Perry's invitation, just months later, was the response. And while Professors Perry and Mitchell pushed me to begin this project, I was blessed to have many scholars and friends who helped me along the way.

I enjoyed sitting down with former teachers, including Tauheedah Baker-Jones, Latosha Guy, Myron Butterfield Humphries, Yvonne Divans Hutchinson, Adimu Madyun, and Carrie Paige Wilson, to interview them about their student experiences and discuss my memories from their classrooms. While all their stories did not make it into the book, they each played an important role in developing the conceptual lens for the project and helped clarify my own connection to the work. I am also grateful to Professors James D. Anderson, Mary Frances Berry, John Bracey, Evelyn Brooks Higginbotham, and Hortense Spillers for their willingness to elaborate on their student experiences when I wrote to them after catching glimpses of their student narratives in public talks or writings. Incorporating their voices into the chorus of student witnessing in this book was an exciting and unexpected addition. What's more, they helped reveal important connections between the history of African American student life and the development of black studies, then and now.

Gathering with friends to talk about our ideas and life—and the relationship between the two—is always a generative experience for me. I usually leave feeling better than when I arrived, with more light, more clarity, and feeling more compelled to get the work done. Friendship, for me, has made the work collaborative and less isolating. Friends like Imani Perry sent text messages with titles of relevant memoirs and autobiographies to read, as well as photos of relevant passages from books as she read them. Others listened for the deeper meaning of *the story* I was telling through *the facts* assembled. Like the time my friend Joshua Bennett listened to me recount stories about black students dressing up to go to school in the late nineteenth century and how they reminded me of the emphasis placed on school clothes in my youth. "You should use that," he said, "School clothes. That's beautiful. And we all know what that means." He encouraged me to think about the stories in this book as cultural armor and equipment for living. Many exchanges like these, long and short, occurred with Charisse Burden-Stelly, Julius Fleming, Roshad Meeks, Timothy Pantoja, kihana ross, Brandon Terry, Jermaine Thibodeaux, Elizabeth Todd-Breland, and Rhaisa Williams—and they all impacted the development of this book. I am also grateful to Therí Pickens and Sarah Watkins for their editorial guidance at key moments. To have such a thoughtful and rigorous group of scholars in my corner has been a wonderful gift.

I enjoyed workshopping early pieces of this book with students enrolled in my fall 2019 doctoral seminar "Black Studies and Education Research" at the Harvard Graduate School of Education. Rebecca Horwitz-Willis, Ashley Ison, Shandra Jones, Kailah McGee, Garry Mitchell, Alyssa Napier, Zenzile Riddick, Edom Tesfa, and Christian Walkes—thank you for the generous yet critical commentary. I am particularly grateful to Christian, who continued to support this project as a research assistant. Anne Korte, member of HGSE's faculty support staff, has also been a tremendous help along the way.

Finally, I am indebted to the long lineage of African Americans who made an intentional decision to bear witness to their educational journeys, those who left a record—written or otherwise—to be revisited and studied in the future. I am tremendously proud of their courage, creativity, and commitment to crafting new visions of possibility for themselves and the world in which they lived. I wrote this book to commemorate the lives of black students—the young people who wrote, and wondered, and sang, and cried, and danced, and dreamed, and joked, and loved, and grew, and taught, anyhow. Their heritage is a worthy one. I dedicate this book to their memory, to our inheritance.

Notes

PREFACE: "SCHOOL CLOTHES" AND THE BLACK VERNACULAR

1. Robert G. O'Meally, "The Vernacular Tradition," in *The Norton Anthology of African American Literature*, ed. Henry Louis Gates Jr. and Nellie McKay, 2nd ed. (New York: Norton, 2004), 3–4.
2. Monica L. Miller, *Slaves to Fashion: Black Dandyism and the Styling of Black Diasporic Identity* (Durham, NC: Duke University Press, 2009), 3.
3. Stuart Hall, "What Is This 'Black' in Black Popular Culture?" *Social Justice* 20, nos. 1/2 (51–52) (1993): 109.
4. Heather Williams, *Self-Taught: African American Education in Slavery and Freedom* (Chapel Hill: University of North Carolina Press, 2007), 177.
5. Mary McLeod Bethune interviewed by Charles S. Johnson, transcript, c. 1940, box 2, folder 1, Mary McLeod Bethune Papers, Fisk University, John Hope and Aurelia E. Franklin Library, Special Collection and Archives.
6. Booker T. Washington, *Up from Slavery: An Autobiography* (Garden City, NY: Doubleday, 1901), 11–12.
7. Wilma King, *Stolen Childhood: Slave Youth in Nineteenth-Century America* (Bloomington: Indiana University Press, 1995).
8. Zora Neale Hurston, "Characteristics of Negro Expression (1934)," in *Hurston: Folklore, Memoirs, and Other Writings*, ed. Cheryl A. Wall (New York: Literary Classics of the United States, 1995), 830–46.
9. Annette Gordon-Reed, *On Juneteenth* (New York: Liveright, 2021), 40.
10. Rachel Devlin, *A Girl Stands at the Door: The Generation of Young Women Who Desegregated America's Schools* (New York: Basic Books, 2018).
11. Christina Sharpe, "Beauty Is a Method," *E-Flux* 105 (December 2019), https://www.e-flux.com/journal/105/303916/beauty-is-a-method/; Tanisha C. Ford, *Dressed in Dreams: A Black Girl's Love Letter to the Power of Fashion* (New York: St. Martin's Press, 2019).

INTRODUCTION: LIVING AND LEARNING BEHIND THE VEIL

1. Toni Cade Bambara, "Deep Sights and Rescue Missions," in *Lure and Loathing: Essays on Race, Identity, and the Ambivalence of Assimilation*, ed. Gerald Lyn Early (New York: Allen Lane/Penguin Press, 1993), 309–10.
2. Melville J. Herskovits, *The Myth of the Negro Past* (New York: Harper & Brothers, 1941), 190; Thomas L Webber, *Deep Like the Rivers: Education in the Slave Quarter Community*, 1831-1865 (New York: Norton, 1978), 10.
3. W. E. B. Du Bois, *The Souls of Black Folk* (1903; rpt. Barnes & Noble Classics, 2003), 8.
4. W. E. B. Du Bois, *Darkwater: Voices from Within the Veil* (1919; rpt. New York: Washington Square Press, 2004), 7.
5. Sylvia Wynter, "No Humans Involved: An Open Letter to My Colleagues," *Forum N.H.I. Knowledge for the 21st Century* 1, no. 1 (Fall 1994): 52.
6. Du Bois, *The Souls of Black Folk*, 3.
7. Du Bois, *The Souls of Black Folk*, 9, 154.
8. Du Bois, *Darkwater*, 9.
9. Kevin Young, *The Grey Album: On the Blackness of Blackness* (Minneapolis: Graywolf Press, 2012), 67.
10. Bambara, "Deep Sights and Rescue Missions," 310.
11. Elizabeth Alexander, *The Trayvon Generation* (New York: Grand Central, 2022), 82.
12. George McDowell Stroud, *Sketch of the Laws Relating to Slavery in the Several States of the United States of America* (1856; rpt. Lavergne, TN: Sagwan Press, 2015), 88, 60.
13. Heather Williams, *Self-Taught: African American Education in Slavery and Freedom* (Chapel Hill: University of North Carolina Press, 2007), 209.
14. Missouri State Archives, "Laws Concerning Slavery in Missouri," Missouri Digital Heritage, accessed November 12, 2020, https://www.sos.mo.gov/archives/education/aahi/earlyslavelaws/slavelaws.
15. Cherokee Nation, *The Constitution and Laws of the Cherokee Nation: Passed at Tahlequah, Cherokee Nation, 1839–51* (Tahlequah, OK: Cherokee Nation, 1852), 55.
16. Henry Louis Gates Jr., *The Trials of Phillis Wheatley: America's First Black Poet and Her Encounters with the Founding Fathers*, rpt. ed. (New York: Civitas Books, 2010), 5 (quotation), 69; Thomas Jefferson, *Notes on the State of Virginia* (Philadelphia: Princhard & Hall, 1787), 149–50. Jefferson wrote, "Comparing them by their

faculties of memory, reason, and imagination, it appears to me, that in memory they are equal to the whites; in reason much inferior, as I think one could scarcely be found capable of tracing and comprehending the investigations of Euclid; and that in imagination they are dull, tasteless, and anomalous. . . . Among the blacks is misery enough, God knows, but no poetry. . . . Religion indeed has produced a Phyllis Wheatley; but it could not produce a poet. The compositions published under her name are below the dignity of criticism."

17. Charles C. Andrews, *The History of the New-York African Free-Schools, from Their Establishment in 1787, to the Present Time; Embracing a Period of More Than Forty Years* (New York: Mahlon Day, 1830), 61–62, italics added.
18. Crystal Lynn Webster, *Beyond the Boundaries of Childhood: African American Children in the Antebellum North* (Chapel Hill: University of North Carolina Press, 2021), 103–4.
19. Andrews, *The History of the New-York African Free-Schools*, 61–62, italics added.
20. Andrews, *The History of the New-York African Free-Schools*, 61–65, italics added.
21. Quoted in Anna Mae Duane, *Educated for Freedom: The Incredible Story of Two Fugitive Schoolboys Who Grew Up to Change a Nation* (New York: NYU Press, 2020), 55.
22. Carter Godwin Woodson, *The Education of the Negro Prior to 1861: A History of the Education of the Colored People of the United States from the Beginning of Slavery to the Civil War* (New York: Putnam & Sons, 1915), 294.
23. Charlotte L. Forten, *The Journal of Charlotte L. Forten*, ed. Ray Allen Billington (New York: W. W. Norton, 1981), 55, italics added.
24. Forten, *The Journal of Charlotte L. Forten*, 76.
25. Campbell F. Scribner, "Surveying the Destruction of African American Schoolhouses in the South, 1864–1876," *Journal of the Civil War Era* 10, no. 4 (December 2020): 469–94.
26. Alice Walker, *Gathering Blossoms Under Fire: The Journals of Alice Walker, 1965–2000*, ed. Valerie Boyd (New York: Simon & Schuster, 2022), 391–92.
27. William Watkins, *The White Architects of Black Education: Ideology and Power in America, 1865–1954* (New York: Teachers College Press, 2001).
28. Horace M. Bond, *Negro Education in Alabama: A Study in Cotton and Steel* (1939; rpt. Tuscaloosa: University of Alabama, 1994), 290.

29. See discussion on "identity resources" and the ecological context of learning and development for students in Na'ilah Nasir, *Racialized Identities: Race and Achievement among African American Youth* (Palo Alto, CA: Stanford University Press, 2011), 29, 110.
30. Vanessa Siddle Walker, *Their Highest Potential: An African American School Community in the Segregated South* (Chapel Hill: University of North Carolina Press, 1996), 10.
31. Tamah Richardson and Annie Rivers, "Progress of the Negro: A Unit of Work for the Third Grade," *Virginia Teachers Bulletin* (May 1936): 3–8.
32. "How We Have Been Helped by the Study of Negro History," and "January," Student Yearbook, 1929, box 312, Nannie Helen Burroughs Papers, Manuscript Division, Library of Congress, Washington, DC.
33. Carter G. Woodson, *The Negro in Our History* (Washington, DC: Associated Publishers, 1922), 179, 226.
34. Carlotta Walls LaNier, interview by Larry Crowe, video, July 8, 2002, HistoryMakers Digital Archive.
35. Du Bois, *Darkwater*, 14.
36. Toni Morrison, "Unspeakable Things Unspoken: The Afro-American Presence in American Literature (1988)," in *The Source of Self-Regard: Selected Essays, Speeches, and Meditations* (New York: Knopf, 2019), 161–97: "But there was never the danger of their 'writing back.' . . . One could even observe them, hold them in prolonged gaze, without encountering the risk of being observed, viewed, or judged in return." See also "oppositional gaze" in bell hooks, "The Oppositional Gaze: Black Female Spectators," in *Black American Cinema*, ed. Manthia Diawara (New York: Routledge, 1993), 294–308.
37. Henry Louis Gates, "Introduction," in *The Classic Slave Narratives* (New York: Penguin, 1987), x. Here, I am following Gates's discussion of imitation and repetition in his analysis of first-person accounts and collective identity in slave narratives.
38. "No given set of casually recorded historical events can in itself constitute a story; the most it might offer the historian are story elements." These elements are made into a story through the distortion and rearrangement of them, which requires "the suppression and subordination of certain of them and the highlighting of others" through various descriptive strategies. This fashioning is indeed a necessary distortion, consisting of the exclusion of some facts but also "the arrangement of events in an order different from the chronological order of their original occurrence, so as to endow them

with different functions in an integrated pattern of meaning." These kinds of narrative strategies are inherent in all historical writing, whether they are acknowledged or not, but they are done with particular intentionality in this text. Hayden White, *Tropics of Discourse: Essays in Cultural Criticism*, rpt. ed. (Baltimore: Johns Hopkins University Press, 1978), 84, 111, "redescription" on 98.

39. Anna Julia Cooper, *A Voice from the South: By a Black Woman from the South* (Xenia, OH: Aldine Printing House, 1892), 31.
40. George Yancy, *Black Bodies, White Gazes: The Continuing Significance of Race* (Rowman & Littlefield, 2008), 65.
41. "Indeed, when the 'I' seeks to give an account of itself, an account that must include the conditions of its own emergence, it must, as a matter of necessity, become a social theorist. The reason for this is that the 'I' has no story of its own that is not also the story of a relation—or set of relations—to a set of norms." Judith Butler, *Giving an Account of Oneself* (New York: Fordham University Press, 2005), 8.
42. "Every generation of African Americans must rediscover the institution of slavery for themselves." Hortense Spillers quoted in Frank B. Wilderson III, "Settler, 'Savage,' Slave: Cinema and the Structure of U.S. Antagonisms" (PhD diss., University of California, Berkeley, 2004), ii.
43. "If slavery persists as an issue in the political life of black America, it is not because of antiquarian obsession with bygone days or the burden of a too-long memory, but because black lives are still imperiled and devalued by a racial calculus and a political arithmetic that were entrenched centuries ago. This is *the afterlife of slavery*—skewed life chances, limited access to health and education, premature death, incarceration, and impoverishment." Saidiya Hartman, *Lose Your Mother: A Journey Along the Atlantic Slave Route*, rpt. ed. (New York: Farrar, Straus & Giroux, 2008), 6.

CHAPTER ONE: GOING TO SCHOOL NORTH OF SLAVERY

1. Alexander Crummell, "Eulogium," in *Africa and America: Addresses and Discourses* (Springfield, MA: Willey, 1891), 274–76.
2. For a detailed account of the 1829 escape, see Crummell, "Eulogium," 274–76; for historical analysis of local Kent County records documenting the ownership and pursuit of the Garnet family, see Amanda Tuttle-Smith and the Historical Society of Kent County, "Henry Highland Garnet—African American History in Kent County" (2020), https://kentcountyhistory.org/history/#African-American-History-in-Kent-County.

3. For reference to George's father, see William J. Simmons and Henry McNeal Turner, *Men of Mark: Eminent, Progressive and Rising* (G. M. Rewell, 1887), 656; Tuttle-Smith and the Historical Society of Kent County, "Henry Highland Garnet."
4. Crummell, "Eulogium," 274–76.
5. The all-girl's class began in 1828 and was run by Julia Andrews, daughter of the white schoolmaster, Charles Andrews. See John L. Rury, "The New York African Free School, 1827–1836: Conflict over Community Control of Black Education," *Phylon* 44, no. 3 (1983): 191.
6. Henry H. Garnet, "From the Voice of Freedom: H. H. Garnet," *Emancipator and Free American* (March 21, 1844): 184; James McCune Smith, "Introduction" to *A Memorial Discourse, by Henry Highland Garnet, Delivered in the Hall of the House of Representatives, Washington City, D.C. on Sabbath, February 12, 1865* (Philadelphia: Joseph M. Wilson, 1865), 25.
7. Leslie M. Harris, *In the Shadow of Slavery: African Americans in New York City, 1626–1863* (Chicago: University of Chicago Press, 2004), 3, 5.
8. Smith, "Introduction," 27.
9. Harris, *In the Shadow of Slavery*, 182.
10. Alexander Crummell, "'Africa and Her People': Lecture Notes," in *Destiny and Race: Selected Writings, 1840–1898*, ed. Wilson Moses, 1st ed. (Amherst: University of Massachusetts Press, 1992), 61.
11. Frederick Douglass, *Narrative of the Life of Frederick Douglass, an American Slave* (Boston: Anti-Slavery Office, 1845), 5. For more on black witnessing, see Elizabeth Alexander, "'Can You Be Black and Look at This?': Reading the Rodney King Video(s)," in *The Black Interior* (Saint Paul, MN: Graywolf Press, 2004), 175–205.
12. Smith, "Introduction," 24–25.
13. Crummell, "Eulogium," 276–77.
14. John Frederick Bell, *Degrees of Equality: Abolitionist Colleges and the Politics of Race* (Baton Rouge: Louisiana State University Press, 2022).
15. Harris, *In the Shadow of Slavery*, 134–35.
16. Davison Douglas, *Jim Crow Moves North: The Battle over Northern School Segregation, 1865–1954* (New York: Cambridge University Press, 2005), 50; Anna Mae Duane, *Educated for Freedom: The Incredible Story of Two Fugitive Schoolboys Who Grew Up to Change a Nation* (New York: New York University Press, 2020).
17. John Hope Franklin and Evelyn Brooks Higginbotham, *From Slavery to Freedom: A History of African Americans*, 9th ed. (New York: McGraw-Hill, 2010), 174.

18. Leon F. Litwack, *North of Slavery: The Negro in the Free States, 1790–1860*, 1st ed. (Chicago: University of Chicago Press, 1965), 137, 115, 134.
19. Crummell, "Eulogium," 278.
20. Crummell, "Eulogium," 300, 277.
21. Crummell, "Eulogium," 278.
22. Booker T. Washington, *Up from Slavery*, ed. William L. Andrews (W. W. Norton, 1996), 25–27.
23. Crummell, "Eulogium," 279–80.
24. Hilary J. Moss, *Schooling Citizens: The Struggle for African American Education in Antebellum America* (Chicago: University of Chicago Press, 2010), 13.
25. Douglas, *Jim Crow Moves North*.
26. Crummell, "Eulogium," 280.
27. Crummell, "Eulogium," 280.
28. Crummell, "Eulogium," 281.
29. Charlotte L. Forten, *The Journal of Charlotte L. Forten*, ed. Ray Allen Billington (New York: W. W. Norton, 1981), 42.
30. See Billington's introduction to *The Journal of Charlotte L. Forten*, 20, 22.
31. George R. Price, "The Roberts Case, the Easton Family, and the Dynamics of the Abolitionist Movement in Massachusetts, 1776–1870," in *Abolitionist Politics and the Coming of the Civil War*, ed. James Brewer Stewart (Amherst: University of Massachusetts Press, 2008), 71.
32. Quoted in Moss, *Schooling Citizens*, 130.
33. Crystal Lynn Webster, *Beyond the Boundaries of Childhood: African American Children in the Antebellum North* (Chapel Hill: University of North Carolina Press, 2021), 112.
34. Litwack, *North of Slavery*, 148, 151.
35. Douglas, *Jim Crow Moves North*, 48–49.
36. Litwack, *North of Slavery*, 137, 151.
37. Forten, *The Journal of Charlotte L. Forten*, 43.
38. Forten, *The Journal of Charlotte L. Forten*, 45.
39. Forten, *The Journal of Charlotte L. Forten*, 46.
40. Forten, *The Journal of Charlotte L. Forten*, 47.
41. On "civic estrangement," see Salamishah Tillet, *Sites of Slavery: Citizenship and Racial Democracy in the Post–Civil Rights Imagination* (Durham, NC: Duke University Press, 2012).
42. Forten, *The Journal of Charlotte L. Forten*, 10.
43. Forten, *The Journal of Charlotte L. Forten*, 58.
44. Webster, *Beyond the Boundaries of Childhood*, 101.

45. Benjamin Quarles and August Meier, *Black Mosaic: Essays in Afro-American History and Historiography*, 1st ed. (Amherst: University of Massachusetts Press, 1988), 11.
46. Forten, *The Journal of Charlotte L. Forten*, 103, 122.

CHAPTER TWO: BECOMING FUGITIVE LEARNERS

1. John W. Blassingame, ed., *Slave Testimony: Two Centuries of Letters, Speeches, Interviews, and Autobiographies*, annotated ed. (Baton Rouge: Louisiana State University Press, 1977), 465.
2. Heather Williams, *Self-Taught: African American Education in Slavery and Freedom* (Chapel Hill: University of North Carolina Press, 2007), 208.
3. Janet Cornelius, "'We Slipped and Learned to Read': Slave Accounts of the Literacy Process, 1830–1865," *Phylon* 44, no. 3 (1983): 174.
4. Williams, *Self-Taught*, 28.
5. Blassingame, *Slave Testimony*, 267, italics added.
6. Kevin Young, *The Grey Album: On the Blackness of Blackness* (Minneapolis: Graywolf Press, 2012), 23.
7. Susie King Taylor, *Reminiscences of My Life in Camp with the 33D United States Colored Troops Late 1st S.C. Volunteers* (Boston, 1902), 5.
8. Wilma King, *Stolen Childhood: Slave Youth in Nineteenth-Century America* (Bloomington: Indiana University Press, 1995).
9. Williams, *Self-Taught*, 204.
10. Stephen Best and Saidiya Hartman, "Fugitive Justice," *Representations* 92, no. 1 (2005): 1–15.
11. James Weldon Johnson, *The Autobiography of an Ex-Coloured Man* (New York: Vintage, 1989), 21–22, 74; Houston A. Baker, "Meditation on Tuskegee: Black Studies Stories and Their Imbrication," *Journal of Blacks in Higher Education* 9 (1995): 53.
12. Nancy Faust Sizer and Theodore Sizer, *The Students Are Watching: Schools and the Moral Contract*, 1st ed. (Boston: Beacon Press, 2000); Jarvis R. Givens, "'There Would Be No Lynching If It Did Not Start in the Schoolroom': Carter G. Woodson and the Occasion of Negro History Week, 1926–1950," *American Educational Research Journal* (January 13, 2019): 13–16.
13. Daphne A. Brooks, *Bodies in Dissent: Spectacular Performances of Race and Freedom, 1850–1910* (Durham, NC: Duke University Press Books, 2006); see also discussion of "embodied learning" in Givens, "'There Would Be No Lynching If It Did Not Start in the Schoolroom.'"
14. The blurring of the line between form and content here is informed by Katherine Dunham's discussion of the relationship between form

of body and function in religious and secular dance in Haiti, "function" meaning what it made possible and opened up through the particular dance/form. Dunham makes clear that what is opened up, accessed, or put to work also determines the form. Katherine Dunham, "Form and Function in Primitive Dance (1941)," in *Kaiso! Writings by and about Katherine Dunham*, ed. VèVè A. Clark and Sara E. Johnson (Madison: University of Wisconsin Press, 2005), 502–7.

15. Tunde Adeleke, *Without Regard to Race: The Other Martin Robison Delany* (Jackson: University Press of Mississippi, 2004), 40–41.
16. Frank A. Rollin, *Life and Public Services of Martin R. Delany, American Negro, His History and Literature* (Boston: Lee & Shepard, 1883), 26–27.
17. "Southampton Affair," *Columbian Register*, September 13, 1831; "From the Albany Evening Journal: Gabriel's Defeat," *Columbian Register*, September 13, 1831.
18. Rita Dove, "David Walker (1785–1830)," *Collected Poems: 1974–2004* (New York: W. W. Norton, 2017), 32.
19. Julius S. Scott, *The Common Wind: Afro-American Currents in the Age of the Haitian Revolution* (London: Verso, 2018), 210.
20. David Walker, *David Walker's Appeal to the Coloured Citizens of the World* (Baltimore: Black Classic Press, 1830).
21. Kenyon Gradert, "The Book That Spooked the South," *Smithsonian*, February 8, 2018, https://www.smithsonianmag.com/history/book-spooked-south-180968101.
22. Birgit Brander Rasmussen, "'Attended with Great Inconveniences': Slave Literacy and the 1740 South Carolina Negro Act," *PMLA* 125, no. 1 (2010): 201–3.
23. Williams, *Self-Taught*, 208.
24. Booker T. Washington, *Up from Slavery: An Autobiography* (Garden City, NY: Doubleday, 1901), 30.
25. Frederick Douglass, *My Bondage and My Freedom* (New York: Miller, Orton & Mulligan, 1855), 199–200, italics added.
26. Douglass, *My Bondage and My Freedom*, 146.
27. Walter Johnson, *Soul by Soul: Life Inside the Antebellum Slave Market* (Cambridge, MA: Harvard University Press, 1999), 19. "Chattel principle" signals both the inheritability of the slave status and the fact that "any slave's identity might be disrupted as easily as a price could be set and a piece of paper passed from one hand to another." Johnson borrows the term from escaped slave and abolitionist James W. C. Pennington.
28. "The birth canal of Black women and women who birth blackness, then, is another kind of domestic Middle Passage; the birth canal,

that passageway from the womb through which a fetus passes during birth. The belly of the ship births blackness; the birth canal remains in, and as, the hold." Christina Sharpe, *In the Wake: On Blackness and Being* (Durham, NC: Duke University Press, 2016), 74.

29. W. S. (William Sanders) Scarborough, *The Autobiography of William Sanders Scarborough: An American Journey from Slavery to Scholarship*, African American Life Series (Detroit: Wayne State University Press, 2005), 27, 31, italics added.
30. Scarborough, *The Autobiography of William Sanders Scarborough*, 40.
31. Scarborough, *The Autobiography of William Sanders Scarborough*, 28.
32. For more on abroad marriages, see Diane Burke, "'Mah Pappy Belong to a Neighbor': The Effects of Abroad Marriages on Missouri Slave Families," in *Searching for Their Places: Women in the South across Four Centuries*, ed. Thomas Appleton and Angela Bosewell (Columbia: University of Missouri Press, 2003), 57–78; Heather Williams, "How Slavery Affected African American Families," Freedom's Story, TeacherServe, National Humanities Center, http://nationalhumanitiescenter.org/tserve/freedom/1609-1865/essays/aafamilies.htm, accessed March 20, 2016.
33. Best and Hartman, "Fugitive Justice," 1–15.
34. Scarborough, *The Autobiography of William Sanders Scarborough*, 31–32.
35. Scarborough, *The Autobiography of William Sanders Scarborough*, 34.
36. Saidiya Hartman, *Wayward Lives, Beautiful Experiments: Intimate Histories of Social Upheaval*, 1st ed. (New York: W. W. Norton, 2019), 17: "I was hungry for images that represented the *experiments in freedom that unfolded within slavery's shadow*, the practice of everyday life and escape subsistence stoked by the liberties of the city. *Beautiful experiments in living free*, urban plots against the plantation flourished, yet were unsustainable or thwarted or criminalized before they could take root."

CHAPTER THREE: LEARNING AND STRIVING IN THE AFTERLIFE OF SLAVERY

1. Elizabeth Hayes Turner, "Juneteenth: Emancipation and Memory," in *Lone Star Pasts: Memory and History in Texas*, ed. Gregg Cantrell and Elizabeth Hayes Turner (College Station: Texas A&M University Press, 2006), 148.
2. William Henry Holtzclaw, *The Black Man's Burden* (New York: Neale, 1915).

3. Toni Morrison, "The Site of Memory," in *Inventing the Truth: The Art and Craft of Memoir*, ed. William Zinsser, 2nd ed. (Boston: Houghton Mifflin Harcourt, 1995), 89.
4. Susie King Taylor, *Reminiscences of My Life in Camp with the 33D United States Colored Troops Late 1st S.C. Volunteers* (Boston, 1902), 9–11.
5. James Anderson, *The Education of Blacks in the South, 1860–1935* (Chapel Hill: University of North Carolina Press, 1988); Heather Williams, *Self-Taught: African American Education in Slavery and Freedom* (Chapel Hill: University of North Carolina Press, 2007).
6. J. W. Alvord, *First Semi-Annual Report on Schools and Finances of Freedmen, January 1, 1866* (Washington, DC: Bureau of Refugees, Freedman and Abandoned Lands, 1868), 9–10.
7. Vincent Harding, *There Is a River: The Black Struggle for Freedom in America* (New York: Harcourt Brace Jovanovich, 1981), 264–65.
8. V. P. Franklin, *Black Self-Determination: A Cultural History of African-American Resistance* (Brooklyn, NY: Lawrence Hill Books, 1992), 147.
9. W. S. (William Sanders) Scarborough, *The Autobiography of William Sanders Scarborough: An American Journey from Slavery to Scholarship*, African American Life Series (Detroit: Wayne State University Press, 2005), 37.
10. Saidiya Hartman, *Scenes of Subjection: Terror, Slavery, and Self-Making in Nineteenth-Century America*, 1st ed. (New York: Oxford University Press, 1997), 128–31; Williams, *Self-Taught*, 136.
11. Anderson, *The Education of Blacks in the South*, 19–20.
12. Alvord, *First Semi-Annual Report on Schools and Finances of Freedmen*, 6.
13. Heather Williams, *Self-Taught: African American Education in Slavery and Freedom* (Chapel Hill: University of North Carolina Press, 2007), 122, 198.
14. Alvord, *First Semi-Annual Report on Schools and Finances of Freedmen*, 5.
15. Campbell F. Scribner, "Surveying the Destruction of African American Schoolhouses in the South, 1864–1876," *Journal of the Civil War Era* 10, no. 4 (December 2020): 470.
16. Williams, *Self-Taught*, 93.
17. Saidiya Hartman, *Lose Your Mother: A Journey Along the Atlantic Slave Route*, rpt. ed. (New York: Farrar, Straus & Giroux, 2008), 6.
18. Williams, *Self-Taught*.

19. Quote taken from Carl Kaestle, *Pillars of the Republic: Common Schools and American Society, 1780–1860*, 1st ed. (New York: Hill & Wang, 1983), 208.
20. My thinking here is informed by philosopher Charles Mills, *The Racial Contract* (Ithaca, NY: Cornell University Press, 1999), 58–59, who writes, "Whiteness is defined in part in respect to an oppositional darkness, so that white self-conceptions of identity, personhood, and self-respect are then intimately tied up with the repudiation of the black Other. No matter how poor one was, one was still able to affirm the whiteness that distinguished one from the subpersons on the other side of the color line"; "hewers of wood and drawers of water" is referencing Carter G. Woodson, *The Mis-Education of the Negro* (ASNLH, 1933/2008), 31.
21. Charisse Burden-Stelly, "Modern U.S. Racial Capitalism: Some Theoretical Insights," *Monthly Review*, July 1, 2020, https://monthlyreview.org/2020/07/01/modern-u-s-racial-capitalism.
22. Walter Johnson, *River of Dark Dreams: Slavery and Empire in the Cotton Kingdom* (Cambridge, MA: Belknap Press / Harvard University Press, 2017), 197, 153.
23. Holtzclaw, *Black Man's Burden*, 16.
24. Some southern whites insisted that teachers be white southerners to ensure control of what blacks were learning; see Williams, *Self-Taught*, 182.
25. Holtzclaw, *Black Man's Burden*, 30.
26. Horace M. Bond, *Negro Education in Alabama: A Study in Cotton and Steel* (1939; rpt. Tuscaloosa: University of Alabama, 1994), 290.
27. Holtzclaw, *Black Man's Burden*, 30, italics added.
28. Richard R. Wright Jr., *87 Years Behind the Black Curtain*, 1st ed. (Philadelphia: Rare Book Co., 1965), 30.
29. Saidiya Hartman, *Wayward Lives, Beautiful Experiments: Intimate Histories of Social Upheaval*, 1st ed. (New York: W. W. Norton, 2019), 47, 206.
30. Robert Jefferson Spencer, interview by Mausiki S. Scales, audiocassettes and transcript, June 20, 1995, Behind the Veil Collection, David M. Rubenstein Rare Book and Manuscript Library, Duke University, 12–13.
31. Benjamin Mays, *Born to Rebel: An Autobiography* (Athens: University of Georgia Press, 2003), 3; for more context on Mays's education, see Randal Maurice Jelks, *Benjamin Elijah Mays, Schoolmaster of the Movement: A Biography* (Chapel Hill: University of North Carolina Press, 2014), 33.
32. Mays, *Born to Rebel*, 3–4.

33. Ralph Ellison, *Shadow and Act* (New York: Random House, 1964), 7.
34. Elizabeth Alexander, *The Black Interior* (Saint Paul, MN: Graywolf, 2004).
35. William Watkins, *The White Architects of Black Education: Ideology and Power in America, 1865–1954* (New York: Teachers College Press, 2001).
36. Zora Neale Hurston, *Mules and Men* (New York: J. B. Lippincott, 1935), 2.
37. Zora Neale Hurston, *Dust Tracks on a Road: An Autobiography* (New York: Harper Collins, 2006), 34–35, italics added.
38. Hurston, *Dust Tracks on a Road*, 34–38.
39. Vanessa Siddle Walker, *The Lost Education of Horace Tate: Uncovering the Hidden Heroes Who Fought for Justice in Schools* (New York: New Press, 2018), 13.
40. Angela Y. Davis, *An Autobiography* (New York: Random House, 1974), 90–93, italics added.
41. See introduction to Hurston, *Mules and Men*, 2.

CHAPTER FOUR: READING IN THE DARK

1. Ira Berlin, Marc Favreau, and Steven F. Miller, *Remembering Slavery: African Americans Talk About Their Personal Experiences of Slavery and Emancipation* (New York: New Press, 2007), 280.
2. James Anderson, *The Education of Blacks in the South, 1860–1935* (Chapel Hill: University of North Carolina Press, 1988), 17.
3. Wayne O'Neil, "Properly Literate," *Harvard Educational Review* 40, no. 2 (1970): 260.
4. "Sojourner Truth on the Press," in *History of Woman Suffrage*, ed. Elizabeth Cady Stanton, Susan B. Anthony, and Matilda Joslyn Gage (Rochester, NY: Charles Mann, 1881), 2:926.
5. Henry Louis Gates Jr., *The Signifying Monkey: A Theory of African-American Literary Criticism*, rpt. ed. (New York: Oxford University Press, 1989), esp. chap. 4: "The Trope of the Talking Book."
6. Gates, "The Trope of the Talking Book," 141.
7. Joshua Bennett, *Being Property Once Myself: Blackness and the End of Man* (Cambridge, MA: Belknap Press / Harvard University Press, 2020), 1.
8. Sam Mchombo, "Linguistic Rights and Conceptual Incarceration in African Education," *Alternation: Interdisciplinary Journal for the Study of the Arts and Humanities in Southern Africa* 24, no. 2 (2017): 191–214; Ngũgĩ wa Thiong'o, *Decolonising the Mind: The Politics of Language in African Literature* (London: J. Currey, 1986).
9. Anderson, *The Education of Blacks in the South*, 156, 184.

10. Jerry Alexander Moore Jr., interview by Janet Sims-Wood, video, April 27, 2007, HistoryMakers Digital Archive.
11. Henry W. Elson, *Modern Times and the Living Past* (New York: American Book Co., 1935), 13.
12. See Mary McLeod Bethune, interview by Charles S. Johnson, transcript, c. 1940, box 2, folder 1, pp. 3–5, Mary McLeod Bethune (1875–1955) Papers, 1928–1943, John Hope and Aurelia E. Franklin Library, Special Collection and Archives, Fisk University.
13. Cheryl Knott, *Not Free, Not for All: Public Libraries in the Age of Jim Crow* (Amherst: University of Massachusetts Press, 2016); Michael Fultz, "Black Public Libraries in the South in the Era of De Jure Segregation," *Libraries and the Cultural Record* 41, no. 3 (2006): 337–59. See also "civic estrangement" in Salamishah Tillet, *Sites of Slavery: Citizenship and Racial Democracy in the Post–Civil Rights Imagination* (Durham, NC: Duke University Press, 2012).
14. Richard Wright, *Black Boy* (1945) (New York: Harper Perennial Modern Classics, 2008), 244–45.
15. The account in this and successive paragraphs comes from Wright, *Black Boy*, 50–54, 174–77.
16. She was turned away at the Oxbridge Library by a "kindly gentleman, who regretted in a low voice as he waved me back that ladies are only admitted to the library if accompanied by a Fellow of the College or furnished with a letter of introduction." Virginia Woolf, *A Room of One's Own* (New York: Harcourt, 1929), 8.
17. Wright, *Black Boy*, 247.
18. The Honorable John Lewis, interviewed by Julieanna L. Richardson, April 25, 2001, A2001.039, HistoryMakers Digital Archive.
19. Michael Fultz, "Black Public Libraries in the South in the Era of De Jure Segregation," *Libraries and the Cultural Record* 41, no. 3 (2006): 342, 346.
20. Ralph Ellison, *Shadow and Act*, reissue ed. (New York: Vintage, 1995), 155.
21. John Hope Franklin, *Mirror to America* (New York: Farrar, Straus & Giroux, 2006), 16–17.
22. "Thompson 'Guarantees' School Board Harmony: Making No Mention of Resignation, Says 'Isms' All Banned; Offensive Text Referred to Lee," *Muskogee Daily Phoenix*, June 2, 1925, Oklahoma Historical Society; see discussion in Jarvis R. Givens, *Fugitive Pedagogy: Carter G. Woodson and the Art of Black Teaching* (Cambridge, MA: Harvard University Press, 2021), 167–68.

23. Franklin, *Mirror to America*, 83.
24. Franklin, *Mirror to America*, 20, 3.
25. Endesha Ida Mae Holland, *From the Mississippi Delta*, 1st ed. (New York: Simon & Schuster, 1997), 32.
26. David Bradley, "Black and American, 1982," *Esquire*, May 1982.
27. Sara Lawrence-Lightfoot, *I've Known Rivers: Lives of Loss and Liberation*, 1st ed. (Reading, MA: Basic Books, 1994), 37–38.
28. William H. Holtzclaw, *The Black Man's Burden* (New York: Neale, 1915).
29. Dorothy Redus Robinson, *The Bell Rings at Four: A Black Teacher's Chronicle of Change*, 1st ed. (Austin, TX: Madrona, 1979), 2–3.
30. See data charts in Anderson, *Education of Blacks in the South*, 194, 200.
31. Holland, *From the Mississippi Delta*, 32.
32. Ellison, *Shadow and Act*, 7.
33. Robinson, *Bell Rings at Four*, 3.
34. Knott, *Not Free, Not for All*, 8.
35. Malcolm X and Alex Haley, *The Autobiography of Malcolm X* (New York: Ballantine Books, 1965), 41–42.
36. Huey P. Newton, *Revolutionary Suicide* (New York: Penguin Classics, 2009), 17–20.
37. Malcolm X and Haley, *The Autobiography of Malcolm X*, 190.
38. Lawrence-Lightfoot, *I've Known Rivers*, 2.
39. Imani Perry, *May We Forever Stand: A History of the Black National Anthem* (Chapel Hill: University of North Carolina Press, 2018), 88–89.
40. Sonia Sanchez, interview by Larry Crowe, April 19, 2003, HistoryMakers Digital Archive.
41. Carter G. Woodson, "My Recollections of Veterans of the Civil War," *Negro History Bulletin*, February 1944.
42. Franklin, *Mirror to America*, 18.
43. Holland, *From the Mississippi Delta*, 43–44.
44. Holland, *From the Mississippi Delta*, 54–63.
45. Tina M. Campt, *A Black Gaze: Artists Changing How We See* (Cambridge, MA: MIT Press, 2021), 8.
46. Gates, *Signifying Monkey*, 141.

CHAPTER FIVE: A SINGING SCHOOL FOR JUSTICE

1. Charlotte L. Forten, *The Journal of Charlotte L. Forten*, ed. Ray Allen Billington (New York: W. W. Norton, 1981), 149–50, 158.

2. Mary McLeod Bethune, interviewed by Charles S. Johnson, transcript, c 1940, box 2, folder 1, Mary McLeod Bethune (1875–1955) Papers, 1928–1943, Fisk University, John Hope and Aurelia E. Franklin Library, Special Collection and Archives.
3. Imani Perry, *May We Forever Stand: A History of the Black National Anthem* (Chapel Hill: University of North Carolina Press, 2018), 12, 8.
4. Albert Murray, *South to a Very Old Place*, rpt. ed. (New York: Vintage, 1991), 87.
5. Sonia Sanchez, interview by Larry Crowe, April 19, 2003, session 1, tape 2, story 1, HistoryMakers Digital Archive.
6. Al Young, *Something about the Blues*, 1st ed. (Naperville, IL: Sourcebooks MediaFusion, 2007), 3.
7. John Bracey, interview by Jarvis R. Givens, University of Massachusetts Amherst, audio, November 21, 2016, personal collection.
8. Bracey interview.
9. Perry, *May We Forever Stand*, 80.
10. Angela Davis, *Angela Davis: An Autobiography* (New York: Random House, 1974), 91.
11. Bracey interview.
12. Hortense J. Spillers to Jarvis R. Givens, email communications, June 24, 27, and 28, 2020.

> June 24:
>
> Looking back over the decades, I don't recall that we were systematic readers of black literature in my childhood, but funny thing! I feel like we were! Let's call it the black effect: because my neighborhood of Orange Mound in Memphis was all black, every inch of it, my whole life world for the first eighteen years of my life was thoroughly shot through with blackness so that everything I was reading then now seems to have reflected my cultural context. Even the King James Bible, so powerful a feature of my human and cultural apprenticeship, is a first layer blackness because those cadences embedded in my memory belong to the faces of black people—my mother and father, the preacher, the one who prays; every time I hear Morgan Freeman's voice, for instance, I'm transported to a very old place! Or Aretha singing, or MLK preaching.
>
> My father was a big reader of Readers Digest and I vaguely recall reading about Mary McLeod Bethune in its pages.
>
> Jarvis, I will pick this up after supper. Excuse me a moment. More soon!
>
> Hjs

June 27:

So what I was trying to identify were early literary influences; they were spotty and hit and miss, but quite consistent in their inclination toward inspirational and oratorical content; somewhere in there, I was exposed to James Weldon Johnson and "God's Trombones," which content perfectly lines up with those tendencies in a religiously ordered household.

Yes, we did celebrate "Negro History Week," but my memory is that such a celebration had two dimensions—either school assemblies, where we heard important speakers, or, newspaper reading in my case.

Hjs

June 28:

What a wonderful email! Thank you for it, especially that story about Merle Epps leading up to Molefi Asante! Who'd have thought? But it makes perfect sense! Where else would Afrocentrism have come from? I love this story!

One of my childhood friends was a girl named Ann Hill whose sister was in my class; Ann was a bit younger than we were, but we were all children of a certain era; our families belonged to the same small Baptist church in Orange Mound, St. John, which my maternal grandfather had help found and build. Anyway, my mother was in charge of the children of our church, primarily, preparing them for Christmas and Easter programs when we recited long poems that we had had to learn to recite— stuff like Wm Cullen Bryant's "Thanatopsis," somebody's "Invictus," and the poem that ends: "Let me live in a house by the side of the road and be a friend to man." Today, these poems and ones like them are appallingly sentimental to us, but we remember them with great fondness and humility because they are an indelible part of our first formal training and made for fantastic oratorical development! How could you beat "I am the master of my fate, I am the captain of my soul" in the mouth of a 10 or 12 year black child in front of her admiring elders? It's worth a movie! Anyway, my mother taught the children these poems from some kind of primer, I suppose, and perhaps even our Sunday School books, which came from religious publishing houses right here in Nashville and which I'd cruise past many years later and almost weep because I'd recall the name of the publisher from 60 years before! Ann Hill was one of those children, primed in the smithy of these devotional adult-led initiatives; but Ann's people took a slightly different tact—They had Ann learn all the books of the

Holy Bible in running order from Genesis to the Revelations! She would recite the order from memory, and it became a performance standard of my early teen years! The recitation was utterly unique to Ann!

I owe you one more answer—soon!

Hjs

13. Maya Angelou, *I Know Why the Caged Bird Sings* (1969), reissue ed. (New York: Random House, 2002), 172.
14. Angelou, *I Know Why the Caged Bird Sings*, 175–76.
15. Angelou, *I Know Why the Caged Bird Sings*, 168, 177–78.
16. Angelou, *I Know Why the Caged Bird Sings*, 179.
17. James D. Anderson, 1962 graduation from George Washington Carver High School in Eutaw, Alabama, interview by Jarvis R. Givens, Zoom video recording, July 11, 2022.
18. Florence Tate and Jake-Ann Jones, *Sometimes Farmgirls Become Revolutionaries: Florence Tate on Black Power, Black Politics and the FBI* (Baltimore: Black Classic Press, 2021), 30–31.
19. Jarvis R. Givens, "'There Would Be No Lynching If It Did Not Start in the Schoolroom': Carter G. Woodson and the Occasion of Negro History Week, 1926–1950," *American Educational Research Journal* 56, no. 4 (2019): 1457–94.
20. William D. Hutchinson to Jarvis R. Givens, email communication, March 10, 2022.

Professor Givens,

A friend and neighbor, a Harvard graduate and a retired professor of theoretical physics at Caltech, shared with me the article about you in the current issue of the Harvard Magazine entitled "Fugitive Pedagogy." Several months ago, I had shared with him memories from my childhood about the efforts made in the racially–segregated public schools of Birmingham, Alabama to provide us Black students with a course that realistically depicted the lives lived by our ancestors under slavery. I explained to him that, as a third-grade student, I had received a course in "Negro History" taught from a textbook written by the Black historian, Dr. Carter G. Woodson. I further explained that the history, as presented by Dr. Woodson, differed significantly from that presented in the text written by the prolific white historian, Henry Steele Commager, that was mandated for our use in the higher grades. It was clear that in the Black schools in Birmingham, the text by Woodson was used surreptitiously.

I appreciate the fact that you have undertaken to lift the veil on the efforts made by Black educators to teach subjects to their students in opposition to the course-work dictated for us by racist school systems and administrators. In many instances it is clear that providing quality educations to Black students was not the intent of the system or the administrators.

I grew up in Birmingham, Alabama and attended the public schools through high school there. I was fortunate to grow up in a neighborhood that was staunchly middle-class. We suffered many bombings by racists in our neighborhood. Many of my fellow students went on after high school to historically Black colleges and Universities. Due to the dedication of our parents, teachers and influences in our neighborhoods, we were well-prepared to become productive citizens. We had role-models who, by their accomplishments, showed what we could achieve. In our neighborhoods, we were exposed to a wide spectrum of others who had prevailed against the constraints we faced.

I was fortunate in coming from a family of achievers. My paternal grandfather was a teacher, a graduate of the Alabama Normal College for Negroes in the nineteenth century. He in fact served as in the 'twenties and 'thirties as the Superintendent of the Sunday School at the Sixteenth Street Baptist Church in Birmingham, where the four girls were killed in the bombing in September 1963. My grandmother was studying at Clark College in Atlanta, Georgia when they married. My father attended prep-school at Morehouse and finished College there in 1926. From there he went on [to] medical School at Meharry, finishing there in 1930. My brother and I finished our undergraduate work at Morehouse finishing, respectively, in 1953 and 1955. My brother finished medical school at Meharry in 1957 and went on to a very successful career as a cardiovascular and thoracic surgeon in New York. I earned a doctorate in chemistry and physics at Caltech in 1960, followed by a career in the aerospace industry as a rocket scientist. We were just two, among many, who thrived as Blacks in the segregated schools in the South. We were trained by dedicated teachers who engaged in the "Fugitive Pedagogy" that is described in the article.

Respectfully,

William D. Hutchinson, Ph.D.,
Altadena, California

21. Freeman Hrabowski, "The Role of Youth in the Civil Rights Movement: Reflections on Birmingham," in *African Americans and Civil*

Rights: A Reappraisal, ed. Larry L. Martin, Diana Beasley, Lorene Lake, and R. Renita Lake (Washington, DC: Associated Publishers, 1996), 5.

22. Hrabowski, "Role of Youth," 7–8.
23. V. P. Franklin, *The Young Crusaders: The Untold Story of the Children and Teenagers Who Galvanized the Civil Rights Movement* (Boston: Beacon Press, 2021), 89, 105.
24. Angela Davis interview featured in Goran Olsson, *The Black Power Mixtape 1967–1975* (MPI Home Video, 2011).
25. Vanessa Siddle Walker, "Research at Risk: Lessons Learned in an African-American Community," *Educational Foundations* 9, no. 1 (1996): 10–11.
26. Davis, *Angela Davis*, 93.
27. This reading is informed by George Yancy's intervention of "the phenomenological return of the Black body" where a white gaze encounters/captures the black body, followed by a perceiving act or gesture reducing it to the instantiations of the white imagination. "During such moments, my body is given back to me in a ludicrous light, where I live the meaning of my body as confiscated." George Yancy, *Black Bodies, White Gazes: The Continuing Significance of Race* (New York: Rowman & Littlefield, 2008), 66–67.
28. Toni Morrison, "The Slavebody and the Blackbody," in *The Source of Self-Regard: Selected Essays, Speeches, and Meditations* (New York: Knopf, 2019), 74–78.
29. Carolyn (C. T.) King-Miller, interview by Larry Crowe, video, March 8, 2011, A2011.009, HistoryMakers Digital Archive.
30. Robert Hudson and Bobby Houston, *Mighty Times: The Children's March*, Teaching Tolerance documentary, 2004.
31. Davis, *Angela Davis*, 100.
32. Hrabowski, "Role of Youth," 3, 5.
33. Hrabowski, "Role of Youth," 7.
34. Lisa Delpit, ed., *Teaching When the World Is on Fire* (New York: New Press, 2019), xi.
35. Franklin, *Young Crusaders*, 94, 88.
36. Franklin, *Young Crusaders*, 88.
37. Franklin, *Young Crusaders*, 2.

CHAPTER 6: SOME OF THEM BECAME SCHOOLTEACHERS

1. Mary McLeod Bethune, interview by Charles S. Johnson, transcript, c 1940, box 2, folder 1, Mary McLeod Bethune (1875–1955) Papers,

1928–1943, Fisk University, John Hope and Aurelia E. Franklin Library, Special Collection and Archives.

2. James Weldon Johnson, *Along This Way: The Autobiography of James Weldon Johnson* (New York: Penguin Classics, 2008), 60.
3. Johnson, *Along This Way*, 155.
4. Mary M. Kennedy, "How We Learn about Teacher Learning," *Review of Research in Education* 43, no. 1 (2019): 139; Dan C. Lortie, *Schoolteacher: A Sociological Study* (Chicago: University of Chicago Press, 1975); Nancy Faust Sizer and Theodore Sizer, *The Students Are Watching: Schools and the Moral Contract*, 1st ed. (Boston: Beacon Press, 2000).
5. Henry Ponder, interview by Denise Gines, video, January 29, 2007, HistoryMakers Digital Archive.
6. Mary McLeod Bethune, "What Does American Democracy Mean to Me?" speech, America's Town Meeting of the Air, New York City, 1939, http://americanradioworks.publicradio.org/features/sayitplain/mmbethune.html.
7. Mary McLeod Bethune, "The Association for the Study of Negro Life and History: Its Contribution to Our Modern Life," *Journal of Negro History* 20, no. 4 (1935): 407–8.
8. Yvonne Hutchinson, interview by Jarvis R. Givens, audio, June 3, 2018, personal collection.
9. Zora Neale Hurston, *Dust Tracks on a Road: An Autobiography* (New York: Harper Collins, 2006), 127.
10. Evelyn Brooks Higginbotham to Jarvis R. Givens, email communication, July 12, 2020.

> Dear Jarvis,
>
> I did grow up with black teachers who played an important role in my life. Most noteworthy was my high school history teacher Helen Blackburn. She also taught Sharon Pratt, the first woman mayor of DC. However, my greatest teacher of black history was my father, even though I did not go to his school. John Bracey was a student at my father's school, however. I recall when black history was being introduced in the schools, Ms. Blackburn asked me for help, so I gave her a lot of materials from the Negro History Bulletin. Dunbar was an important school in my family's history because my aunt Julia Brooks was a vice-principal there. Most of the alums of the 1930s have passed on now, but they would always tell me about Miss Julia Brooks. Some even said I looked a bit like her. Also, at the college level, I went to Howard,

> did not finish the B.A. there, however. I came back to Howard for my M.A. and studied under Rayford W. Logan. Logan had gone to M St. with my father and even in the same class.
>
> Evelyn

11. Hutchinson interview.
12. Yvonne Divans Hutchinson, "Typed Reproduction of 'Letter Back Home,'" October 12, 1951, reprinted copy in author's possession. Hutchinson reproduced this letter and incorporated it into assignments for her students over the years. The details of Miss Hutch's encounter with *Jet* magazine did not appear in the original letter, but she included this memory because *Jet* quickly became one of her favorite things to read within her first year in Los Angeles.
13. Hutchinson interview.
14. Yvonne Hutchinson, "Who Loses If She Gets Transferred? Her Students: This Black Teacher Wants to Stay in Watts," *Los Angeles Times*, June 3, 1976.
15. Hutchinson interview.
16. Hutchinson, "Who Loses If She Gets Transferred?"
17. Hutchinson, "Who Loses If She Gets Transferred?"
18. Hutchinson interview.
19. Hutchinson, "Who Loses If She Gets Transferred?"
20. Hutchinson interview.
21. Hutchinson interview.
22. Hutchinson, "Who Loses If She Gets Transferred?"
23. Hutchinson, "Who Loses If She Gets Transferred?"
24. Yvonne Hutchinson, "Letters to the Times: Teaching in the Inner City," *Los Angeles Times*, June 24, 1985.
25. Mike Rose, *Possible Lives: The Promise of Public Education in America*, 1st ed. (Boston: Houghton Mifflin, 1995) 9, 16–17.
26. Maya Angelou, *The Complete Poetry*, illustrated ed. (New York: Random House, 2015), 265.
27. Rose, *Possible Lives*, 17.
28. Rose, *Possible Lives*, 17.
29. Erin J. Aubry, "Book Lovers' Bash," *Los Angeles Times*, January 3, 1995.

CONCLUSION: HIEROGLYPHICS OF THE BLACK STUDENT BODY

1. "And so you are trying now to free yourself. And what I want to suggest to you is that in your freeing yourself, you have to free the human itself. And that can only be done, literally, by what I propose;

the science of origin stories. Because we are hybrid, both bios and mythoi." Sylvia Wynter, Joshua Bennett, and Jarvis R. Givens, "'A Greater Truth than Any Other Truth You Know': A Conversation with Professor Sylvia Wynter on Origin Stories," *Souls* 22, no. 1 (2020): 128.

2. William H. Holtzclaw, *The Black Man's Burden* (New York: Neale, 1915), 28–29.
3. Zora Neale Hurston, "Characteristics of Negro Expression (1934)," in *Folklore, Memoirs, and Other Writings* (New York: Literary Classics of the United States, 1995), 831.
4. On "decorating a decoration," see Hurston, "Characteristics of Negro Expression," 834.
5. "In my text, the weather is the totality of our environments; the weather is the total climate; and the climate is antiblack." Christina Sharpe, *In the Wake: On Blackness and Being*, rpt. ed. (Durham, NC: Duke University Press Books, 2016), 104.
6. Heather Williams, *Self-Taught: African American Education in Slavery and Freedom* (Chapel Hill: University of North Carolina Press, 2007), 143.
7. W. E. B. Du Bois, *The Souls of Black Folk* (New York: Barnes & Noble Classics, 2005), 15.
8. Hortense J. Spillers, "Mama's Baby, Papa's Maybe: An American Grammar Book," *Diacritics* 17, no. 2, special issue, "Culture and Countermemory: The 'American' Connection" (1987): 64–81.
9. Davison Douglas, *Jim Crow Moves North: The Battle over Northern School Segregation, 1865–1954* (New York: Cambridge University Press, 2005), 49.
10. On Detroit, see Douglas, *Jim Crow Moves North*, 155; on Marrs, see Williams, *Self-Taught*, 122; see also Campbell F. Scribner, "Surveying the Destruction of African American Schoolhouses in the South, 1864–1876," *Journal of the Civil War Era* 10, no. 4 (December 2020): 469–94.
11. Quoted in Stephen G. Hall, *A Faithful Account of the Race: African American Historical Writing in Nineteenth-Century America* (Chapel Hill: University of North Carolina Press, 2009), 49.
12. James W. C. Pennington, *Text Book of the Origin and History of the Colored People* (Hartford, CT: L. Skinner, 1841); on "chattel principle," see James W. C. Pennington, *The Fugitive Blacksmith; or, Events in the History of James W. C. Pennington, Pastor of a Presbyterian Church, New York, Formerly a Slave in the State of Maryland, United States* (London: Charles Gilpin, 1849), iv.

13. James Weldon Johnson, *Along This Way: The Autobiography of James Weldon Johnson* (New York: Penguin Classics, 2008), 163.
14. Quintard Taylor, *In Search of the Racial Frontier: African Americans in the American West, 1528–1990* (New York: W. W. Norton, 1999), 217.
15. Madeline Stratton Morris, interview by Larry Crowe, video, August 28, 2003, A2003.209, session 1, tape 3, story 3, HistoryMakers Digital Archive.
16. James Anderson, *The Education of Blacks in the South, 1860–1935*, 1st ed. (Chapel Hill: University of North Carolina Press, 1988); W. E. B. Du Bois, *Black Reconstruction in America, 1860–1880* (New York: Free Press, 1998), 638.
17. Endesha Ida Mae Holland, *From the Mississippi Delta*, 1st ed. (New York: Simon & Schuster, 1997), 31.
18. V. P. Franklin, *The Young Crusaders: The Untold Story of the Children and Teenagers Who Galvanized the Civil Rights Movement* (Boston: Beacon Press, 2021), 105.
19. Bob Smith, *They Closed Their Schools: Prince Edward County, Virginia, 1951–1964* (Farmville, VA: M. E. Forrester Council of Women, 1996).
20. Rachel Devlin, *A Girl Stands at the Door: The Generation of Young Women Who Desegregated America's Schools* (New York: Basic Books, 2018).
21. Katherine Mellen Charron, *Freedom's Teacher: The Life of Septima Clark* (Chapel Hill: University of North Carolina Press, 2012).
22. "Sept. 2, 1966: Grenada, Miss. School Desegregation Battle," Zinn Education Project, https://www.zinnedproject.org/news/tdih/grenada-ms-school-desegregation, accessed April 2, 2021.
23. This is *the afterlife of slavery*—skewed life chances, limited access to health and education, premature death, incarceration, and impoverishment." Saidiya Hartman, *Lose Your Mother: A Journey Along the Atlantic Slave Route*, rpt. ed. (New York: Farrar, Straus & Giroux, 2008), 6.

Image Credits

Page 34: New York African Free School: New York Public Library

Page 36: Alexander Crummell: New York Public Library

Page 37: Henry Highland Garnet: National Portrait Gallery, Smithsonian Institution

Page 40: "Noyes Academy Removal": Canaan Historical Society

Page 45: Charlotte Forten: New York Public Library

Page 57: Susie King Taylor: Liljenquist Family Collection of Civil War Photographs (Library of Congress)

Page 67: Photo of W. S. Scarborough: New York Public Library

Page 142: African American students escorted to jail: AP Photo/Bill Hudson

Page 159: Henry Ponder: Photo of the HistoryMakers

Page 160: Mary McLeod Bethune with three African American male students: Mary McLeod Bethune Papers, Amistad Research Center, Tulane University, New Orleans, Louisiana

Page 161: Mary McLeod Bethune with two African American male students: Afro Newspaper/Gado/Archive Photos via Getty Images

Page 172: Elizabeth Eckford: Francis Miller/The LIFE Picture Collection/Shutterstock.com

Page 180: Yvonne Divans Hutchinson: Robert Gauthier copyright © 1995. *Los Angeles Times*. Used with permission.

Page 181: From *Los Angeles Times* article: Robert Gauthier copyright © 1995. Los Angeles Times. Used with permission.

Index

Page numbers in italics refer to photographs.

Teaching Guide for *School Clothes*

Overview

This guide was designed to support engaged study of *School Clothes* through meaningful writing activities, critical discussions, self-reflection, and creative projects. The guide is organized into four units of study, each consisting of two to three chapters. Units include guiding questions, key concepts, and potential activities. The key concepts offer detailed explanations of terms and ideas appearing in the text, and they should inform your engagement with guiding questions and potential activities.

To access the more extensive teaching guide, please use the QR code on the back of the book or visit beacon.org/GivensGuide.

Unit 1 | Preface & Introduction

Guiding Questions:

- How do the stories we inherit about education shape who we are and who we will become?
- What do we stand to learn from reviewing first person accounts of black students?
- Reflecting on your prior knowledge, what are two to three distinct topics or features that come to mind when thinking about the history of African American students, and why do they stand out for you?
- What concerns or possibilities pertaining to African American education are you bringing with you as you engage with *School Clothes*?
- What does the metaphor of "school clothes" mean to you?

Key Concepts:

1. **Black Vernacular & "School Clothes":** African American (or black) vernacular refers to the language and cultural practices developed internally among African American communities,

including ways of saying things in the context of African American Vernacular English (AAVE). The words and linguistic traditions embedded in black vernacular culture carry symbolic representations connected to the historical experiences of African Americans. Givens presents "school clothes," for instance, as a distinct concept within African American vernacular culture (see p. vii), while also reflecting on the historical significance of literal clothing procured by African American learners after slavery. He then further unpacks the phrase "school clothes," from its literal meaning to its metaphorical and symbolic meaning, arguing that *school clothes are both the physical items students wear that symbolize the communal value of black education as well as the lessons regarding education black families and communities passed on to young people to adorn and cover themselves as they went to school and navigated an antiblack world.*

2. **The Black Student Body & Fugitive Learning:** The black student body is defined as "a distinct constituency of learners whose shared past of criminalized education, then confinement in materially inferior segregated schools, and finally contemporary experiences of school violence and neglect, engenders a suspicion and necessary vigilance of the 'official' curriculum and protocols of the American education system" (p. 21). In order to pursue meaningful, liberatory education within this context, these learners often engage in practices of fugitive learning: "a countervailing educational tradition set against an antiblack status quo in American schooling" (p. 7). Throughout *School Clothes*, black students engage in a variety of fugitive learning practices that challenged restrictions imposed on black education and that defied prevailing assumptions that black people were intellectually inferior. This shared oppression and collective resistance made African American students a distinct community of learners in the American school.
3. **Collective Memoir:** *School Clothes* takes the form of "collective memoir," a narrative based on an assembly of documented accounts of individual people pertaining to significant events, experiences, or memories shared by a distinguishable group or community, whereby the narrative reflects their shared histories or identities. Collective memoir must be based on the first-person accounts of those whose narratives are represented, and it is necessarily autobiographical, engaging the personal experiences of the author in relation to the collective historical record.

Potential Activities:

1. **School Clothes: An Autobiographical Essay** — Reflect on the stories you have inherited about schooling. These do not have to be your own experiences. They can include stories you've seen on TV, read in books, or those shared by loved ones, etc. How do these stories shape your understanding of education?
2. **The Black Student Body: Discussion or Written Reflection** — Reflect on Givens's description of this student body as being made up of a *distinct* group of learners. In doing so, consider how racial ideas about black people and education are read onto the literal bodies of African American youth. How do you understand your relationship to the "black student body" as it is defined? How would you add to, revise, or expand the definition?
3. **Locating African American Student Voices: An Activity** — Identify one space or cultural artifact (film, poem, song, social media thread, etc.) where the black student voices are prominently featured. What are they saying? What questions do they invite?

Unit 2 | Chapters 1 & 2

Guiding Questions:

- Why is it useful to zoom in on the details of individual students' narratives while studying the broader history of African American education?
- What is the "color line"? How have the student narratives in *School Clothes* referred to the color line, directly or indirectly?
- What stories in these chapters best reflect the literal *and* metaphorical meaning of fugitive learning?
- How did "the white gaze" shape educational experiences of black students during the antebellum era?
- What fugitive learning strategies and spaces did black students develop to resist and subvert the white gaze? What ideas and conversations did black students express in these spaces?
- What does the history of anti-literacy laws teach us about the historical and political significance of black literacy and African American literature/studies?

- How did black students create, claim, and demonstrate "agency" in the antebellum South and North? Why is it important to think about black agency when studying the complex history of racial oppression?

Key Concepts:

1. **Black Education in Northern Free States:** In chapter 1, Givens traces the educational experiences of black students in northern states during the antebellum period, including the sparse and segregated schools for black children, the oppressive philosophies of white reformers controlling black education, and the destruction of schools such as Noyes Academy. By illustrating how antiblackness in education was national in scope, Givens points out the unstable nature of boundaries typically drawn between "slave states" and "free states."
2. **Witnessing & Shared Vulnerability During Slavery:** The act of witnessing for African American learners "involves coming into awareness of how the violence and mistreatment of other individual black people could potentially be visited on oneself" (p. 32). Such witnessing made them aware of a "shared vulnerability" between their individual selves, as black students, and black people as a collective group subjected to distinct forms of racial persecution. It is in this context of shared vulnerability that the concept of freedom—*and the value of education*—takes on collective meaning for African Americans.
3. **Fugitive Learning in the Context of Slavery:** For black people, reading and writing was an act of "fugitive justice" in a context where their education was criminalized, whereby African Americans defied black codes, anti-literacy laws, and key features of the US legal institution of slavery because they deemed them to be illegitimate. This was a countervailing vision of educational justice from the position of the enslaved (p. 58). Thus, "*fugitive learning was constituted by the secret and subtle forms of educational resistance that black students enacted, even as they performed staged acts of compliance in the coercive presence of white authoritative power*" (p. 55, emphasis added).

Potential Activities:

1. **Fugitive Learning: What Does It Mean?** — In your own words, define fugitive learning and analyze two examples covered in the book that best represent some aspect of the term's meaning.
2. **African American Literature & Anti-Literacy Laws: An Analytical Essay** — How might we interpret the tradition of African American literature as a response to, and critique of, anti-literacy laws that criminalized black education? To place anti-literacy laws in conversation with black literature, select an excerpt of African American literature written before 1865 (e.g., slave narratives, black poetry, a speech) to be referenced and included in your essay.

Unit 3 | Chapters 3 & 4

Guiding Questions:

- What is meant by "the afterlife of slavery" (p. 24)? How does framing the history of black education after the Civil War as situated within the afterlife of slavery invite us to think about education and freedom in new ways?
- What does it mean to say that freedom is a process, not an event? How do the stories in *School Clothes* exemplify the relationship between literacy and the process of freedom?
- What is racial capitalism, and how has it shaped the lives of black learners in the past as well as the present? (See p. 80.)
- How did practices of fugitive learning and resistance to "the white gaze" continue to evolve in the afterlife of slavery?
- What different meanings and purposes have literacy carried in the context of black educational history? What did it mean for black learners to be "properly literate" (p. 94) during the afterlife of slavery?
- What connections do you see between the barriers of accessing books during the Jim Crow era (see chapter 4) and contemporary book bans?

Key Concepts:

1. **Black Education in the Afterlife of Slavery**: Thinking with Saidiya Hartman's (in *Lose Your Mother*, 2008) notion of "the afterlife of slavery" in mind, whereby "black lives are still imperiled and devalued by a racial calculus and a political arithmetic that were entrenched centuries ago" (p. 201n43), Givens frames black education after emancipation as an ongoing process of pursuing freedom. He explains, "Even after slavery was abolished, black people's educational visions continued to be patterned by fugitive learning, because they continued to be met by violent white opposition and northern paternalism" (p. 79).
2. **The White Gaze in the Black Schoolhouse**: A phrase popularized by Toni Morrison, "the white gaze" refers to the act of being seen by and responding to a white observer. In *School Clothes*, the white gaze is represented by the white reformers who determined that black students should receive an industrial and agricultural education (see p. 86) as well as by the white surveillance of black school life. This prompted students and teachers to engage in "staged moments of compliance," which doubled as acts of refusal (p. 91).
3. **Black Literacy, Reading the Word & the World**: While "literacy" conventionally describes the ability to read and write, for black learners who were often barred from such activity, literacy is an expansive term: *Black literacy requires not only being able to read and write words on paper but also being able to understand the racial and social context that shapes black access to the written word, as well as the antiblack content of written works. In this way, black learners must read the word and the world. Both were texts.*

Potential Activities:

1. **The White Gaze: Discussion Prompts** — What is the "white gaze," and how does it connect to the "color line"? How do black people in the text respond to the presence of the white gaze? What spaces did black students seek out or create to operate outside of the white gaze? What are black students saying and doing in these spaces?
2. **Reading "Black Literacy"** — How do discussions of literacy in *School Clothes* align with or stretch your prior understandings of the concept? What lessons about "black literacy" do we learn from

people like Sojourner Truth and Papa Dallas, who were technically illiterate? Identify a text (written text, cultural object, image, or historical event)—one featured in the book or elsewhere—and explain how the tradition of "black literacy" might inform how we read or analyze it.

Unit 4 | Chapters 5, 6 & Conclusion

Guiding Questions:

- What is the black interior? What is black formalism? What can studying black formal practices (such as the singing of "Lift Every Voice and Sing") teach us about the African American experience and African American culture?
- How do you understand the distinctions between "black formalism" (or black formal culture) and black vernacular culture, as introduced in unit 1? (See pp. 131—33.)
- How did the events, experiences, understandings, and historical realities of the 1960s shape black students' acts of fugitive learning and civic engagement during that time?
- What connections can be drawn between black student experiences in and surrounding school and their decision to become teachers?
- What roles did black teachers and students play in the long black freedom struggle?
- What lessons can we glean from photographic representations of black education? What is the significance of historical images in the archive?
- What does the history of the black student experience teach us about the larger society we live in? What do we learn about African American history by centering the voices of African American students?

Key Concepts:

1. **Black Formalism and "Lift Every Voice and Sing":** African American studies scholar Imani Perry refers to "black formalism"

as the traditions, rituals, and routines engaged in formal black spaces (like church, school, and civic organizations) that consisted of "ways of doing and being conditioned by internally held values, aesthetics, and cultural norms" (p. 131). Black formalism involves African American communities cultivating "their own norms, rituals, and ideas about what constituted a purposeful education for students" (p. 133). "Lift Every Voice and Sing" became an iconic example of black formalism, as the Negro national anthem, in African American education. Black students and communities asserted and sustained dignity and pride through such black formalist traditions.

Potential Activities:

1. **Memory Is a Collective Enterprise: Educational Oral Histories** — Interview two people in your family or community about their educational experiences. Develop a list of six to ten questions, building from those listed below:

    - What is your earliest memory as a student?
    - What do you remember about your school clothes? What meaning did they carry?
    - Who had the biggest impact on your educational journey?
    - How, if at all, did ideas about race come up in your educational experiences? (What do you remember about the race of the students and teachers?)
    - What assignment, book, or class was most transformative in your K–12 education?

    If possible, interview one subject who is an elder. Be thoughtful about the questions you will ask and the way you intend to preserve their narrative.

    Consider filming or recording the interviews if possible.
2. **Bearing Witness: A Letter-Writing Activity** — For this activity, you will be writing a letter to the author, Professor Jarvis Givens. Introduce yourself and answer the following: What questions do you have after reading the book? What stories did you want to know more about, and why? If he was to add a new chapter to the book, what would you want him to write about?